Better Homes and Gardens®

Eat Healthy, Lose Weight

Volume 2

Meredith® Consumer Marketing
Des Moines, Iowa

Better Homes and Gardens®
Eat Healthy, Lose Weight, Volume 2

Meredith Corporation Consumer Marketing
Senior Vice President, Consumer Marketing: David Ball
Consumer Product Marketing Director: Kathi Prien
Consumer Product Marketing Manager: Amanda Werts
Business Manager: Ron Clingman
Senior Supply Chain Manager: Al Rodruck

Waterbury Publications, Inc.
Editorial Director: Lisa Kingsley
Creative Director: Ken Carlson
Associate Editor: Tricia Laning
Associate Design Director: Doug Samuelson
Contributing Editor: Lois White
Contributing Designer: Chad Jewell
Contributing Copy Editors: Terri Fredrickson,
    Gretchen Kauffman, M. Peg Smith
Contributing Indexer: Elizabeth Parson

Better Homes and Gardens® **Magazine**
Editor in Chief: Gayle Goodson Butler
Deputy Editor, Food and Entertaining: Nancy Hopkins

Meredith Publishing Group
President: Tom Harty
Executive Vice President: Andy Sareyan
Vice President, Manufacturing: Bruce Heston

Meredith Corporation
President and Chief Executive Officer: Stephen M. Lacy

In Memoriam: E. T. Meredith III (1933–2003)

Test Kitchen

Our seal assures you that every recipe
in *Eat Healthy, Lose Weight,* Volume
2 has been tested in the Better
Homes and Gardens® Test Kitchen.
This means that each recipe is
practical and reliable, and meets our
high standards of taste appeal. We
guarantee your satisfaction with this
book for as long as you own it.

All of us at Meredith® Consumer Marketing are dedicated
to providing you with the information and ideas you need
to create delicious foods. We welcome your comments and
suggestions. Write to us at: Meredith Consumer Marketing,
1716 Locust St., Des Moines, IA 50309-3023.

CONTENTS

Blueberry-Cornmeal Pancakes,
Page 28

Asian Flank Steak,
Page 115

Mocha Cake,
Page 241

THIS IS DIET FOOD?

Dieters usually want to know which foods will help them drop weight quickly. Because there are no magic foods, the answer is to eat foods that offer the most nutrients and that are the least processed. Do that to eat fewer calories than there are in high-calorie processed foods and you will feel full and begin to lose weight.

That simple method was used to develop more than 270 delicious recipes of wholesome, basic ingredients that include whole grains, lean protein, nutrient-rich fruits and vegetables, and healthful fats. All the recipes in *Eat Healthy, Lose Weight,* Volume 2 were developed and tested by registered dietitians in the Better Homes and Gardens® Test Kitchen to ensure that each one is delicious and satisfying. The dishes are so good that many taste testers were surprised these are foods that will help people lose and maintain weight.

As a bonus, the shortcut dinner chapter has recipes for superfast meals. Although the recipes call for convenience foods, they are the best of the bunch, such as frozen vegetable blends, vegetarian products, and spice blends.

Because many dieters eat out and want some of the same flavors for meals at home, this book also has a chapter that features restaurant entrées. Re-create your favorite dishes from some of the most popular chain restaurants in versions that are lower in calories, fat, and sodium—and the more healthful versions taste great!

Welcome to *Eat Healthy, Lose Weight,* Volume 2—a dieter's best friend for preparing fresh, wholesome, appetizing dishes. Get cooking, lose weight, and feel great!

Chapter 1

Weight Loss Guide

THE NO-DIET DIET

At any given time, millions of Americans claim to be "on a diet." And there are almost as many diets as there are people who want to lose weight. The methods dieters choose to lose weight or gain control of what they eat is the difference between successful or unsuccessful weight loss. When deciding on which route to take to lose extra pounds, be well informed. Typical strict and restrictive weight loss diets are unlikely to help you reach and maintain healthy weight. Why? Consider these points:

• An estimated 95 percent of people who lose weight by restrictive dieting gain back the weight—and often a few additional pounds—within five years.

• People often view dieting as a temporary situation to endure until they lose weight, then resume old patterns, which caused weight gain in the first place.

• With dieting comes the false hope that losing weight is magically life-changing. Many people believe that if they lose weight, they will look like a fashion model, find love, or be promoted. The reality is that they'll still be the same people living the same lives. The only difference is that they will wear a smaller size.

• Because diets dictate when, what, and how much to eat, they undermine inborn signals of hunger and fullness. Listening to these signals is the best gauge for how much food your body needs.

• Some diets are hazardous to your health because they forbid consumption of certain foods or food groups, making it difficult to get the nutrients you need.

If the old-fashioned restrictive diets don't work, then what does? The surest route to healthy weight is to take gradual, permanent steps toward changing the way you eat and how much physical activity you get. In this guide, you'll find the information and tools you need to do just that. Most important, you'll discover a no-diet way to lose pounds and maintain a healthful weight.

Are You Ready to Lose Weight?

This may seem like a silly question, but the fact is that many people don't stay motivated because the reasons for losing weight aren't clear in their minds or because they're trying to lose for the wrong reasons.

• Are your reasons specific and meaningful? A vague reason, such as "I know I should," is not as motivating as "I want to feel more energetic" or "I want to lower my blood pressure in hopes of reducing my medication."

• Are you doing it just for you? Losing weight to please someone else isn't likely to be enough motivation to reach your goal.

• Are you ready to do the work? Succeeding at weight loss requires a firm commitment to change eating and exercise habits. You must be willing to develop and carry out an action plan.

• Are you in it for the long haul? Losing weight for a wedding or class reunion is short-term motivation. Consider how you'll stick with your plan afterwards.

WHAT'S CAUSING AMERICA'S WEIGHT PROBLEM?

According to a recent government survey, nearly two out of three (64.5 percent) American adults age 20 years and older are classified as overweight or obese, and this number is rising steadily.

In the simplest terms, people gain weight when they eat more calories than they burn off. Consuming just 100 extra calories per day—the amount in a cookie, a handful of potato chips, or an 8-ounce soft drink—can add up to a 10-pound weight gain in a year. That's a simple calculation, but the factors fueling caloric imbalance are complex and specific to each individual.

Some factors are as basic as being surrounded by bountiful food portions, eating everything on the plates when full, and living sedentary lifestyles. Today people drive short distances that are more appropriate for walking and use laborsaving devices, such as elevators and escalators, power lawn mowers, and leaf blowers, that eliminate everyday calorie-burning activities.

Individual differences in metabolism and genetic makeup also influence the tendency to gain weight. In addition, researchers are examining the body's complex system of hormones that control appetite to determine its role in making weight loss more difficult for some people.

What's Your Healthy Weight?

Are you overweight or obese? The answer to this question is not as clear-cut as you may think. Perhaps a better question is "Are you 'overfat'?" Extra body weight from fat increases risk for developing health problems, such as high blood pressure, heart disease, diabetes, and some cancers.

How do you know if you are overfat? The number you see on the scale provides only one piece of the puzzle because it doesn't tell you how much weight is fat, muscle, bone, or fluid. Consulting a weight chart offers another clue, but most charts don't account for individual characteristics, such as age and frame size. In addition, like the scale, charts can't tell whether you carry an unhealthful amount of fat. Use these tools as general guidelines only.

Two reliable guidelines to assess weight are the body mass index (BMI) and your waist measurement. Health experts say the higher the BMI and waist measurement, the higher the potential for developing weight-related health problems, especially with one or more risk factors.

For instance, risks may be greater if close relatives have heart disease or type 2 diabetes. If you already have a health condition associated with obesity, such as high cholesterol, high blood pressure, diabetes, or heart disease, risk of heart attack or stroke is increased, especially for those who are overweight or obese. Being sedentary and a smoker also increases your risk.

To calculate BMI and waist measurement and evaluate whether weight is a health risk, see "Evaluate Your Weight," page 9.

Setting a Goal Weight

If your BMI or waist measurement suggests that you need to lose weight, the next step is to set a realistic and healthful goal weight.

The best weight for you is as individual as your fingerprints. To make sure your goal is reasonable and realistic, ask these questions:

• Am I relying on a weight chart to find the best weight for me? Because weight charts offer only general guidelines, the best weight for you may be higher or lower than the chart indicates.

• Is my goal weight realistic and achievable for me? Few people have the build of tall, willowy fashion models. Set a goal that suits your particular build.

• Can I comfortably maintain my goal weight without constant dieting and exercising? A healthful weight is one that you can maintain by eating moderate portions of a wide variety of foods and by getting moderate amounts of physical activity. To begin, set your goal at the lowest adult weight you've comfortably maintained for one year or more. When you reach the goal, re-evaluate whether you are happy with the weight or want to set a lower goal weight.

Ask your doctor or a registered dietitian help you assess your need to lose weight and set the most healthful goal weight for you.

How Many Calories Do You Need?

How many calories do you need each day to reach your healthful goal weight? It depends on several factors, including age, body size, and activity level. Although obsessive calorie counting is not the goal, knowing the approximate number of calories that your body requires to fuel your activities throughout the day is helpful in determining why you weigh what you do. To get an idea of how many calories you need a

day, see "Calculate Your Calorie Needs," page 10.

A pound of body fat contains approximately 3,500 calories (about the same as a pound of butter or margarine). Think of it this way: If, over time, you eat 3,500 fewer calories than your body uses, you will shed about 1 pound. Take in 7,000 fewer calories—or use up 7,000 extra calories—and you will lose about 2 pounds. (Most nutrition experts do not recommend losing more than 2 pounds per week.) Remember, if you eat too few calories, you risk slowing your metabolism, which makes losing weight more difficult. To lose weight faster, follow an exercise program to burn body fat and calories.

How does all this translate into everyday living? By eating 500 fewer calories each day, you should lose about 1 pound a week. Or cut only 250 calories each day and lose half a pound a week. Perform some kind of physical activity to burn the other half of the calories.

EVALUATE YOUR WEIGHT

Grab a calculator and a tape measure, then follow the steps below to evaluate whether your weight puts your health at risk.

To calculate your BMI:
The body mass index (BMI) measures weight in relation to height. People with a high BMI tend to have a high risk of developing long-term health problems. (One discrepancy is for muscular people, who may have a high BMI without any health risks.) Use the formula below to calculate your BMI.
BMI = [Weight in pounds ÷ Height in inches x Height in inches] x 703

For example, a 145-pound woman who stands 5'6" (66") tall has a BMI of 23, which falls into the "healthy weight" category.
BMI = [145 pounds ÷ 66"x 66"] x 703 = 23

Once you calculate your BMI, check the chart below to see which category it falls into.

Body Mass Index (BMI)	Category
18.5 to 24.9	Healthy weight
25 to 29.9	Overweight
30 or higher	Obese

Source: Report of the Dietary Guidelines Advisory Committee on the Dietary Guidelines for Americans, 2005 Edition, Figure E-1.

To calculate your waist measurement:
Excess abdominal fat may increase your risk for health problems, even if your BMI is in the healthy weight range. While standing, measure around your waist, just above your hipbones. A measurement of greater than 35 inches for women or 40 inches for men indicates greater risk for health problems.

CALCULATE YOUR CALORIE NEEDS

Figuring out how many calories you need in a day can be complicated. It depends on your age, gender, muscle mass, activity level, and the metabolism you inherited. Following is a basic calculation to help estimate appropriate calorie level.

1. Multiply your weight in pounds by 10. This covers your basal metabolic needs—what you need to breathe and perform other basic bodily functions (also called resting metabolic rate, or RMR).

2. Add 10% for digestion. Eating and digesting food takes energy. The more often you eat, the harder your body works, which is why many diets suggest eating five mini meals a day rather than three big meals.

3. Add 10% for light activity level. Add 20% for moderate activity level. Add 30% for high-intensity activity level. Activity level varies by person; large people burn more calories than small people doing the same activity. The add-on for activity calories is not precise, but it works as an estimate. If you move a little during the day doing basic household tasks, use the light activity number. If you stay fairly active all day and include a little exercise as well, that's moderate. If you do an intense workout each day or have a very active job, add the 30%.

To lose half to 1 pound a week, subtract 250 to 500 calories a day from the total for maintenance calories. Create a daily deficit of 500 calories per day by eating fewer calories, burning off calories with physical activity, or both in different ways. For example, each day you could eat 400 fewer calories and burn off 100 extra calories with physical activity, or eat 300 fewer calories and burn off 200 extra calories. Choose which combination works for you.

Do not cut calories severely! It is very difficult to get all the nutrients needed when you eat fewer than 1,200 calories per day. Most nutrition experts warn that calorie intake should never go below resting metabolic rate (RMR) and, ideally, should be at least 150 calories above (see "Calculate Your Calorie Needs" at left). If you delve lower than 1,200 calories, enlist the supervision of your doctor.

The Food Factor

Now that you have your goal weight and an estimate of calorie needs for weight loss, what foods should you eat? The chart "What to Eat," page 17, recommends daily food choices for good health. The following help you put these guidelines into practice.

Be calorie conscious. Don't obsess about every calorie down to the last digit, but educate yourself about calories and nutrients in foods to help set a calorie level and make informed healthful food choices. To learn how many calories are in the foods you eat, read food labels for serving sizes and the number of calories per serving. Weigh and measure foods until you learn what a serving looks like (you may be surprised). The Nutrition Facts with all recipes in this book also provide useful information.

Use easy calorie-trimming tricks. Allow yourself leeway to include other foods within your calorie budget. Grill, bake, or broil foods instead of frying. Trim fat off meat and the skin off poultry; use half the usual amount of butter or margarine on your toast. Choose reduced-fat milk and cheese; reduced-calorie versions of salad dressing, mayonnaise, and sour cream; fruit canned in water or juice instead of syrup; and diet soft drinks or water instead of regular soft drinks.

Downsize mountainous portions. Spoon reasonable portions onto plates rather than put serving bowls on the table. Family members can request seconds when hunger persists. Put snacks in a small bowl rather than eating out of a box or bag. At fast-food restaurants, shun supersizes in favor of small options. In sit-down restaurants, ask for take-home containers before you eat so you can immediately put half the meal away for another meal.

Tackle trouble spots. Develop tactics to deal with situations in which you repeatedly overeat. For example, if every afternoon a sweet tooth sends you to a vending machine for a candy bar, stock your desk or fridge with small candy bars (and stop at just one) or mini boxes of raisins, small cartons of fruit yogurt, or single-serving pudding cups.

Snack to your advantage. A healthful snack between meals keeps you fueled, energizes you for late-afternoon workouts, and prevents munchies while preparing dinner. Include snacks within your daily calorie total and plan ahead. Keep fruit, cheese sticks, whole grain crackers, small handfuls of nuts, or cartons of yogurt available.

Enjoy your favorite foods. An eating plan that you enjoy is an eating plan you'll stick with. Saying "never again" to favorites such as cake, cookies, or chocolate is unrealistic and often backfires, spurring a binge. Occasionally include treats in reasonable portions—and savor every bite.

Trust your inner signals. Rather than eat by the clock or eat everything on your plate, tune in to your body's signals for hunger and fullness, those natural gauges for when and how much to eat. It may take some practice, but with patience and gentle persistence, listening and responding to inner signals will become second nature and guide you to eat the right amount of food to achieve weight that is healthful and easy to maintain.

List strategies to stop emotional eating. In this hectic and stressful world, people often turn to food to soothe, comfort, or cheer them. Rather than use food to cope, write a list of 10 things you like to do and keep it handy. When emotions unravel, read the list and do one activity rather than eat. Journal, take a quick nap, read, or deep breathe to center and calm yourself without food.

Enlist support. Support and encouragement from family and friends strengthen your motivation and reinforce positive changes. Involve loved ones in planning and preparing healthful meals and in enjoyable physical activities. It's good for them too!

Eat, enjoy, and savor good food! Eating is something everyone does, and most find pleasure in doing so. By choosing foods wisely, you can be slimmer and healthier. The recipes in *Eat Healthy, Lose Weight,* Vol. 2 are tools to help you reach your goal. Restrictive dieting creates an ongoing battle between dieter and food, but a relationship between you and food has to exist in order for you to live! Make it a peaceful relationship.

Are You Fat Phobic? Get Over It!

Remember the fat-free craze of the 1990s? Not long ago many people thought the surest route to good health and weight loss was to drastically reduce the amount of fat in their diets. As a result, a whole population of people embraced fat-free (and often flavor-free) products, such as chips, cake, and ice cream, without realizing that fat-free wasn't calorie-free. In fact, because of increased sugar content, some reduced-fat and fat-free foods contain as many or more calories than regular versions.

Thank goodness those days are over. Dietary guidelines recommend a diet that is moderate in total fat (no more than 35 percent of daily caloric intake). The good news is that the inclusion of some fat in meals and snacks may help weight loss because fat is digested more slowly, so you feel full longer. Fat also brings delicious, satisfying flavor to foods.

The type of fats is important because some fats are more healthful than others. The unsaturated fats in olive, canola, peanut, corn, safflower, and soybean oils help lower blood cholesterol levels. The omega-3 fatty acids in fatty fish such as salmon and tuna, nuts and seeds, and canola, soybean, and flaxseed oils may reduce risks for heart attack and hardening of the arteries.

Eating too much saturated fat (in fatty meats, poultry skin, butter, and full-fat cheese, milk, and ice cream) and trans fatty acids (in foods containing partially hydrogenated oils, such as hard margarines and some fried and baked foods) may raise blood cholesterol and increase risks for heart disease. "Too much" translates to more than 10 percent of the total caloric intake (18 grams for an 1,800 calorie diet). Eating too much of any type of fat is linked to increased risks for various cancers and may promote weight gain because all fats and oils are calorie-dense.

The bottom line: Enjoy some fats, oils, and high-fat foods because they add to the enjoyment of eating. Just don't go overboard. (Note that many recipes in this book include ingredients such as butter or cream that typically were forbidden in other diets. Used in moderation, these foods are not harmful.)

Living the Active Life Leads to a Healthy Weight—and Much More

How much would you pay for an elixir that could …
· Help you lose weight and keep it off.
· Increase physical fitness.
· Strengthen bones, muscles, and joints.
· Build endurance and strength.
· Reduce the risk for heart disease, high blood pressure, colon cancer, and type 2 diabetes.
· Promote a sense of well-being and reduce feelings of depression or anxiety.

Most people would be willing to pay a premium. These benefits are yours free when you live a physically active lifestyle.

To reap the benefits, you don't have to spend hours sweating in a gym or huffing and puffing around a track. The Dietary Guidelines for Americans recommend physical activity that is moderate. Adults should accumulate at least 30 minutes of moderate physical activity most days of the week, preferably every day. That 30 minutes can be separated into short chunks of time—10 minutes, 20 minutes. What could be easier? Besides, good health is worth 30 minutes of moderate exercise each day.

A moderate physical activity is one that requires about as much energy as walking two miles in 30 minutes. In addition to walking, activities such as jogging, swimming, biking, and exercise classes are a terrific way to meet your daily physical activity quota. Everyday activities count toward the quota as well. If you're new to exercise, daily activities, including chores, are one way to start when time is limited. Here's a sampling of what counts.
· Short walks to a store, from bus stop to work, and around a mall.
· Climbing stairs instead of riding an elevator or escalator.
· Housecleaning, such as washing windows, mopping, scrubbing, and vacuuming.
· Outdoor tasks, such as gardening, mowing, raking, and shoveling.
· Actively playing, romping, dancing, wrestling, jumping, and running with kids.

The Triple Crown of Fitness

Ready to step up the pace? Once you get hooked on how good 30 minutes of daily physical activity makes you feel, begin a more structured, consistent program. People who maintain healthy weight tend to get at least one hour of moderate-intensity physical activity daily, according to the Institute of Medicine of the National Academies.

The American Council on Exercise (ACE) reports that a complete fitness program includes three components: aerobic exercise, strength training, and flexibility training. (For more ACE information and safety guidelines, go to the ACE website at acefitness.org.)

Aerobic exercise promotes a healthy cardiovascular system and healthy weight. Do any activity that gets your heart pumping faster, such as brisk walking, jogging, jumping rope, dancing, kickboxing, cycling (outdoors or indoors on stationary bikes), and swimming. For good health, do aerobic exercise three to four days each week for 20 minutes or more. To promote weight loss, gradually build up to four or more weekly sessions (with at least one day off) of 45 minutes or more. If you have injured or weak or delicate joints, choose low-impact activities; walk, swim, or cycle at low intensity.

Strength training (also called weight training or muscular conditioning) strengthens muscles, reduces risks for injury, and aids weight control. With the benefits attributed to weight training, it is worth including it in weight control plans because it:

• Increases bone strength and reduces risks of osteoporosis.

• Prevents joint injuries by strengthening connective tissues.

• Increases lean muscle mass and decreases body fat.

• Increases metabolism to burn more calories (a huge bonus!).

• Improves recreational sports performance, which means more fun.

Strength training programs utilize weight machines, free weights, exercise tubing and bands, and calisthenics. A good program covers all major muscle groups. Do strength training at least twice a week, with at least one day off between workouts.

Flexibility training maintains range of motion in joints, improves posture, promotes relaxation, and reduces risks of injury and muscle soreness. Examples are stretching exercises, yoga, Pilates, and tai chi. Do flexibility exercises at least 30 minutes, three times a week. At minimum, stretch for a few minutes before and after aerobic exercise or strength training.

Note: If you have health problems, are a man over age 40, or a woman over age 50, consult your doctor before beginning a new physical activity program.

Frequently Asked Questions

Making changes in exercise and eating habits always raises questions about why some things work and others don't, or common concerns about the results of those changes. Here are the answers to some of the most frequently asked questions.

Q: Instead of exercising, why can't I simply cut back on calories to lose weight?

A: Severely cutting calories may seem like an easy route to take. And it may work initially. Over time this strategy backfires. When you restrict calories severely, your body kicks into starvation mode and triggers slower metabolism to burn fewer calories. Eating a reasonable number of calories each day (at least 1,200) plus getting some physical activity is the safest and surest route to weight loss and keeping it off.

Q: As a woman, won't lifting weights make me bulk up too much and make me look masculine?

A: This is a common worry among women, but it needn't be. The women who build huge muscles are body builders who lift superheavy weights, follow special diets, and often take steroids. For the average woman, strengthening muscles by lifting weights results in a lean appearance because muscle is more compact than fat. Women who strength train look more toned and less flabby. More good news: The more muscle you have, the more calories your body burns.

Q: My doctor says I should lose weight to improve my health, but I have a lot to lose and I feel overwhelmed! How much do I have to lose before I recognize overall health benefits?

A: Even modest weight loss yields big benefits. Losing just 5 to 10 percent of your initial body weight reduces risks for heart

NO TIME FOR HEALTHY EATING AND EXERCISE?

Why aren't you doing more to eat better and get more exercise? If you said you don't have time, you're not alone. A shortage of time is one of the top reasons cited by respondents in the American Dietetic Association's nutrition trends survey. The following tactics can help you tackle the time challenge.

Enlist the supermarket as your kitchen assistant. A wealth of washed, chopped, sliced, and diced fruits and vegetables is available to pick. Salad bars are a source of ready-to-use recipe ingredients, such as chopped veggies for stir-fry or fruit salad for dessert. Swing by the deli for roasted chicken and salads or other premade side dishes. It doesn't take extra time to pick up good-for-you whole grain bread, cereal, and pasta, lean cuts of meat, skinless and boneless chicken breasts, and reduced-fat dairy products.

Don't be caught shorthanded. When you try to eat right, the last thing you want to do is run out of food and resort to fast, fat-laden meals. Instead, stock up on quick fixings for healthful meals and snacks. Combine precooked chicken strips, canned beans, a variety of pastas, quick-cooking brown rice, bagged salad mixes, frozen vegetables, and canned and dried fruit in a variety of ways. On weekends, cook a big casserole or pot of hearty soup or chili so you'll have several meals for the week and some to freeze.

Search for quick-and-easy recipes (see Shortcut Meals chapter, page 251) to get healthful meals on the table when time is short.

When there's no getting around fast food, choose small burgers, grilled chicken sandwiches, baked potatoes, salads with reduced-calorie dressing, low-fat milk, bottled water, or diet soft drinks. To save about 100 calories per serving, ask to have mayo or sauce left off of sandwiches. If you simply can't resist french fries, share an order or two with the whole family.

Schedule exercise classes or walking dates with a friend into your calendar or appointment book just as you would any important appointment. Pedal an exercise bike, lift light hand weights, or stretch while watching TV. Pop in an exercise video when you have a few free minutes. It all adds up, so use short snatches of time to take a quick walk or put on some favorite music and move!

---

disease, high blood pressure, and type 2 diabetes. If your starting weight is 200 pounds, losing 10 to 20 pounds and keeping them off puts you on the path to better health right away.

Making Change Permanent

Follow these guidelines to help stick to new hard-earned, healthful habits.

• Break it down in small steps. Rather than change everything at once, change eating and physical activity habits gradually. You're more likely to maintain new habits when you adopt them one or two at a time. Similarly, set short-term goals for weight loss in addition to your long-term goal. As you reach each short-term goal, you'll feel motivated to continue.

• Be specific. Rather than set vague goals, such as eating more fruit or walking more each day, take concrete action. Pack an apple for an afternoon snack or schedule a class after work or a 30-minute walk over your lunch hour.

• Help yourself succeed. Reaching goals takes thought and preparation. Stock up on foods you need for your eating plan. Pack a gym bag or walking shoes the night before so you can get to the gym during your lunch hour.

• Make it noteworthy. Keep a journal to outline goals, track progress, devise solutions to difficult situations, and highlight successes.

• Celebrate your successes. Reward progress with something other than food. Treat yourself to flowers, new walking shoes, or a manicure when you reach a short-term goal. Splurge on a new outfit or a complete makeover when you reach a long-term goal.

• Think progress, not perfection. It can take three to six months to establish a new habit. Don't be discouraged if you eat a bit too much or skip your walk one day. Just make sure you get right back on track.

Keeping It Off: Lessons from Successful Losers

For many people, losing weight is the easy part. Keeping it off is another story. If you can identify with this problem, take heart because there are plenty of long-term success stories. A collection of nearly 5,000 of them resides in the National Weight Control Registry, a database established in 1993 by researchers at the University of Colorado and University of Pittsburgh.

Registry members have maintained a weight loss of at least 30 pounds for at least one year. The average member has lost more than 60 pounds and kept it off for about five years. How each reached weight goals varies. Some created their own eating and exercise plan; others used methods such as joining a weight loss group, following a liquid diet, or receiving counseling from a doctor or registered dietitian. Though they reached their goals in different ways, their techniques for keeping off the weight are strikingly similar. Registry members tend to
• Modify fat intake and keep calories in check. On average, members get 24 percent of their calories from fat and consume 1,400 calories per day.
• Keep a watchful eye on their weight.
• Prepare for action. When weight creeps up, they immediately take steps to return to their goal weight. This usually means trimming food intake or increasing exercise.
• Make exercise a daily habit. Members burn about 2,800 calories per week by exercising one hour per day. Walking is the favorite activity.
• Eat breakfast. Nearly 8 out of 10 members eat breakfast every day. Researchers speculate that eating breakfast helps stave off overeating later in the day and provides the necessary energy to be physically active.
• Enjoy their new healthful lifestyle. The

longer members maintain their weight loss, the less effort it seems to take.

What's New in the Weight Loss World?

While eating fewer calories and being more physically active make up the foundation for a successful weight management plan, researchers continually unearth clues to tweak plans for better success. Stay tuned as research continues to unfold.

High or low protein? Middle-of-the-road may be the way to go. Researchers from the University of Illinois compared overweight women who consumed a balanced, higher-protein diet (10 ounces of meat daily) to overweight women who consumed a balanced, high-carbohydrate, lower-protein diet (about 5 ounces of meat daily). Both groups ate about 1,700 calories per day. After 10 weeks, both groups lost about 16 pounds, but the higher-protein group lost more body fat and retained more muscle mass. Researchers think the amino acid leucine, found in high-quality protein foods, such as beef, poultry, fish, eggs, and dairy products, is responsible for the beneficial effect.

Calcium flicks the fat-burning switch. Extensive research shows that consuming more calcium as part of a calorie-controlled weight-management plan may help burn more fat. Calcium turns on fat-burning machinery. Consuming 1,000 mg of calcium per day from dairy foods, such as milk, yogurt, and cheese, is more effective than taking calcium as pills. Choose two to three daily servings of fat-free or reduced-fat dairy products.

Go for oats. Research shows that people who eat oatmeal for breakfast experience less hunger during the morning and eat less at lunchtime than people who eat sugared cornflakes for breakfast. The fiber in oatmeal slows down the digestion process so you feel full longer.

Watery foods cut calories and soup up satisfaction. Research at Pennsylvania State University shows that humans tend to eat the same weight of food each day, regardless of calories. Eating more water-heavy foods, such as fruits, vegetables, cooked cereal, pasta and grains, stews and soups, may aid weight loss because these foods are filling and the high water content makes them less calorie-dense than some other foods. Take note: Drinking a glass of water with your meal doesn't seem to have the same effect. For best results, choose watery foods.

Kids and Weight: Cause for Alarm

More than 15 percent of American children and adolescents are overweight, according to recent government surveys. Alarmingly, that means about twice as many children and three times as many adolescents are overweight today compared to the number who tipped the scale only two decades ago.

Along with these sharp increases come worrisome signs of chronic diseases that were once common only among adults. Nearly 70 percent of overweight children exhibit one risk factor for heart disease, such as high blood cholesterol or high blood pressure; 39 percent of obese children exhibit two or more risk factors. Even type 2 diabetes (formerly called adult onset diabetes) is appearing more frequently in children.

Like adults, children carry around excess weight because they burn off fewer calories than they consume. While experts can't point to one particular reason for this caloric imbalance, frequent fast-food meals and high-calorie snacks and soft drink consumption are cited as culprits. Certainly the immobile lifestyle of many children is a contributor. Although the Dietary Guidelines for Americans recommends that children get at least 60 minutes of moderate physical activity daily, many get far less. What's keeping kids from exercising? Some blame little or no physical education at school; others fault too many hours spent daily watching TV or on computer or other electronic screens. According to the National Institute on

Media and the Family, kids ages 8 to 18 watch TV, play video games, and use the computer an average of nearly six and a half hours daily.

Is It OK to Put Kids on a Diet?

Restrictive diets are not generally recommended for overweight children. Children need sufficient calories and nutrients to grow and develop. Instead, experts usually promote healthful eating and physical activity. Good eating habits and exercise will help a child grow into his or her weight.

To determine the extent of a child's weight problem, the child's doctor can calculate BMI (see page 9) and plot the result on a sex-specific growth chart for children ages 2 to 20. When a child is seriously overweight, the doctor may recommend a treatment program that includes lifestyle counseling from a pediatrician, a registered dietitian, an exercise physiologist, and a psychologist.

What's a Parent to Do?
10 Food and Fitness Tips for a Healthy Family

Children see, children do, say health experts. A parent's job as a role model is the most important influence on children's eating and exercise habits. If you eat wisely and exercise, they'll be more likely to as well. Follow/enlist these tips to help you and your family.

1. Don't forbid favorite foods. Doing so will backfire. Kids like fast food, ice cream, candy, and soft drinks. If you forbid these foods, kids will most likely find another way to get them, and they may binge when they do. It's fine for children to enjoy these foods occasionally as long as portion size is small and frequency is occasional.

2. Don't go to the opposite extreme and allow a food free-for-all. Provide well-balanced meals and snacks that include a variety of

nutrient-dense foods. Decide whether it's OK to have ice cream for dessert or whether it's fresh fruit night.

3. Have fruits and veggies available. Stock an array of easy-to-eat produce for snack time. Baby carrots, red pepper strips, zucchini or cucumber slices, and broccoli florets are colorful and crunchy options to dip in reduced-fat salad dressing. Young children love the sweetness and novelty of frozen grapes or banana slices. Keep a bowl of favorite fruits in sight on the kitchen counter.

4. Get kids cooking. Children love to help in the kitchen. They take pride in their creations and are more likely to eat what they prepare. It's fun to cook together too.

5. Make yours an active family. Have fun together by practicing the latest dance steps, riding bikes, playing touch football, shooting hoops, swimming, or taking a walk after dinner. Treat kids to a trip to the zoo, museum, or a guided nature hike where they can learn, have fun, and be active.

6. Encourage foot and pedal power. Rather than drive kids everywhere, encourage them to walk or bike to school, to a friend's house, or to the convenience store if it's a safe, reasonable distance.

7. Assign kids active household chores, such as vacuuming, mopping, sweeping, dusting, pulling weeds, raking leaves, and walking the dog.

8. Strive to outstep each other. Fitness experts say that for good health, individuals should take 10,000 steps every day. Kids and adults enjoy tracking steps by wearing a step counter throughout the day. Step counters are available at sporting goods stores in a variety of price ranges. Get one for each family member and have a friendly competition to outstep each other.

WHAT TO EAT: A DAILY FOOD GUIDE

An eating plan that promotes good health is built on a foundation of whole grains, fruits, vegetables, lean meats, and low-fat dairy products. This chart outlines a healthful daily eating plan, what to eat—and how much.

What to Eat	Serving Sizes
5 to 11 servings of whole grain breads, cereals, rice, and pasta	1 slice bread; 1 ounce ready-to-eat cereal; 1/2 cup cooked cereal, rice, or pasta; 6-inch tortilla
3 to 5 servings of vegetables	2 cups raw leafy vegetables; 1 cup other cooked or raw vegetables; 1 cup vegetable juice
2 to 4 servings of fruit	1 medium piece whole fresh fruit; 1 cup chopped, cooked, frozen, or canned fruit; 1 cup fruit juice; 1/2 cup berries or cut-up fruit; 1/2 cup dried fruit
3 servings of fat-free milk, low-fat yogurt, and cheese	1 cup milk or yogurt; 1 1/2 ounces natural cheese; 2 ounces processed cheese
5 to 6 servings of lean meat, poultry, fish, dry beans, eggs, nuts, and soy foods	One serving is 1 ounce cooked lean meat, poultry, or fish. Count the following as 1 ounce: 1/4 cup cooked dry beans; 1 egg; 1 tablespoon peanut butter; 1/2 ounce nuts; 1/4 cup tofu; 1 ounce tempeh; 2 tablespoons hummus

9. Slash screen time. The American Academy of Pediatrics recommends that parents limit children's time spent watching TV, playing video games, and using the computer to one to two hours daily. Allow your child to decide how to use the alotted time.

10. People, including kids, resist change. Start small. Even one change a month amounts to many healthful new habits over time.

Web Resources

These websites provide more information about weight management.

cdc.gov Access extensive information about weight management and other health issues at the Centers for Disease Control and Prevention (CDC) website.

eatright.org For customized weight-management counseling, you can find a registered dietitian (R.D.) near you at the American Dietetic Association website.

acefitness.org The American Council on Exercise (ACE) website helps you find an ACE-certified personal trainer or fitness instructor in your area. Also check out the Fit Facts section for articles on safe and effective exercise.

bam.gov This CDC-sponsored website answers kids' questions about healthy eating, physical activity, and other health topics.

kidnetic.com This interactive, educational website for children and parents, sponsored by the International Food Information Council, promotes healthful eating and physical activity in fun ways.

win.niddk.nih.gov The Weight-Control Information Network (WIN) is a service of the National Institutes of Health. WIN was established in 1994 to raise awareness and provide up-to-date, science-based information on obesity, physical activity, weight control, and other related nutritional issues.

obesity.org The American Obesity Society focuses on changing public policy and perceptions about obesity and stresses education, research, and prevention of obesity.

Chapter 2

Breakfast

On the opener: Blueberry-Cornmeal Pancakes *(see recipe, page 28)*

EGGS & CHEESE

PANCAKES, WAFFLES & TOAST

HOT & COLD CEREAL

FRUIT & SMOOTHIES

- 2 tablespoons sliced almonds
- 1 yellow sweet pepper, cut in thin bite-size strips
- 1 fresh jalapeño chile pepper, seeded and chopped (see note, page 263)
- 1 tablespoon olive oil or cooking oil
- 4 medium tomatoes (about 1¼ pounds), peeled and chopped
- 1½ to 2 teaspoons purchased or homemade Mexican seasoning*
- ¼ teaspoon salt
- 4 eggs
  Salt (optional)
  Black pepper (optional)
- 1 medium ripe avocado, seeded, peeled, and sliced (optional)

1 Spread almonds in a large skillet. Cook, stirring occasionally, over medium heat for 4 to 5 minutes or until lightly browned. Remove toasted almonds from skillet; set aside. In the same skillet cook sweet pepper and jalapeño pepper in hot oil about 2 minutes or until tender. Stir in tomatoes, Mexican seasoning, and the ¼ teaspoon salt. Bring to boiling; reduce heat. Simmer, covered, for 5 minutes.

2 Break 1 of the eggs into a measuring cup. Carefully slide the egg into simmering tomato mixture. Repeat with remaining eggs. If desired, sprinkle the eggs lightly with additional salt and black pepper.

3 Cover and simmer the eggs over medium-low heat for 3 to 5 minutes or until the whites are completely set and yolks begin to thicken but are not hard. If desired, top with avocado slices. Sprinkle with the toasted almonds.

*Note: For homemade Mexican seasoning, combine 1 to 1½ teaspoons chili powder and ½ teaspoon ground cumin.

Southwest Skillet

START TO FINISH: 25 minutes
MAKES: 4 servings

NUTRITION FACTS per serving:

CALORIES 171
TOTAL FAT 11 g total fat (2 g sat. fat)
CHOLESTEROL 213 mg
PROTEIN 9 g
CARBOHYDRATE 11 g
FIBER 3 g
SODIUM 289 mg

EXCHANGES 2 Vegetable, 1 Meat, 1 Fat

Nonstick cooking spray

1 large onion, halved and thinly sliced

1 15-ounce can chunky chili-style tomato sauce

1 fresh jalapeño chile pepper, seeded and chopped (see note, page 263)

3 tablespoons snipped fresh cilantro

6 eggs

¼ teaspoon salt

⅛ teaspoon black pepper

¾ cup shredded Monterey Jack or cheddar cheese (3 ounces)

6 8-inch flour tortillas, warmed, or 6 slices bread, toasted

Ranch Eggs

PREP: 15 minutes   **BAKE:** 16 minutes
OVEN: 400°F   **MAKES:** 6 servings

NUTRITION FACTS per serving:

CALORIES 250
TOTAL FAT 12 g total fat (5 g sat. fat)
CHOLESTEROL 225 mg
PROTEIN 12 g
CARBOHYDRATE 22 g
FIBER 2 g
SODIUM 717 mg

EXCHANGES 1 Vegetable, 1 Starch, 1½ Meat

1 Coat a 12-inch ovenproof skillet with nonstick cooking spray. Preheat skillet over medium-high heat. Cook onion in hot skillet for 4 to 5 minutes or until tender. Remove from heat.

2 In a small bowl stir together the tomato sauce, jalapeño pepper, and cilantro. Pour sauce mixture over onions in skillet. Break 1 of the eggs into a measuring cup. Carefully slide the egg into simmering tomato sauce mixture. Repeat with remaining eggs. Sprinkle eggs with salt and black pepper.

3 Bake, uncovered, in a 400°F oven for 15 to 20 minutes or until eggs are set. Sprinkle with cheese; bake for 1 minute more. Serve with warmed tortillas or toast.

- ½ a medium onion, cut in very thin wedges
- 1 teaspoon olive oil
- 1 cup sliced fresh mushrooms
- 2 cloves garlic, minced
- ¼ teaspoon dried thyme, crushed
- 1 8-ounce can (about 1 cup) stewed tomatoes, drained
- 1 cup refrigerated or frozen egg product, thawed, or 2 eggs plus 2 egg whites
- 2 tablespoons water
- ¼ teaspoon coarsely ground black pepper
  Dash salt
  Nonstick cooking spray
- 1 teaspoon olive oil
- 2 tablespoons finely shredded Asiago or Parmesan cheese

Provençal Omelet

START TO FINISH: 30 minutes
MAKES: 2 servings

NUTRITION FACTS per serving:

CALORIES 214
TOTAL FAT 9 g total fat (2 g sat. fat)
CHOLESTEROL 8 mg
PROTEIN 17 g
CARBOHYDRATE 16 g
FIBER 1 g
SODIUM 557 mg

EXCHANGES 3 Vegetable, 2 Meat, ½ Fat

1 In a small skillet cook and stir onion in 1 teaspoon hot oil over medium heat for 3 minutes. Add mushrooms, garlic, and thyme; cook and stir for 3 minutes more. Add tomatoes. Bring to boiling; reduce heat. Simmer, uncovered, for 5 minutes.

2 Meanwhile, in a medium bowl beat together egg product or eggs and egg whites, the water, pepper, and salt. Coat a 10-inch nonstick skillet with sloped sides with nonstick cooking spray. Preheat over medium heat. Add 1 teaspoon oil, swirling to coat skillet. Add egg mixture. Immediately begin stirring egg mixture gently and continuously with a wooden or plastic spatula until mixture resembles small pieces of cooked egg surrounded by liquid egg. Stop stirring. Cook 30 to 60 seconds more or until egg mixture is set yet shiny.

3 Spoon half the tomato mixture on half the omelet; sprinkle with some of the cheese. Using a wide spatula, fold omelet in half. Cut omelet in half. Spoon remaining tomato mixture on omelet halves. Top with remaining cheese.

Poached Eggs with Polenta and Black Beans

START TO FINISH: 35 minutes
MAKES: 4 servings

NUTRITION FACTS per serving:

CALORIES 258
TOTAL FAT 10 g total fat (2 g sat. fat)
CHOLESTEROL 213 mg
PROTEIN 11 g
CARBOHYDRATE 30 g
FIBER 5 g
SODIUM 610 mg

EXCHANGES 2 Starch, 1 Meat, ½ Fat

3	medium roma tomatoes, seeded and chopped
½	cup canned black beans, rinsed and drained
2	tablespoons chopped red onion
1	fresh jalapeño chile pepper, seeded and finely chopped (see note, page 263)
1	tablespoon snipped fresh cilantro
2	teaspoons lime juice
1	teaspoon olive oil
⅛	teaspoon black pepper
1	16-ounce tube refrigerated cooked polenta, cut into 12 slices
1	tablespoon olive oil
4	eggs
	Salt (optional)
	Black pepper (optional)
2	teaspoons snipped fresh cilantro
	Fresh cilantro sprigs (optional)
	Lime wedges

1 For salsa, in a small bowl combine the tomatoes, black beans, red onion, jalapeño pepper, the 1 tablespoon cilantro, lime juice, 1 teaspoon oil, and ⅛ teaspoon black pepper. Set aside.

2 In a 12-inch nonstick skillet cook the polenta slices in the 1 tablespoon hot oil over medium heat for 14 to 16 minutes or until polenta is browned; turn once.

3 Meanwhile, fill a large skillet half full with water. Bring to boiling; reduce heat to simmering. Break 1 of the eggs into a measuring cup. Carefully slide egg into simmering water, holding the lip of the cup as close to the water as possible. Repeat with the remaining eggs. If desired, sprinkle with salt and black pepper. Simmer, uncovered, for 3 to 5 minutes or until the egg whites are completely set and yolks begin to thicken but are not hard. Using a slotted spoon, remove eggs.

4 To serve, divide the polenta slices among 4 dinner plates. Top with eggs and salsa. Sprinkle with snipped cilantro. If desired, garnish with cilantro sprigs. Serve with lime wedges.

1   16-ounce container refrigerated egg product or 8 slightly beaten eggs

¼   cup milk

¼   cup thinly sliced green onions (2)

¼   teaspoon garlic salt

¼   teaspoon black pepper

1   tablespoon butter or margarine

1   cup refrigerated shredded hash brown potatoes

½   cup diced low-fat, reduced-sodium cooked boneless ham (2 ounces)

⅓   cup shredded reduced-fat cheddar cheese

1 In a medium bowl beat together egg product or eggs, milk, green onions, garlic salt, and pepper; set aside. In a large nonstick skillet heat butter over medium heat until melted. Add potatoes and ham to skillet. Cook for 6 to 8 minutes or until light brown, stirring occasionally. Add egg mixture. Cook over medium heat, without stirring, until mixture begins to set on the bottom and around edge.

2 With a spatula or large spoon, lift and fold the partially cooked egg product mixture so the uncooked portion flows underneath. Continue cooking for 2 to 3 minutes more or until egg product mixture is cooked through yet is still glossy and moist. Remove from heat immediately. Sprinkle with shredded cheese. Serve warm.

Ham and Potato Scramble

START TO FINISH: 25 minutes
MAKES: 4 servings

NUTRITION FACTS per serving:

CALORIES 175
TOTAL FAT 6 g total fat (3 g sat. fat)
CHOLESTEROL 23 mg
PROTEIN 19 g
CARBOHYDRATE 10 g
FIBER 1 g
SODIUM 593 mg

EXCHANGES ½ Starch, 2½ Meat

1½ pounds fresh asparagus or two 9- or 10-ounce packages frozen cut asparagus

1 medium yellow sweet pepper, cut into ¼-inch-wide strips

⅓ cup chopped onion (1 small)

1 small zucchini, halved lengthwise and cut into ¼-inch slices (about 1 cup)

10 slightly beaten eggs

1 cup milk

2 tablespoons snipped fresh flat-leaf parsley

1¼ teaspoons salt

¼ to ½ teaspoon black pepper

Vegetable Frittata

PREP: 30 minutes **BAKE:** 35 minutes
OVEN: 350°F **STAND:** 10 minutes
MAKES: 8 servings

NUTRITION FACTS per serving:

CALORIES 130
TOTAL FAT 7 g total fat (2 g sat. fat)
CHOLESTEROL 268 mg
PROTEIN 10 g
CARBOHYDRATE 7 g
FIBER 1 g
SODIUM 460 mg

EXCHANGES 1 Vegetable, 1 Meat

1 Butter a 2-quart rectangular baking dish; set aside.

2 If using fresh asparagus, snap off and discard woody bases. If desired, scrape off scales. Cut into 1-inch pieces.

3 In a large saucepan bring about 1 inch water to boiling. Add asparagus, pepper strips, and onion. Bring just to boiling; reduce heat slightly. Cover and boil about 1 minute or until vegetables are crisp-tender. Drain well. Stir zucchini into vegetable mixture; spread vegetables evenly in prepared baking dish.

4 In a large bowl combine eggs, milk, parsley, salt, and black pepper. Pour over vegetables in baking dish. Bake, uncovered, in a 350°F oven about 35 minutes or until a knife inserted near the center comes out clean. Let stand for 10 minutes before serving.

Nonstick cooking spray

- 3 eggs
- ½ cup all-purpose flour
- ½ cup milk
- ¼ teaspoon salt
- ¼ cup orange marmalade
- 3 cups sliced fresh fruit (such as strawberries, peeled kiwifruit, nectarines, pears, or peeled peaches)

1 Lightly coat six 5-inch individual baking dishes, 4½-inch pie plates, or 10-ounce custard cups with nonstick cooking spray; set aside.

2 For batter, in a medium bowl use a wire whisk or rotary beater to beat eggs until combined. Add flour, milk, and salt; beat until mixture is smooth. Immediately pour batter into prepared baking dishes. Bake in a 400°F oven for 20 to 25 minutes or until puffed and brown.

3 Meanwhile, in a small saucepan melt the orange marmalade over low heat. To serve, top pancakes with fruit; spoon melted marmalade over fruit. Serve warm.

Large Puffed Oven Pancake: Place 2 tablespoons butter or margarine in a 10-inch ovenproof skillet. Place skillet in a 400°F oven for 3 to 5 minutes or until butter melts. Meanwhile, prepare batter as above. Immediately pour batter into the hot skillet. Bake in the 400°F oven for 20 to 25 minutes or until puffed and brown. Serve as above.

Individual Puffed Oven Pancakes

PREP: 10 minutes **BAKE:** 20 minutes
OVEN: 400°F **MAKES:** 6 servings

NUTRITION FACTS per serving:

CALORIES 140
TOTAL FAT 3 g total fat (1 g sat. fat)
CHOLESTEROL 108 mg
PROTEIN 5 g
CARBOHYDRATE 23 g
FIBER 2 g
SODIUM 147 mg

EXCHANGES 1½ Fruit, 1 Meat

1 cup all-purpose flour
2 tablespoons cornmeal
1 tablespoon granulated sugar
1 teaspoon baking powder
½ teaspoon baking soda
¼ teaspoon salt
¼ teaspoon ground cinnamon
1 beaten egg
1 cup buttermilk or sour milk*
2 tablespoons cooking oil
1 cup fresh or frozen blueberries
Sifted powdered sugar (optional)
Maple or blueberry-flavored syrup (optional)

Blueberry-Cornmeal Pancakes

PREP: 10 minutes
COOK: 4 minutes per batch
MAKES: 4 or 5 servings

NUTRITION FACTS per serving:

CALORIES 253
TOTAL FAT 9 g total fat (2 g sat. fat)
CHOLESTEROL 56 mg
PROTEIN 7 g
CARBOHYDRATE 35 g
FIBER 3 g
SODIUM 484 mg

EXCHANGES 1 Starch, 1½ Other Carbo., 1 Fat

1 In a medium bowl combine flour, cornmeal, granulated sugar, baking powder, baking soda, salt, and cinnamon. Make a well in center of flour mixture; set aside.

2 In another medium bowl stir together the egg, buttermilk, and oil. Add egg mixture all at once to flour mixture. Stir just until moistened (batter should be lumpy). Gently fold in blueberries.

3 For each pancake, pour or spread about ¼ cup of the batter into a 4-inch circle onto a hot, lightly greased griddle or heavy skillet. Cook over medium heat about 2 minutes on each side or until pancakes are golden brown, turning when pancakes have bubbly surfaces and edges are slightly dry. Serve warm. If desired, sprinkle with powdered sugar. If desired, pass syrup.

*Note: To make 1 cup sour milk, place 1 tablespoon lemon juice or vinegar in a glass measuring cup. Add enough milk to equal 1 cup total liquid; stir. Let the mixture stand for 5 minutes before using it in a recipe.

- 2   cups all-purpose flour
- 2   tablespoons brown sugar
- 1   tablespoon baking powder
- ½   teaspoon salt
- ½   teaspoon pumpkin pie spice
- 1½   cups fat-free milk
- 1   cup canned pumpkin
- ½   cup refrigerated or frozen egg product, thawed
- 2   tablespoons cooking oil
- 1   recipe Orange Syrup
- 1   orange, peeled and sectioned (optional)

1 In a medium bowl stir together the flour, brown sugar, baking powder, salt, and pumpkin pie spice. Make a well in the center of the flour mixture.

2 In another medium bowl combine the milk, pumpkin, egg product, and oil. Add milk mixture all at once to flour mixture. Stir just until moistened (batter should be lumpy).

3 Pour about ¾ cup batter onto grids of a preheated, lightly greased waffle baker. Close lid quickly. Bake until waffle maker signals or until waffle is golden brown. When done, use a fork to lift waffle off grids. Repeat with remaining batter. Serve waffles warm with Orange Syrup and, if desired, orange sections.

Orange Syrup: In a small saucepan stir together 1 cup orange juice, 2 tablespoons honey, 2½ teaspoons cornstarch, and ¼ teaspoon ground cinnamon. Cook and stir until thickened and bubbly. Cook and stir for 2 minutes more. Serve warm. Makes about 1 cup.

Pumpkin Waffles with Orange Syrup

PREP: 10 minutes
BAKE: per waffle baker directions
MAKES: 10 waffles

NUTRITION FACTS per serving:

CALORIES 173
TOTAL FAT 3 g total fat (1 g sat. fat)
CHOLESTEROL 1 mg
PROTEIN 5 g
CARBOHYDRATE 31 g
FIBER 1 g
SODIUM 279 mg

EXCHANGES 2 Starch

Banana French Toast

PREP: 25 minutes **CHILL:** 6 to 24 hours
BAKE: 25 minutes **STAND:** 10 minutes
OVEN: 425°F/ 325°F
MAKES: 6 servings

NUTRITION FACTS per serving:

CALORIES 325
TOTAL FAT 9 g total fat (3 g sat. fat)
CHOLESTEROL 73 mg
PROTEIN 10 g
CARBOHYDRATE 51 g
FIBER 3 g
SODIUM 342 mg

EXCHANGES 1½ Fruit, 2 Starch, ½ Meat, 1 Fat

2 medium ripe bananas, cut into ¼-inch slices (about 1⅓ cups)
1 tablespoon lemon juice
12 ½-inch slices French bread
¼ cup miniature semisweet chocolate pieces
2 beaten eggs
¾ cup milk
2 tablespoons honey
½ teaspoon vanilla
¼ teaspoon ground cinnamon
¼ cup sliced almonds
1 teaspoon sugar
   Maple-flavored syrup (optional)

1 In a small bowl gently toss bananas with lemon juice. Grease a 2-quart square baking dish. Arrange half of the bread slices in the prepared baking dish. Layer bananas over bread in baking dish. Top with chocolate pieces and remaining bread slices.

2 In a medium bowl combine eggs, milk, honey, vanilla, and cinnamon. Pour liquid slowly over bread to coat evenly. Cover and chill for at least 6 hours or up to 24 hours.

3 Uncover the baking dish. Sprinkle bread with almonds and sugar. Bake in a 425°F oven for 5 minutes. Reduce oven temperature to 325°F. Bake for 20 to 25 minutes more or until knife inserted near the center comes out clean and top of French toast is light brown. Let stand for 10 minutes before serving. If desired, serve with maple-flavored syrup.

2   1-ounce envelopes instant oatmeal (plain)

1   medium banana, peeled and sliced

Desired fresh fruit (such as blueberries, sliced strawberries, and/or sliced peaches)

2   tablespoons chopped pecans, toasted

2   teaspoons caramel-flavored ice cream topping

Milk (optional)

1 In two microwave-safe bowls prepare oatmeal according to package directions. Top each serving with banana slices, fresh fruit, and pecans. Drizzle with ice cream topping. If desired, heat in microwave on 100% power (high) for 30 seconds. If desired, serve with milk.

Fruit and Caramel Oatmeal

START TO FINISH: 10 minutes
MAKES: 2 servings

NUTRITION FACTS per serving:

CALORIES 231
TOTAL FAT 7 g total fat (1 g sat. fat)
CHOLESTEROL 0 mg
PROTEIN 6 g
CARBOHYDRATE 39 g
FIBER 6 g
SODIUM 302 mg

EXCHANGES 1½ Fruit, 1 Starch, 1 Fat

Honey Granola with Yogurt

PREP: 15 minutes   **BAKE:** 30 minutes
OVEN: 325°F   **MAKES:** 12 servings

NUTRITION FACTS per serving:

CALORIES 244
TOTAL FAT 4 g total fat (1 g sat. fat)
CHOLESTEROL 2 mg
PROTEIN 11 g
CARBOHYDRATE 44 g
FIBER 5 g
SODIUM 96 mg

EXCHANGES 1 Milk, ½ Fruit, 1½ Starch, ½ Fat

Nonstick cooking spray
2½ cups regular rolled oats
1 cup wheat flakes
⅓ cup toasted wheat germ
⅓ cup sliced almonds or pecan pieces
⅓ cup unsweetened pineapple juice or apple juice
⅓ cup honey
¼ teaspoon ground allspice
¼ teaspoon ground cinnamon
6 cups desired fat-free yogurt
4 cups fresh fruit (such as blueberries, seedless green grapes, raspberries, sliced strawberries, and/or chopped peaches)

1 Coat a 15×10×1-inch baking pan with nonstick cooking spray; set aside. In a large bowl stir together the oats, wheat flakes, wheat germ, and nuts. In a small saucepan stir together juice, honey, allspice, and cinnamon. Cook and stir just until boiling. Remove from heat. Pour over oat mixture, tossing just until coated.

2 Spread the oat mixture evenly in prepared pan. Bake in a 325°F oven for 30 to 35 minutes or until oats are lightly browned, stirring twice. Remove from oven. Immediately turn oats mixture out onto a large piece of foil; cool completely.

3 For each serving, spoon ½ cup of the yogurt into a bowl. Top with ⅓ cup of the oat mixture and ⅓ cup desired fruit.

Make-ahead directions: Prepare as above through step 2. Cover and chill for up to 2 weeks. For longer storage, seal in freezer bags and freeze for up to 3 months.

- 1 lemon
- 1 orange or tangerine
- 1 lime
- ⅓ cup sugar
- 2 large pears, cored and sliced
- 2 medium papayas, peeled, seeded, and cubed
- 1 cup seedless red grapes, halved

1 Halve lemon, orange, and lime; squeeze out all of the juices (about ¾ cup total), reserving citrus shells. In a small saucepan combine the juices, sugar, and half of the citrus shells; bring to boiling. Discard remaining shells. Cook and stir until sugar dissolves; reduce heat. Simmer, uncovered, for 5 minutes. Carefully remove shells; discard.

2 Place pears, papayas, and grapes in a large bowl. Pour hot juice mixture over fruit, gently stirring to mix. Cover and chill for at least 1 hour or up to 4 hours.

Sunrise Fruit Compote

PREP: 20 minutes   **CHILL:** 1 to 4 hours
MAKES: 6 servings

NUTRITION FACTS per serving:

CALORIES 159
TOTAL FAT 1 g total fat (0 g sat. fat)
CHOLESTEROL 0 mg
PROTEIN 1 g
CARBOHYDRATE 40 g
FIBER 4 g
SODIUM 7 mg

EXCHANGES 2½ Fruit

1 cup vanilla-flavored soymilk or
1 cup light or low-fat milk plus
¼ teaspoon vanilla

¼ cup orange juice

¼ cup refrigerated or frozen egg
product, thawed

1 to 2 tablespoons honey

½ cup chopped mango

½ cup frozen strawberries,
raspberries, blueberries, or
boysenberries

Fresh mint sprigs (optional)

1 In a blender container combine soymilk, orange juice, egg product, and honey. Cover and blend for 10 seconds.

2 Add mango and frozen berries. Cover and blend until smooth. Immediately pour into two glasses. If desired, garnish with fresh mint.

Berry-Mango Soy Smoothie

START TO FINISH: 10 minutes
MAKES: 2 (10-ounce) servings

NUTRITION FACTS per serving:

- -

CALORIES 168
TOTAL FAT 2 g total fat (0 g sat. fat)
CHOLESTEROL 0 mg
PROTEIN 7 g
CARBOHYDRATE 31 g
FIBER 3 g
SODIUM 117 mg

EXCHANGES ½ Milk, 1½ Fruit, ½ Meat

On the opener: Apple-Cherry-Filled Rolls (see recipe, page 45)

QUICK BREADS

YEAST BREADS

1¾ cups all-purpose flour

½ cup sugar

2 teaspoons baking powder

¼ teaspoon salt

1 slightly beaten egg white

¾ cup fat-free milk

3 tablespoons cooking oil

1 teaspoon finely shredded
     orange peel

½ cup snipped dried tart cherries

2 tablespoons chopped walnuts

1 Line twelve 2½-inch muffin pans with paper bake cups; set aside. In a medium bowl stir together flour, sugar, baking powder, and salt. Make a well in center of flour mixture; set aside.

2 In another bowl combine egg white, milk, oil, and orange peel. Add milk mixture all at once to flour mixture. Stir just until moistened (batter should be lumpy). Gently fold in cherries and nuts.

3 Spoon batter into prepared muffin cups, filling each two-thirds full. Bake in a 400°F oven for 18 to 20 minutes or until golden and a wooden toothpick inserted in centers comes out clean. Cool in muffin cups on wire rack for 5 minutes. Remove from muffin cups; serve warm.

Cherry-Nut Muffins

PREP: 15 minutes   **BAKE:** 18 minutes
OVEN: 400°F   **STAND:** 5 minutes
MAKES: 12 muffins

NUTRITION FACTS per muffin:

CALORIES 154
TOTAL FAT 4 g total fat (1g sat. fat)
CHOLESTEROL 0 mg
PROTEIN 3 g
CARBOHYDRATE 26 g
FIBER 1 g
SODIUM 128 mg

EXCHANGES 1½ Starch, ½ Fat

Nonstick cooking spray

1½	cups all-purpose flour
⅓	cup sugar
1	teaspoon baking powder
1	teaspoon ground cinnamon
¼	teaspoon baking soda
⅛	teaspoon salt
⅔	cup buttermilk or sour milk*
1	egg or ¼ cup refrigerated or frozen egg product, thawed
3	tablespoons cooking oil
¼	cup apricot, peach, or raspberry spread

1 Coat twelve 2½-inch muffin cups with nonstick cooking spray or line with paper bake cups; set aside. In a medium bowl stir together flour, sugar, baking powder, cinnamon, baking soda, and salt. Make a well in the center of the flour mixture; set aside.

2 In a small bowl stir together buttermilk, egg or egg product, and oil. Add buttermilk mixture all at once to flour mixture. Stir just until moistened (batter should be lumpy).

3 Spoon batter into prepared muffin cups, filling each about one-fourth full. Place 1 teaspoon of the spreadable fruit in center of each. Add remaining batter.

4 Bake in a 400°F oven for 18 to 20 minutes or until golden. Cool in muffin cups on a wire rack for 5 minutes. Remove from muffin cups. Serve warm.

*Note: To make ⅔ cup sour milk, place 2 teaspoons lemon juice or vinegar in a glass measuring cup. Add enough milk to equal ⅔ cup total liquid; stir. Let mixture stand for 5 minutes before using.

Fruit-Filled Muffins

PREP: 20 minutes **BAKE:** 18 minutes
OVEN: 400°F **MAKES:** 12 muffins

NUTRITION FACTS per muffin:

CALORIES 129
TOTAL FAT 4 g total fat (1 g sat. fat)
CHOLESTEROL 18 mg
PROTEIN 2 g
CARBOHYDRATE 21 g
FIBER 0 g
SODIUM 104 mg

EXCHANGES ½ Fruit, 1 Starch, ½ Fat

1	cup fresh cranberries
2	tablespoons sugar
2	cups all-purpose flour
¼	to ½ cup sugar
4	teaspoons baking powder
1	teaspoon finely shredded orange peel
½	teaspoon salt
1	beaten egg
¾	cup milk
¼	cup butter, melted

1 Grease twelve to fourteen 2½-inch muffin cups or line with paper bake cups. Set aside. In a medium bowl toss cranberries with the 2 tablespoons sugar. Set aside.

2 In a large bowl combine flour, the ¼ to ½ cup sugar, the baking powder, orange peel, and salt. Stir well. In a small bowl combine egg, milk, and butter. Make a well in the center of the flour mixture; add egg mixture and cranberries. Stir just until moistened (batter should be lumpy). Spoon into prepared muffin cups, filling each about two-thirds full.

3 Bake in a 400°F oven about 15 minutes or until golden. Cool in muffin cups on a wire rack for 5 minutes. Remove from muffin cups. Serve warm.

Cranberry Muffins

PREP: 20 minutes   **BAKE:** 15 minutes
OVEN: 400°F
MAKES: 12 to 14 muffins

NUTRITION FACTS per muffin:

CALORIES 147
TOTAL FAT 5 g total fat (3 g sat. fat)
CHOLESTEROL 30 mg
PROTEIN 3 g
CARBOHYDRATE 22 g
FIBER 1 g fiber
SODIUM 285 mg

EXCHANGES 1½ Starch, ½ Fat

2 cups all-purpose flour

4 teaspoons baking powder

½ teaspoon cream of tartar

¼ teaspoon salt

¼ cup shortening

¾ cup fat-free milk

2 tablespoons sugar

1 teaspoon ground cinnamon

Sugar and Spice Biscuits

PREP: 15 minutes **BAKE:** 10 minutes
OVEN: 450°F **MAKES:** 12 biscuits

NUTRITION FACTS per biscuit:

CALORIES 121
TOTAL FAT 4 g total fat (1 g sat. fat)
CHOLESTEROL 0 mg
PROTEIN 3 g
CARBOHYDRATE 18 g
FIBER 1 g
SODIUM 190 mg

EXCHANGES 1 Starch, 1 Fat

1 Grease twelve 2½-inch muffin cups; set aside. In a large bowl stir together flour, baking powder, cream of tartar, and salt. Using a pastry blender, cut in shortening until mixture resembles coarse crumbs. Make a well in the center; add milk. Stir just until dough clings together.

2 Turn dough out onto a lightly floured surface. Knead by folding and gently pressing dough for 10 to 12 strokes or until dough is nearly smooth. Divide dough in half. Roll one portion into a 12×10-inch rectangle. In a small bowl combine the sugar and cinnamon. Sprinkle some of the sugar mixture over the rectangle.

3 Cut rectangle into five 12×2-inch strips. Stack the strips on top of each other. Cut into six 2-inch-square stacks. Place each stack, cut sides down, in a prepared muffin cup. Repeat with remaining dough and sugar mixture.

4 Bake in a 450°F oven for 10 to 12 minutes or until golden. Serve warm.

- 2 cups all-purpose flour
- 2½ teaspoons baking powder
- ¼ teaspoon salt
- 6 tablespoons butter
- ¾ cup small-curd cream-style cottage cheese
- ⅔ cup milk
- 2 tablespoons snipped fresh chives or thinly sliced green onion tops

1 Line a baking sheet with parchment paper; set aside.

2 In a medium bowl stir together flour, baking powder, and salt. Using a pastry blender, cut in butter until mixture resembles coarse crumbs. Make a well in the center of flour mixture; set aside.

3 In a small bowl combine cottage cheese, milk, and chives or green onion tops. Add mixture all at once to flour mixture. Using a fork, stir just until moistened.

4 Drop dough by generous tablespoonfuls onto prepared baking sheet. Bake in a 425°F oven for 15 to 18 minutes or until golden. Remove from parchment to wire rack; serve warm.

Cottage Cheese-Chive Biscuits

PREP: 20 minutes
BAKE: 15 minutes
OVEN: 425°F
MAKES: 12 biscuits

NUTRITION FACTS per biscuit:

CALORIES 144
TOTAL FAT 7 g total fat (4 g sat. fat)
CHOLESTEROL 19 mg
PROTEIN 4 g
CARBOHYDRATE 16 g
FIBER 1 g
SODIUM 254 mg

EXCHANGES 1 Starch, 1½ Fat

1½ cups all-purpose flour

1 teaspoon ground cinnamon

½ teaspoon baking soda

½ teaspoon salt

¼ teaspoon baking powder

¼ teaspoon ground nutmeg

1 beaten egg

1 cup sugar

1 cup finely shredded, unpeeled zucchini

¼ cup cooking oil

½ cup chopped walnuts or pecans, toasted

Zucchini Bread

PREP: 20 minutes   **BAKE:** 50 minutes
OVEN: 350°F   **STAND:** Overnight
MAKES: 1 loaf (16 servings)

NUTRITION FACTS per serving:

CALORIES 146
TOTAL FAT 6 g total fat (1 g sat. fat)
CHOLESTEROL 13 mg
PROTEIN 2 g
CARBOHYDRATE 21 g
FIBER 1 g
SODIUM 23 mg

EXCHANGES 1½ Starch, ½ Fat

1 Grease the bottom and ½ inch up sides of an 8×4×2-inch loaf pan; set aside. In a medium bowl stir together flour, cinnamon, baking soda, salt, baking powder, and nutmeg. Make a well in center of flour mixture; set aside.

2 In another medium bowl stir together egg, sugar, shredded zucchini, and oil. Add zucchini mixture all at once to flour mixture. Stir just until moistened (batter should be lumpy). Fold in nuts. Spoon batter into prepared pan.

3 Bake in a 350°F oven for 50 to 55 minutes or until a wooden toothpick inserted near center comes out clean. Cool in pan on a wire rack for 10 minutes. Remove from pan. Cool completely on a wire rack. Wrap and store overnight before slicing.

- 1½ cups buttermilk
- ⅔ cup water
- ¼ cup sugar
- 2 tablespoons butter or margarine
- 1½ teaspoons salt
- ¾ cup instant mashed potato flakes
- 2 tablespoons snipped fresh sage or 2 teaspoons dried sage, crushed
- 4¼ to 4¾ cups all-purpose flour
- 2 packages active dry yeast

1 In a medium saucepan bring buttermilk, water, sugar, butter, and salt just to boiling. (Mixture may appear curdled.) Remove from heat. Stir in potato flakes; let stand until temperature is 120°F to 130°F (about 15 minutes). Stir in sage.

2 In a large mixing bowl stir together 1½ cups of the all-purpose flour and the yeast. Add potato mixture. Beat with an electric mixer on low to medium speed for 30 seconds, scraping side of bowl constantly. Beat on high speed for 3 minutes. Using a wooden spoon, stir in as much of the remaining flour as you can.

3 Turn out dough onto a lightly floured surface. Knead in enough of the remaining flour to make a moderately stiff dough that is smooth and elastic (6 to 8 minutes total). Shape into a ball. Place in a lightly greased bowl; turn once to grease the surface of dough. Cover and let rise in a warm place until double in size (45 to 60 minutes).

4 Punch dough down. Turn out onto a lightly floured surface. Divide in half. Cover and let rest for 10 minutes. Grease 2 large baking sheets; set aside. Divide each half of the dough into 12 pieces. Shape pieces into balls. Arrange on prepared baking sheets about 2 inches apart. Loosely cover; let rise until nearly double in size (about 30 minutes).

5 Bake rolls in a 350°F oven about 12 minutes or until golden. Remove rolls from baking sheets; cool slightly on wire racks. Serve warm.

Potato Rolls

PREP: 45 minutes   **RISE:** 1¼ hours
BAKE: 12 minutes   **OVEN:** 350°F
MAKES: 24 rolls

NUTRITION FACTS per roll:

CALORIES 104
TOTAL FAT 1 g total fat (1 g sat. fat)
CHOLESTEROL 3 mg
PROTEIN 3 g
CARBOHYDRATE 20 g
FIBER 1 g
SODIUM 174 mg

EXCHANGES 1½ Starch

Nonstick cooking spray

2	cups all-purpose flour
1	package active dry yeast
½	cup cream-style cottage cheese
½	cup water
1	tablespoon sugar
1	tablespoon butter
2	teaspoons fennel seeds, crushed
1	teaspoon dried minced onion
½	teaspoon salt
¼	teaspoon coarsely ground black pepper
1	egg
½	cup toasted wheat germ

Fennel Batter Rolls

PREP: 20 minutes   **RISE:** 50 minutes
BAKE: 15 minutes   **OVEN:** 375°F
MAKES: 12 rolls

NUTRITION FACTS per roll:

CALORIES 119
TOTAL FAT 3 g total fat (1 g sat. fat)
CHOLESTEROL 22 mg
PROTEIN 5 g
CARBOHYDRATE 19 g
FIBER 1 g
SODIUM 149 mg

EXCHANGES 1½ Starch

1 Lightly coat twelve 2½-inch muffin cups with nonstick cooking spray; set aside. In a medium mixing bowl stir together 1 cup of the flour and the yeast.

2 In a small saucepan heat and stir cottage cheese, the water, sugar, butter, fennel seeds, dried onion, salt, and pepper just until warm (120°F to 130°F) and butter almost melts. Add cottage cheese mixture to flour mixture; add egg. Beat with an electric mixer on low to medium speed for 30 seconds, scraping bowl constantly. Beat on high speed for 3 minutes. Using a wooden spoon, stir in the remaining 1 cup flour and the wheat germ (batter will be stiff).

3 Spoon the batter into the prepared muffin cups. Cover and let rise in a warm place until nearly double in size (50 to 60 minutes).

4 Bake in a 375°F oven for 15 to 20 minutes or until golden. Immediately remove from muffin cups. Serve warm or cool.

Nonstick cooking spray

1 16-ounce package hot roll mix
1 cup chopped, peeled apple
¼ cup dried tart cherries
2 tablespoons brown sugar
½ teaspoon ground cinnamon
1 recipe Orange Icing

1 Lightly coat 2 baking sheets with nonstick cooking spray; set aside.

2 Prepare hot roll mix according to package directions through the resting step. Meanwhile, for filling, in a small bowl stir together apple, dried cherries, brown sugar, and cinnamon.

3 Divide dough in 16 portions. Flatten one portion of dough to a 4-inch circle; spoon 1 rounded teaspoon of filling onto the dough. Shape the dough around the filling to enclose, pulling dough until smooth and rounded. Place, rounded side up, on prepared baking sheet. Repeat with remaining dough and filling. Cover; let rise until double (about 30 minutes).

4 Bake in a 375°F oven for 13 to 15 minutes or until golden. Cool slightly on a wire rack. Drizzle with Orange Icing. Serve warm.

Orange Icing: In a small bowl stir together 1 cup sifted powdered sugar and enough orange juice (1 to 2 tablespoons) to make of drizzling consistency.

Apple-Cherry-Filled Rolls

PREP: 30 minutes **RISE:** 30 minutes
BAKE: 13 minutes **OVEN:** 375°F
MAKES: 16 rolls

NUTRITION FACTS per roll:

CALORIES 165
TOTAL FAT 2 g total fat (0 g sat. fat)
CHOLESTEROL 13 mg
PROTEIN 4 g
CARBOHYDRATE 33 g
FIBER 0 g
SODIUM 186 mg

EXCHANGES ½ Fruit, 1½ Starch

1¼ cups all-purpose flour

2 teaspoons sugar

1½ teaspoons baking powder

½ teaspoon salt

½ cup milk

2 tablespoons butter, melted

2 teaspoons sesame seeds

1 In a medium bowl stir together the flour, sugar, baking powder, and salt. Add milk, stirring just until moistened. Turn dough out onto a well-floured surface; knead gently three to five times. Pat or roll dough into a 10×5-inch rectangle. Cut crosswise in 12 sticks, flouring knife between cuts.

2 Add melted butter to a 13×9×2-inch baking pan; tilt pan to coat bottom. Place breadsticks in pan, turning once to coat with butter; arrange evenly in pan. Sprinkle with sesame seeds. Bake in a 450°F oven for 14 to 16 minutes or until golden. Serve warm.

Soft Breadsticks

PREP: 15 minutes

OVEN: 450°F

BAKE: 14 minutes

MAKES: 12 breadsticks

NUTRITION FACTS per breadstick:

CALORIES 72

TOTAL FAT 3 g total fat (1 g sat. fat)

CHOLESTEROL 6 mg

PROTEIN 2 g

CARBOHYDRATE 10 g

FIBER 0 g

SODIUM 173 mg

EXCHANGES ½ Starch, ½ Fat

- 2¾ to 3¼ cups all-purpose flour
- 1 package active dry yeast
- ¼ cup grated Parmesan cheese
- 1 teaspoon dried Italian seasoning, crushed
- ¾ teaspoon salt
- ½ teaspoon cracked black pepper
- 1 cup warm water (120°F to 130°F)
- ½ cup shredded Monterey Jack cheese with jalapeño peppers or shredded Monterey Jack cheese (2 ounces)
- 2 tablespoons cooking oil

1 In a large mixing bowl combine 1¼ cups of the flour, the yeast, Parmesan cheese, Italian seasoning, salt, and black pepper. Add the warm water, Monterey Jack cheese, and oil. Beat with an electric mixer on low to medium speed for 30 seconds, scraping bowl constantly. Beat on high speed for 3 minutes. Using a wooden spoon, stir in as much of the remaining flour as you can.

2 Turn out dough onto a lightly floured surface. Knead in enough of the remaining flour to make a moderately stiff dough that is smooth and elastic (6 to 8 minutes total). Shape dough into a ball. Place in a lightly greased bowl; turn once. Cover; let rise in a warm place until double (about 1 hour). Punch dough down.

3 Turn out dough onto lightly floured surface; cover and let rest for 10 minutes. Grease baking sheets; set aside. Divide the dough in thirds. On a lightly floured surface, roll each portion in a 14×10-inch rectangle. Using a pizza cutter or sharp knife, cut the dough lengthwise in ½-inch strips.

4 For each breadstick, pick up two dough strips together and twist several times; press ends together. Place breadsticks ½ inch apart on prepared baking sheets.

5 Bake in a 400°F oven for 10 to 12 minutes or until golden. Remove from baking sheets; cool on wire racks.

Pepper Cheese Breadsticks

PREP: 40 minutes   **RISE:** 1 hour
BAKE: 10 minutes   **OVEN:** 400°F
MAKES: 30 breadsticks

NUTRITION FACTS per breadstick:

CALORIES 57
TOTAL FAT 2 g total fat (1 g sat. fat)
CHOLESTEROL 2 mg
PROTEIN 2 g
CARBOHYDRATE 8 g
FIBER 0 g
SODIUM 81 mg

EXCHANGES ½ Starch

Parmesan and Pine Nut Focaccia

PREP: 20 minutes   **RISE:** 30 minutes
BAKE: 15 minutes   **COOL:** 10 minutes
OVEN: 375°F   **MAKES:** 24 servings

NUTRITION FACTS per serving:

CALORIES 95
TOTAL FAT 3 g total fat (0 g sat. fat)
CHOLESTEROL 9 mg
PROTEIN 4 g
CARBOHYDRATE 15 g
FIBER 0 g
SODIUM 121 mg

EXCHANGES 1 Starch, ½ Fat

Nonstick cooking spray
1 16-ounce package hot roll mix
1 egg
2 tablespoons olive oil
1 beaten egg white
2 tablespoons water
¼ cup pine nuts
2 tablespoons finely shredded Parmesan cheese

1 Coat a 15×10×1-inch baking pan or a 12- to 14-inch pizza pan with nonstick cooking spray. Set aside.

2 Prepare the hot roll mix according to package directions for the basic dough, except use the 1 egg and substitute the olive oil for the margarine. Knead dough; allow to rest as directed. If using the baking pan, roll dough in a 15×10-inch rectangle and carefully transfer to prepared pan. If using the pizza pan, roll dough in a 12-inch circle and carefully transfer to prepared pan.

3 With fingertips, press indentations every inch or so in dough. In a small bowl stir together egg white and the water; brush over dough. Sprinkle with pine nuts, pressing lightly into dough; sprinkle with Parmesan cheese. Cover; let rise in a warm place until nearly double (about 30 minutes).

4 Bake in a 375°F oven for 15 to 20 minutes or until golden. Cool 10 minutes on a wire rack. Remove focaccia from pan; cool completely on rack.

- 3½ to 4 cups all-purpose flour
- 1 package active dry yeast
- 1 teaspoon salt
- 1¼ cups warm water (120°F to 130°F)
- 2 tablespoons olive oil
- ⅔ cup shredded Swiss cheese
- ⅓ cup finely chopped almonds
- ½ teaspoon cracked black pepper
- ½ teaspoon coarse sea salt

1 In a large bowl stir together 1¼ cups of the flour, the yeast, and salt. Add the warm water and 1 tablespoon of the oil. Beat with an electric mixer on low to medium speed for 30 seconds, scraping sides of bowl. Beat on high speed for 3 minutes. Stir in as much of the remaining flour as you can with a wooden spoon.

2 Turn out dough onto a lightly floured surface. Knead in enough remaining flour to make a stiff dough that is smooth and elastic (8 to 10 minutes total). Shape dough in a ball. Place in a lightly greased bowl; turn once to grease surface. Cover; let rise in a warm place until double in size (about 1 hour).

3 Punch dough down. Turn out onto a lightly floured surface. Divide in half. Lightly oil 2 baking sheets. Shape each half in a ball. Place on prepared baking sheets. Cover and let rest for 10 minutes. Flatten each ball into a circle about 9 inches in diameter. Press ½-inch-deep indentations about 2 inches apart into the surface with your fingers. Brush with the remaining 1 tablespoon olive oil. Sprinkle with cheese, nuts, pepper, and coarse salt. Cover; let rise in a warm place until nearly double (about 20 minutes).

4 Bake in a 375°F oven for 25 to 30 minutes or until golden. Remove from baking sheets; cool on wire racks.

Swiss Cheese-Almond Flatbread

PREP: 40 minutes **RISE:** 1⅓ hours
BAKE: 25 minutes **OVEN:** 375°F
MAKES: 2 rounds (12 servings per round)

NUTRITION FACTS per serving:

CALORIES 96
TOTAL FAT 3 g total fat (1 g sat. fat)
CHOLESTEROL 3 mg
PROTEIN 3 g
CARBOHYDRATE 13 g
FIBER 1 g
SODIUM 141 mg

EXCHANGES 1 Starch, ½ Fat

1¾ to 2¼ cups all-purpose flour
1 package active dry yeast
1 teaspoon sugar
1 teaspoon salt
1 cup warm water (120°F to 130°F)
⅓ cup olive oil
1¼ cups semolina
  Semolina

1 In a large mixing bowl stir together 1¼ cups of the all-purpose flour, the yeast, sugar, and salt. Add warm water and oil. Beat with an electric mixer on low speed for 30 seconds, scraping sides of bowl. Beat on high speed for 3 minutes. Stir in the 1¼ cups semolina and as much of the remaining all-purpose flour as you can with a wooden spoon.

2 Turn out dough onto a lightly floured surface. Knead in enough remaining all-purpose flour to make a moderately stiff dough that is smooth and elastic (6 to 8 minutes total). Shape dough into a ball. Place in a greased bowl; turn once to grease surface. Cover; let rise in a warm place until double (about 1 hour).

3 Punch dough down. Turn out onto a lightly floured surface. Divide in half. Cover and let rest 10 minutes. Grease two baking sheets. Shape each half into a ball. Place balls on the prepared baking sheets. Flatten each ball to about 6½ inches in diameter. Cover and let rise until nearly double (30 to 45 minutes).

4 Rub loaves lightly with additional semolina. Cut a crisscross in the top of each loaf. Bake in a 375°F oven about 25 minutes or until golden and the bread sounds hollow when lightly tapped. Remove from baking sheets; cool on wire racks.

Country-Style Semolina Loaves

PREP: 40 minutes   **RISE:** 1½ hours
BAKE: 25 minutes   **OVEN:** 375°F
MAKES: 2 loaves (8 servings per loaf)

NUTRITION FACTS per serving:

CALORIES 134
TOTAL FAT 5 g total fat (1 g sat. fat)
CHOLESTEROL 0 mg
PROTEIN 3 g
CARBOHYDRATE 20 g
FIBER 1 g
SODIUM 146 mg

EXCHANGES ½ Starch, ½ Fat

- 4 to 4¼ cups all-purpose flour
- ½ cup warm water (105°F to 115°F)
- 1 teaspoon active dry yeast
- 1 cup warm water (105°F to 115°F)
- 2 teaspoons salt
  Cornmeal (optional)
- 1 tablespoon olive oil
  Snipped fresh rosemary
  Coarse salt
  Shredded Parmesan cheese
  (optional)

1 In a large bowl combine ½ cup of the flour, the ½ cup warm water, and the yeast. Beat with a wooden spoon until smooth. Cover loosely with plastic wrap. Let stand overnight at room temperature to ferment.

2 Gradually stir in the 1 cup warm water, the 2 teaspoons salt, and just enough of the remaining flour to make a dough that pulls away from the side of the bowl. Turn out onto a lightly floured surface. Knead in enough of the remaining flour to make a stiff dough that is smooth and elastic (8 to 10 minutes total). Place in a lightly greased bowl; turn once. Cover; let rise in a warm place until double (about 1 hour).

3 Divide dough in fourths; place dough portions onto a well-floured surface. Cover; let stand for 30 minutes. Grease two large baking sheets. If desired, sprinkle with cornmeal; set aside.

4 Place two dough portions on each prepared baking sheet; shape each portion into a 6-inch circle by pulling and pressing with your fingertips. (Don't stretch dough too roughly or the dough will deflate; you want to keep air bubbles intact.)

5 Dust your fingers with flour and press into dough to make ½-inch indentations about 2 inches apart. Brush dough with olive oil; sprinkle with rosemary, coarse salt, and, if desired, Parmesan cheese.

6 Bake in a 475°F oven about 20 minutes or until golden, checking after 8 minutes and popping any large air bubbles with a sharp knife. Remove from baking sheets. Cool focaccia on wire racks for 15 minutes. Serve warm.

Focaccia

PREP: 30 minutes
STAND: Overnight + 30 minutes
RISE: 1 hour   **BAKE:** 20 minutes
OVEN: 475°F   **COOL:** 15 minutes
MAKES: 16 servings

NUTRITION FACTS per serving:

CALORIES 113
TOTAL FAT 1 g total fat (0 g sat. fat)
CHOLESTEROL 0 mg
PROTEIN 3 g
CARBOHYDRATE 22 g
FIBER 1 g
SODIUM 413 mg

EXCHANGES 1½ Starch

Seven-Grain Bread

PREP: 30 minutes
RISE: 1 hour + 30 minutes
BAKE: 40 minutes **OVEN:** 375°F
MAKES: 1 loaf (16 servings)

NUTRITION FACTS per serving:

CALORIES 111
TOTAL FAT 2 g total fat (0 g sat. fat)
CHOLESTEROL 13 mg
PROTEIN 4 g
CARBOHYDRATE 20 g
FIBER 2 g
SODIUM 151 mg

EXCHANGES 1½ Starch

¾ to 1¼ cups all-purpose flour
½ cup seven-grain cereal
1 package active dry yeast
⅔ cup water
⅓ cup applesauce
2 tablespoons honey
1 teaspoon salt
1 egg
⅓ cup shelled sunflower seeds
1¾ cups whole wheat flour

1 In a large mixing bowl stir together ¾ cup of the all-purpose flour, the ½ cup cereal, and yeast; set aside.

2 In a medium saucepan combine the water, applesauce, honey, and salt; heat and stir just until warm (120°F to 130°F). Add applesauce mixture and egg to flour mixture. Beat with an electric mixer on low to medium speed for 30 seconds, scraping bowl constantly. Beat on high speed for 3 minutes. Using a wooden spoon, stir in the ⅓ cup sunflower seeds, the whole wheat flour, and as much of the remaining all-purpose flour as you can.

3 Turn out dough onto a lightly floured surface. Knead in enough of the remaining all-purpose flour to make a moderately stiff dough that is smooth and elastic (6 to 8 minutes total). Shape dough into a ball. Place in a lightly greased bowl; turn once. Cover; let rise in a warm place until double (1 to 1½ hours).

4 Punch dough down. Turn out onto a lightly floured surface; cover and let rest for 10 minutes. Lightly grease an 8×4×2-inch loaf pan.

5 Shape dough in a loaf. Place in prepared pan. Cover and let rise in a warm place until nearly double (30 to 45 minutes).

6 Bake in a 375°F oven for 40 to 45 minutes or until bread sounds hollow when lightly tapped. (If necessary to prevent overbrowning, cover loosely with foil the last 10 minutes of baking.) Immediately remove bread from pan. Cool on a wire rack.

- 1 cup water
- ¼ cup cracked wheat
- ¾ cup milk
- 1 tablespoon olive oil
- ¾ teaspoon salt
- 3½ to 4 cups all-purpose flour
- ¼ cup finely shredded Parmesan cheese (1 ounce)
- 1 package active dry yeast
- 1 egg
  Cracked wheat
  All-purpose flour

1 In a small saucepan bring the water to boiling; remove from heat. Stir in the ¼ cup cracked wheat. Let stand for 3 minutes; drain well. Add milk, oil, and salt to drained cracked wheat; let stand until cooled to lukewarm (120°F to 130°F).

2 In a large mixing bowl stir together 1½ cups of the flour, the cheese, and yeast. Add warm milk mixture and egg. Beat with an electric mixer on low to medium speed for 30 seconds, scraping bowl constantly. Beat on high speed for 3 minutes. Using a wooden spoon, stir in as much of the remaining flour as you can.

3 Turn out dough onto a lightly floured surface. Knead in enough of the remaining flour to make a moderately stiff dough that is smooth and elastic (6 to 8 minutes total). Shape dough into a ball. Place in a lightly greased bowl; turn once. Cover; let rise in a warm place until double (45 to 60 minutes).

4 Punch dough down. Turn out dough onto a lightly floured surface. Cover and let rest for 10 minutes. Grease a baking sheet.

5 Shape dough in a 6-inch round. Place on prepared baking sheet. Cover and let rise in a warm place until nearly double (30 to 40 minutes). Using a sharp knife, cut two or three slashes on top of loaf in each direction to make a diamond pattern. Brush with water; sprinkle additional cracked wheat and flour.

6 Bake in a 375°F oven for 25 to 30 minutes or until loaf sounds hollow when tapped.

Italian Peasant Loaf

PREP: 25 minutes
RISE: 45 minutes + 30 minutes
BAKE: 25 minutes   **OVEN:** 375°F
MAKES: 1 loaf (16 servings)

NUTRITION FACTS per serving:

CALORIES 130
TOTAL FAT 2 g total fat (1 g sat. fat)
CHOLESTEROL 16 mg
PROTEIN 5 g
CARBOHYDRATE 23 g
FIBER 1 g
SODIUM 140 mg

EXCHANGES 1½ Starch

English Muffin Bread

PREP: 20 minutes   **RISE:** 45 minutes
BAKE: 25 minutes   **OVEN:** 400°F
MAKES: 2 loaves (32 servings)

NUTRITION FACTS per serving:

CALORIES 90
TOTAL FAT 1 g total fat (0 g sat. fat)
CHOLESTEROL 1 mg
PROTEIN 3 g
CARBOHYDRATE 18 g
FIBER 1 g
SODIUM 91 mg

EXCHANGES 1 Starch

Cornmeal

6	cups all-purpose flour
2	packages active dry yeast
¼	teaspoon baking soda
2	cups milk
½	cup water
1	tablespoon sugar
1	teaspoon salt

1 Grease two 8×4×2-inch loaf pans. Lightly sprinkle pans with cornmeal to coat bottoms and sides; set pans aside.

2 In a large bowl combine 3 cups of the flour, the yeast, and baking soda; set aside. In a medium saucepan heat and stir the milk, water, sugar, and salt just until warm (120°F to 130°F). Using a wooden spoon, stir milk mixture into flour mixture. Stir in remaining flour.

3 Divide dough in half. Place dough in prepared pans. Sprinkle tops with additional cornmeal. Cover; let rise in a warm place until double (about 45 minutes).

4 Bake in a 400°F oven about 25 minutes or until golden. Immediately remove bread from pans. Cool on wire racks.

3	to 3½ cups all-purpose flour
4	teaspoons unsweetened cocoa powder
1	package active dry yeast
1	cup milk
3	tablespoons brown sugar
1	tablespoon butter
¾	teaspoon salt
1	egg
1½	teaspoons vanilla
1	tablespoon light-color corn syrup
½	cup miniature semisweet chocolate pieces
	Sifted powdered sugar (optional)

1 In a large mixing bowl stir together 1¼ cups of the flour, the cocoa powder, and yeast; set aside. In a saucepan heat and stir the milk, brown sugar, butter, and salt until warm (120°F to 130°F). Add to flour mixture; add egg and vanilla. Beat with an electric mixer on low to medium speed for 30 seconds, scraping bowl constantly. Beat on high speed for 3 minutes. Stir in as much of the remaining flour as you can.

2 Turn out dough onto a lightly floured surface. Knead in enough of the remaining flour to make a moderately soft dough that is smooth and elastic (3 to 5 minutes total). Shape dough in a ball. Place in a greased bowl; turn once. Cover; let rise in a warm place until double (about 1 hour).

3 Punch dough down. Turn out onto a lightly floured surface. Cover; let rest for 10 minutes. Lightly grease an 8×4×2-inch loaf pan. Roll dough in a 12×8-inch rectangle. Brush with corn syrup. Sprinkle with chocolate pieces; press lightly into dough. Starting from a short side, roll up in a spiral. Seal seam and ends. Place in prepared pan, seam side down. Cover; let rise in a warm place until nearly double (about 30 minutes).

4 Bake in a 375°F oven for 25 to 30 minutes or until bread sounds hollow when tapped. If necessary, to prevent overbrowning cover with foil after 20 minutes. Remove from pan; cool on a rack. If desired, sprinkle with powdered sugar.

Double-Chocolate Swirl

PREP: 30 minutes
RISE: 1 hour + 30 minutes
BAKE: 25 minutes   **OVEN:** 375°F
MAKES: 1 loaf (16 servings)

NUTRITION FACTS per serving:

CALORIES 139
TOTAL FAT 3 g total fat (2 g sat. fat)
CHOLESTEROL 17 mg
PROTEIN 4 g
CARBOHYDRATE 25 g
FIBER 1 g
SODIUM 131 mg

EXCHANGES 1½ Starch, ½ Fat

1   cup whole wheat flour
1   cup all-purpose flour
1   teaspoon baking powder
½   teaspoon baking soda
¼   teaspoon salt
3   tablespoons butter
2   beaten eggs
¾   cup buttermilk or sour milk*
2   tablespoons brown sugar
⅓   cup dried tart cherries or raisins

Irish Soda Bread

PREP: 20 minutes   **BAKE:** 35 minutes
OVEN: 375°F
MAKES: 1 loaf (10 servings)

NUTRITION FACTS per serving:

CALORIES 161
TOTAL FAT 5 g total fat (3 g sat. fat)
CHOLESTEROL 53 mg
PROTEIN 5 g
CARBOHYDRATE 25 g
FIBER 2 g
SODIUM 232 mg

EXCHANGES 1½ Starch, ½ Fat

1 Grease a baking sheet; set aside. In a medium bowl combine whole wheat flour, all-purpose flour, baking powder, baking soda, and salt. Using a pastry blender, cut in butter until mixture resembles coarse crumbs. Make a well in center of flour mixture; set aside.

2 In a small bowl stir together 1 of the eggs, the buttermilk, brown sugar, and dried cherries. Add egg mixture all at once to flour mixture. Stir just until moistened.

3 Turn out dough onto a lightly floured surface. Knead dough by folding and gently pressing dough for 10 to 12 strokes or until dough is nearly smooth. Shape in a 6-inch round loaf. Cut a 4-inch cross, ½ inch deep, on the top. Place on prepared baking sheet. Brush with the remaining egg.

4 Bake in a 375°F oven about 35 minutes or until golden. Serve warm.

*Note: To make ¾ cup sour milk, place 2¼ teaspoons lemon juice or vinegar in a glass measuring cup. Add enough milk to equal ¾ cup total liquid; stir. Let mixture stand for 5 minutes before using.

On the opener: Five-Spice Steak Wraps *(see recipe, page 60)*

12	ounces beef flank steak
3	tablespoons frozen orange juice concentrate, thawed
3	tablespoons water
2	tablespoons lime juice
1	teaspoon grated fresh ginger
½	teaspoon dried oregano, crushed
⅛	teaspoon salt
⅛	teaspoon cayenne pepper
1	clove garlic, minced
4	8- to 10-inch garden vegetable flour tortillas
¾	cup red and/or yellow sweet pepper strips
1	small onion, sliced and separated in rings
¼	cup hoisin or plum sauce
1	cup shredded napa cabbage

1 Score meat by making shallow cuts at 1-inch intervals diagonally across steak in a diamond pattern. Repeat on each side. Place meat in a plastic bag set in a shallow dish. For marinade, in a small bowl combine orange juice concentrate, the water, lime juice, ginger, oregano, salt, cayenne pepper, and garlic. Pour over meat; seal bag. Marinate in the refrigerator for at least 30 minutes or up to 4 hours, turning bag occasionally.

2 Preheat broiler. Drain meat, reserving marinade. Place meat on the unheated rack of a broiler pan. Broil 3 to 4 inches from the heat for 15 to 18 minutes or until medium doneness (160°F), turning once. Thinly slice meat diagonally across the grain.

3 Wrap tortillas in foil. Place beside the broiler pan for the last 8 minutes of broiling meat. Meanwhile, pour reserved marinade into a medium saucepan. Stir in sweet pepper and onion. Bring to boiling; reduce heat. Simmer, covered, for 5 to 8 minutes or until vegetables are tender. To serve, spread each tortilla with some of the hoisin sauce. Top with napa cabbage and beef. Using a slotted spoon, spoon pepper mixture over beef. Roll up.

Asian Flank Steak Roll-Ups

PREP: 15 minutes
MARINATE: 30 minutes to 4 hours
BROIL: 15 minutes   **MAKES:** 4 servings

NUTRITION FACTS per serving:

CALORIES 411
TOTAL FAT 11 g total fat (4 g sat. fat)
CHOLESTEROL 34 mg
PROTEIN 26 g
CARBOHYDRATE 50 g
FIBER 5 g
SODIUM 673 mg

EXCHANGES 1 Vegetable, 1 Fruit, 2 Starch, 3 Meat

Five-Spice Steak Wraps

START TO FINISH: 25 minutes
MAKES: 4 servings

NUTRITION FACTS per serving:

CALORIES 237
TOTAL FAT 7 g total fat (2 g sat. fat)
CHOLESTEROL 51 mg
PROTEIN 22 g
CARBOHYDRATE 20 g
FIBER 2 g
SODIUM 329 mg

EXCHANGES 1 Vegetable, 1 Starch, 2 Meat

12	ounces boneless beef round steak
2	cups packaged shredded cabbage with carrot (coleslaw mix)
¼	cup red and/or green sweet pepper cut in thin bite-size strips
¼	cup carrot cut in thin bite-size strips
¼	cup snipped fresh chives
2	tablespoons rice vinegar
½	teaspoon toasted sesame oil
½	teaspoon five-spice powder
¼	teaspoon salt
	Nonstick cooking spray
¼	cup plain low-fat yogurt or light dairy sour cream
4	8-inch flour tortillas

1 If desired, partially freeze steak for easier slicing. In a medium bowl combine coleslaw mix, sweet pepper, carrot, and chives. In a small bowl combine vinegar and sesame oil. Pour vinegar mixture over coleslaw mixture; toss to coat. Set aside.

2 Trim fat from steak. Thinly slice steak across the grain into bite-size strips. Sprinkle steak with five-spice powder and salt. Coat an unheated large nonstick skillet with nonstick cooking spray. Preheat over medium-high heat. Add steak strips; stir-fry for 3 to 4 minutes or until browned.

3 To assemble, spread 1 tablespoon of the yogurt down the center of each tortilla. Top with steak strips. Stir coleslaw mixture; spoon over steak. Fold in sides of tortillas. If desired, secure with wooden toothpicks.

12	ounces boneless beef top sirloin steak, cut ½ inch thick
½	cup reduced-fat, reduced-calorie bottled balsamic-, raspberry-, or Italian-flavored vinaigrette
½	teaspoon crushed red pepper
1	clove garlic, minced
¼	cup low-fat mayonnaise dressing
1	small red onion, thinly sliced
2	teaspoons cooking oil
4	hoagie rolls (about 2 ounces each), split and toasted
1¼	cups small lettuce leaves
⅔	cup fresh basil leaves, thinly sliced

1 If desired, partially freeze steak for easier slicing. Trim fat from steak. Thinly slice steak across the grain into bite-size strips. In a medium bowl combine vinaigrette, red pepper, and garlic. In a small bowl combine 1 tablespoon of the vinaigrette mixture and the mayonnaise dressing. Cover and chill.

2 Add steak strips to the remaining vinaigrette mixture; stir to coat evenly. Cover and marinate in the refrigerator for 1 hour. Drain steak strips, discarding the marinade.

3 In a large nonstick skillet cook steak strips and onion in hot oil over medium-high heat for 2 to 3 minutes or until meat is browned and onion is crisp-tender.

4 To assemble, spread mayonnaise dressing-vinaigrette mixture evenly onto cut sides of hoagie rolls. Top roll bottoms with lettuce and basil. With a slotted spoon, divide steak and onion mixture among the roll bottoms. Add roll tops.

Vinaigrette-Dressed Steak Sandwich

PREP: 25 minutes **MARINATE:** 1 hour
MAKES: 4 servings

NUTRITION FACTS per serving:

CALORIES 397
TOTAL FAT 12 g total fat (2 g sat. fat)
CHOLESTEROL 55 mg
PROTEIN 23 g
CARBOHYDRATE 48 g carbo
FIBER 3 g
SODIUM 500 mg

EXCHANGES 2 Vegetable, 2½ Starch, 2 Meat, ½ Fat

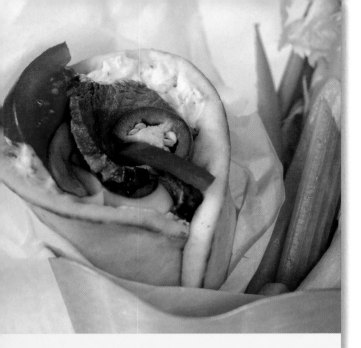

1 head garlic

1 teaspoon olive oil

½ of an 8-ounce package reduced-fat cream cheese (Neufchâtel), softened

1 tablespoon fat-free milk

¾ teaspoon herb-pepper seasoning

4 small pita bread rounds

1 small zucchini, thinly sliced lengthwise

1 medium tomato, halved and thinly slices

1 small fresh jalapeño chile pepper, sliced (see note, page 263), or 2 tablespoons finely chopped green sweet pepper

6 ounces thinly sliced cooked beef

Beef and Garlic Pita Roll-Ups

PREP: 20 minutes　　**BAKE:** 25 minutes
OVEN: 425°F　　**MAKES:** 4 servings

NUTRITION FACTS per serving:
- -

CALORIES 346
TOTAL FAT 11 g total fat (5 g sat. fat)
CHOLESTEROL 51 mg
PROTEIN 22 g
CARBOHYDRATE 41 g
FIBER 2 g
SODIUM 469 mg

EXCHANGES 1 Vegetable, 2½ Starch, 1½ Meat

1 Peel away the dry outer layers of peel from the head of garlic, leaving skins and cloves intact. Cut off the pointed top portion (about ¼ inch), leaving the bulb intact but exposing the individual cloves. Place the garlic head, cut side up, in a muffin cup or custard cup. Drizzle with oil. Cover with foil. Bake in a 425°F oven for 25 to 35 minutes or until the cloves feel soft when pressed. Set aside just until cool enough to handle. Squeeze out the garlic paste from individual cloves.

2 In a small mixing bowl combine garlic paste, cream cheese, milk, and herb-pepper seasoning. Beat with an electric mixer or stir by hand until mixture is smooth.

3 For roll-ups, spread cream cheese mixture over 1 side of each pita bread round. Top each with some of the zucchini, tomato, and jalapeño pepper. Top with cooked beef. Roll up pita bread rounds, securing with wooden picks if necessary.

- ⅓ cup light dairy sour cream
- 2 tablespoons snipped fresh chives
- 2 tablespoons spicy brown mustard
- 1 teaspoon prepared horseradish
- ½ teaspoon sugar
- ¼ teaspoon salt
- 1 cup packaged shredded broccoli (broccoli slaw mix)
- 8 ounces thinly sliced cooked roast beef
- 8 ½-inch slices sourdough bread, toasted

1 In a medium bowl combine sour cream, chives, brown mustard, horseradish, sugar, and salt. Add shredded broccoli; toss to coat.

2 To assemble, divide roast beef among 4 of the bread slices. Top with broccoli mixture. Top with remaining bread slices. If desired, secure sandwiches with wooden toothpicks.

Beef Sandwich with Horseradish Slaw

START TO FINISH: 15 minutes
MAKES: 4 servings

NUTRITION FACTS per serving:

CALORIES 315
TOTAL FAT 11 g total fat (4 g sat. fat)
CHOLESTEROL 53 mg
PROTEIN 23 g
CARBOHYDRATE 30 g
FIBER 2 g
SODIUM 630 mg

EXCHANGES 2 Starch, 2 Meat, ½ Fat

4 uncooked turkey bratwurst

½ cup water

1 small onion, thinly sliced

1 small red or green sweet pepper, cut into thin strips

¼ teaspoon black pepper

⅛ teaspoon salt

2 teaspoons butter or margarine

4 bratwurst buns, split and toasted

3 tablespoons spicy brown mustard

Brats with Onion-Pepper Relish

PREP: 15 minutes   **COOK:** 15 minutes
MAKES: 4 servings

NUTRITION FACTS per serving:

CALORIES 284
TOTAL FAT 12 g total fat (4 g sat. fat)
CHOLESTEROL 43 mg
PROTEIN 17 g
CARBOHYDRATE 27 g
FIBER 2 g
SODIUM 1,100 mg

EXCHANGES 1 Vegetable, 1½ Starch, 1½ Meat, ½ Fat

1 In a large nonstick skillet cook bratwurst over medium heat about 5 minutes or until brown, turning frequently. Carefully add the water. Bring to boiling; reduce heat. Simmer, covered, for 15 to 20 minutes or until internal temperature registers 165°F on an instant-read thermometer. Drain on paper towels.

2 Meanwhile, in a covered medium saucepan cook onion, sweet pepper, black pepper, and salt in hot butter for 3 minutes. Stir onion mixture. Cook, covered, for 3 to 4 minutes more or until onion is golden.

3 Spread cut sides of toasted buns with the mustard. Serve bratwurst in buns topped with onion mixture.

Grill method: Prepare as above, except arrange medium-hot coals around a drip pan in a covered grill. Test for medium heat above the pan. Place bratwurst on grill over the pan. Cover and grill for 20 to 25 minutes or until internal temperature registers 165°F on an instant-read thermometer, turning bratwurst once halfway through grilling. Cook onion mixture and serve as above.

- 4 slices firm white bread or sourdough bread
- 4 teaspoons cranberry or raspberry mustard
- 2 ounces very thinly sliced reduced-sodium cooked ham
- 2 slices reduced-fat Swiss cheese (2 ounces)
- ¼ cup reduced-fat milk
- 1 egg white
  Butter-flavor nonstick cooking spray
- 1 teaspoon butter or margarine
  Sifted powdered sugar (optional)
  Raspberry preserves (optional)

1 Spread one side of each bread slice lightly with mustard. Layer ham and cheese between the mustard-spread sides of the bread slices. In a shallow bowl or pie plate beat together milk and egg white.

2 Coat an unheated nonstick griddle or large skillet with nonstick cooking spray. Preheat griddle over medium heat. Melt butter on griddle. Dip each sandwich in milk mixture, turning to coat. Place in skillet; cook for 1 to 2 minutes per side or until golden and cheese is melted. If desired, sprinkle with powdered sugar and serve with preserves.

Classic Monte Cristo Sandwiches

START TO FINISH: 15 minutes
MAKES: 2 servings

NUTRITION FACTS per serving:

CALORIES 314
TOTAL FAT 10 g total fat (4 g sat. fat)
CHOLESTEROL 41 mg
PROTEIN 21 g
CARBOHYDRATE 33 g
FIBER 0 g
SODIUM 606 mg

EXCHANGES 2 Starch, 2 Meat, ½ Fat

Pork Sandwiches with Mojo Sauce

START TO FINISH: 35 minutes
MAKES: 4 servings

NUTRITION FACTS per serving:

CALORIES 316
TOTAL FAT 11 g total fat (4 g sat. fat)
CHOLESTEROL 54 mg
PROTEIN 24 g
CARBOHYDRATE 28 g
FIBER 3 g
SODIUM 490 mg

EXCHANGES 1 Vegetable, 1½ Starch, 2½ Meat

¾	cup finely chopped red and/or yellow sweet pepper
4	large cloves garlic, minced
1	teaspoon olive oil
¼	cup orange juice
1	tablespoon lime juice
1	teaspoon ground cumin
1	teaspoon dried oregano, crushed
¼	teaspoon salt
¼	teaspoon black pepper
2	ounces mozzarella cheese, thinly sliced
4	small rolls, toasted if desired
8	ounces cooked pork loin, thinly sliced
1	cup packaged shredded cabbage with carrot (coleslaw mix)

1 For mojo sauce, in a small saucepan cook sweet pepper and garlic in hot oil until tender. Stir in orange juice, lime juice, cumin, oregano, salt, and black pepper. Bring to boiling; reduce heat. Boil gently for 1 minute. Cool to room temperature. (If desired, store tightly covered in the refrigerator for up to 1 week.)

2 For sandwiches, divide cheese among roll bottoms. Top each with one-quarter of the pork slices and ¼ cup of the cabbage. Spoon 2 tablespoons of the mojo sauce onto each sandwich. Top with roll tops.

- 1 16-ounce loaf frozen wheat or white bread dough, thawed
- 8 ounces lean ham, thinly sliced
- ¼ cup pitted ripe olives, coarsely chopped
- ¼ cup pimiento-stuffed green olives, coarsely chopped
- ¼ cup shredded mozzarella cheese (1 ounce)
- ⅛ teaspoon crushed red pepper flakes
- 1 tablespoon reduced-fat milk
- 1 tablespoon shredded Parmesan cheese (optional)

1 Line a 15×10×1-inch baking pan with foil; grease foil. Set aside. On a lightly floured surface, roll bread dough to a 15×8-inch rectangle. (If dough is difficult to roll out, cover and let rest a few minutes.) Top dough rectangle with ham to within ½ inch of the edges. Top ham with olives, mozzarella cheese, and crushed red pepper flakes. Brush edges with water.

2 Starting with a long end, roll into a spiral, pinching edges to seal. Pinch ends and tuck under. Place, seam side down, on prepared baking pan. Brush surface with milk. Using a sharp knife, make shallow cuts diagonally at 2-inch intervals along the top to allow steam to escape. If desired, sprinkle with Parmesan cheese.

3 Bake in a 375°F oven for 25 to 30 minutes or until brown. (If necessary, cover loosely with foil after 20 minutes of baking to prevent overbrowning.)

Quick Stromboli

PREP: 20 minutes   **BAKE:** 25 minutes
OVEN: 375°F   **MAKES:** 8 servings

NUTRITION FACTS per serving:

CALORIES 206
TOTAL FAT 5 g total fat (1 g sat. fat)
CHOLESTEROL 16 mg
PROTEIN 14 g
CARBOHYDRATE 28 g
FIBER 2 g
SODIUM 878 mg

EXCHANGES 2 Starch, 1 Meat

1/3   cup fine dry bread crumbs

2   teaspoons dried Italian seasoning, crushed

2   turkey tenderloins (about 1 pound total)

2   teaspoons olive oil

2   tablespoons snipped fresh basil

1/4   cup light mayonnaise dressing or salad dressing

8   1/2-inch slices Italian bread, toasted

1   cup bottled roasted red and/or yellow sweet peppers, cut into thin strips

   Fresh basil leaves (optional)

Italian Turkey Sandwiches

START TO FINISH: 20 minutes
MAKES: 4 sandwiches

NUTRITION FACTS per serving:

CALORIES 399
TOTAL FAT 11 g total fat (2 g sat. fat)
CHOLESTEROL 73 mg
PROTEIN 33 g
CARBOHYDRATE 40 g
FIBER 3 g
SODIUM 671 mg

EXCHANGES 1/2 Vegetable, 1 1/2 Starch, 3 1/2 Meat, 1 1/2 Fat

1 In a large plastic bag combine the bread crumbs and Italian seasoning. Slice each turkey tenderloin in half horizontally to make 1/2-inch steaks. Place a turkey tenderloin steak in bag; seal and shake to coat. Repeat with remaining steaks.

2 In a 12-inch nonstick skillet cook steaks in hot oil over medium heat about 10 minutes or until tender and no longer pink (170°F); turn once.

3 In a small bowl stir 1 tablespoon of the snipped basil into the mayonnaise dressing. Spread dressing mixture on one side of 4 bread slices. Top bread slices with turkey steaks, sweet pepper strips, and the remaining snipped basil. If desired, garnish with basil leaves. Top with remaining bread slices.

- 1 beaten egg
- ¼ cup fine dry bread crumbs
- 1 teaspoon Thai seasoning
- 1 pound uncooked ground turkey
- 4 kaiser rolls or hamburger buns, split and toasted
- ¾ cup fresh basil leaves
- 2 tablespoons purchased peanut dipping sauce

  Green onions, bias-sliced (optional)

1 Preheat broiler. In a medium bowl combine egg, bread crumbs, and Thai seasoning. Add ground turkey; mix well. Shape mixture into four ¾-inch patties.

2 Place patties on the unheated rack of broiler pan. Broil 3 to 4 inches from the heat for 14 to 18 minutes or until internal temperature registers 165°F on an instant-read thermometer; turn once.

3 To serve burgers, top bottom half of each bun with some of the basil. Add patties. Spoon peanut dipping sauce over patties. If desired, garnish with green onions. Add bun tops.

Thai Turkey Burgers

PREP: 15 minutes   **BROIL:** 14 minutes
MAKES: 4 servings

NUTRITION FACTS per serving:

CALORIES 389
TOTAL FAT 13 g total fat (3 g sat. fat)
CHOLESTEROL 123 mg
PROTEIN 31 g
CARBOHYDRATE 36 g
FIBER 2 g
SODIUM 739 mg

EXCHANGES 2½ Starch, 3½ Meat

¼ cup fat-free plain yogurt

3 tablespoons horseradish mustard

8 slices multigrain bread, toasted

12 lettuce leaves

8 to 12 ounces deli-sliced cooked turkey breast

1 tomato, sliced

1 yellow sweet pepper, sliced

1 cup fresh pea pods

1 In a small bowl stir together yogurt and horseradish mustard. Spread yogurt mixture on four of the toasted bread slices.

2 Top the remaining bread slices with lettuce, turkey, tomato, sweet pepper, and pea pods. Top with remaining bread slices, spread sides down.

Tall Turkey Sandwiches

START TO FINISH: 15 minutes
MAKES: 4 servings

NUTRITION FACTS per serving:

CALORIES 235
TOTAL FAT 3 g total fat (0 g sat. fat)
CHOLESTEROL 23 mg
PROTEIN 22 g
CARBOHYDRATE 34 g
FIBER 6 g
SODIUM 1,163 mg

EXCHANGES 1 Vegetable, 2 Starch, 2 Meat

4   fresh or frozen fish fillets (such as cod, orange roughy, or pike), about ½ inch thick (about 1 pound)

Nonstick cooking spray

¼   cup fine dry bread crumbs

¼   teaspoon ground ginger

⅛   teaspoon salt

⅛   teaspoon cayenne pepper

2   tablespoons butter or margarine, melted

4   lettuce leaves

4   baguette-style rolls, hamburger buns, or kaiser rolls, split and toasted

1   recipe Ginger Topper

1 Thaw fish, if frozen. Rinse fish; pat dry with paper towels.

2 Lightly coat a shallow baking pan with nonstick cooking spray; set aside. In a small bowl combine bread crumbs, ginger, salt, and cayenne pepper; set aside. Place fish fillets on waxed paper. Brush tops and sides of the fish with melted butter; coat tops and sides with crumb mixture.

3 Arrange the fish fillets in a single layer, crumb sides up, in prepared baking pan. Bake, uncovered, in a 450°F oven for 4 to 6 minutes or until fish flakes easily when tested with a fork.

4 To serve, top bottoms of rolls with lettuce, fish, and Ginger Topper. Add roll tops.

Ginger Topper: In a small bowl stir together ¼ cup low-fat mayonnaise dressing, 1 teaspoon orange marmalade, and ¼ teaspoon ground ginger.

Fish Sandwich with Ginger Mayonnaise

START TO FINISH: 15 minutes
OVEN: 450°F   **MAKES:** 4 servings

NUTRITION FACTS per serving:

CALORIES 319
TOTAL FAT 10 g total fat (5 g sat. fat)
CHOLESTEROL 68 mg
PROTEIN 25 g
CARBOHYDRATE 31 g
FIBER 2 g
SODIUM 711 mg

EXCHANGES 2 Starch, 3 Meat

1 medium cucumber, seeded and chopped

1 cup cooked or canned black beans, rinsed and drained

¼ cup snipped fresh cilantro

2 tablespoons cider vinegar

1 tablespoon olive oil

1 pickled jalapeño chile pepper, finely chopped (see note, page 263)

½ to 1 teaspoon chili powder

1 clove garlic, minced

Salt

Black pepper

3 large tomatoes, halved

1 large sweet onion (such as Vidalia, Maui, Texas Sweet, or Walla Walla), sliced ½ inch thick

1 loaf French bread

Gazpacho Sandwiches

PREP: 20 minutes   **GRILL:** 13 minutes
MAKES: 6 servings

NUTRITION FACTS per serving:

CALORIES 295
TOTAL FAT 5 g total fat (1 g sat. fat)
CHOLESTEROL 0 mg
PROTEIN 11 g
CARBOHYDRATE 54 g
FIBER 6 g
SODIUM 671 mg

EXCHANGES 2 Vegetable, 3 Starch, ½ Fat

1 In a medium bowl combine the cucumber, beans, cilantro, vinegar, oil, jalapeño pepper, chili powder, and garlic. Season to taste with salt and black pepper. Set aside.

2 Place the tomatoes and onion slices on the lightly greased rack of an grill directly over medium coals. Grill for 12 to 15 minutes or until lightly charred, turning onion slices once. Transfer vegetables to a cutting board; cool slightly and coarsely chop. Add chopped vegetables to the cucumber mixture; toss to combine.

3 Meanwhile, halve the French bread lengthwise. Cut each bread half crosswise into 3 pieces. Using a fork, hollow out the bread pieces slightly. Place the bread pieces, cut sides down, on the rack of the grill directly over medium coals. Grill about 1 minute or until toasted. Spoon the bean mixture into the grilled bread pieces.

- 1   15-ounce can black-eyed peas, rinsed and drained
- 1   13¾- to 14-ounce can artichoke hearts, drained and cut up
- ½   cup torn mixed salad greens
- ¼   cup bottled creamy garlic salad dressing
- ¼   teaspoon cracked black pepper
- 3   pita bread rounds, halved crosswise
- 1   small tomato, sliced

1 In a medium bowl combine black-eyed peas, artichoke hearts, mixed greens, salad dressing, and pepper. Line pita bread halves with tomato slices. Spoon artichoke mixture into pita bread halves.

Peppery Artichoke Pitas

START TO FINISH: 20 minutes
MAKES: 6 servings

NUTRITION FACTS per serving:

CALORIES 189
TOTAL FAT 4 g total fat (1 g sat. fat)
CHOLESTEROL 0 mg
PROTEIN 7 g
CARBOHYDRATE 31 g
FIBER 5 g
SODIUM 632 mg

EXCHANGES 1 Vegetable, 1½ Starch, ½ Fat

1 cup torn arugula

2 teaspoons red wine vinegar

1 teaspoon olive oil

1/3 cup seasoned fine dry bread crumbs

2 tablespoons grated Pecorino Romano cheese or Parmesan cheese

1 egg

1 tablespoon milk

2 tablespoons all-purpose flour

1/2 teaspoon salt

1 medium eggplant, cut crosswise into 1/2-inch slices

1 tablespoon olive oil

3 ounces fresh mozzarella cheese, thinly sliced

6 individual focaccia rolls or one 12-inch plain or seasoned Italian flatbread (focaccia),* halved horizontally

1 large tomato, thinly sliced

Eggplant Panini

START TO FINISH: 25 minutes
MAKES: 6 servings

NUTRITION FACTS per serving:

- -

CALORIES 271
TOTAL FAT 10 g total fat (3 g sat. fat)
CHOLESTEROL 53 mg
PROTEIN 12 g
CARBOHYDRATE 37 g
FIBER 3 g
SODIUM 687 mg

EXCHANGES 1 Vegetable, 2 Starch, 1 Meat, 1/2 Fat

1 In a small bowl toss together the arugula, red wine vinegar, and the 1 teaspoon oil; set aside. In a shallow dish stir together the bread crumbs and Romano cheese. In another shallow dish beat together the egg and milk. In a third shallow dish stir together the flour and salt. Dip the eggplant slices into flour mixture to coat. Dip the slices into egg mixture; coat both sides with bread crumb mixture.

2 In a 12-inch nonstick skillet heat the 1 tablespoon oil over medium heat. Add eggplant slices; cook for 6 to 8 minutes or until lightly browned, turning once. (Add more oil as necessary during cooking.) Top the eggplant with mozzarella cheese; reduce heat to low. Cook, covered, just until cheese begins to melt.

3 To serve, place the tomato slices on bottom halves of rolls. Top with eggplant slices, cheese sides up; the arugula mixture; and top halves of rolls. (Or place tomato slices on bottom half of bread. Top with eggplant slices, arugula mixture, and top half of bread. Cut into wedges.)

*Note: For easier slicing, purchase focaccia that is at least 2 1/2 inches thick.

On the opener: Chicken and Rice Salad *(see recipe, page 82)*

BEEF

PORK

CHICKEN & TURKEY

FISH & SEAFOOD

MEATLESS

- 8 ounces boneless beef top sirloin steak
- 8 cups torn mixed salad greens
  Nonstick cooking spray
- ¼ cup finely shredded fresh basil
  Salt (optional)
  Black pepper (optional)
- 2 medium carrots, cut into thin bite-size strips
- 1 medium yellow sweet pepper, cut into thin bite-size strips
- 1 cup yellow and/or red pear-shaped tomatoes, halved
- 1 recipe Buttermilk Dressing

1 If desired, partially freeze steak for easier slicing. Arrange salad greens on 4 dinner plates. Set aside. Trim fat from steak. Cut steak across the grain into thin bite-size strips.

2 Lightly coat an unheated large skillet with nonstick cooking spray. Preheat over medium-high heat. Add steak strips. Cook and stir for 2 to 3 minutes or until meat is browned. Remove from heat. Stir in basil. If desired, lightly sprinkle with salt and black pepper to taste.

3 To serve, spoon the warm meat mixture over greens. Top with carrots, sweet pepper, and tomatoes. Drizzle with Buttermilk Dressing. Serve immediately.

Buttermilk Dressing: In a small bowl combine ½ cup plain low-fat yogurt; ⅓ cup buttermilk; 3 tablespoons freshly grated Parmesan cheese; 3 tablespoons finely chopped red onion; 3 tablespoons low-fat mayonnaise dressing; 2 tablespoons snipped fresh parsley; 1 tablespoon white wine vinegar or lemon juice; 1 clove garlic, minced; ¼ teaspoon salt; and ⅛ teaspoon black pepper. Cover and refrigerate for at least 30 minutes or up to 24 hours.

Steak Salad with Buttermilk Dressing

START TO FINISH: 35 minutes
MAKES: 4 servings

NUTRITION FACTS per serving:

CALORIES 187
TOTAL FAT 5 g total fat (2 g sat. fat)
CHOLESTEROL 35 mg
PROTEIN 19 g
CARBOHYDRATE 18 g
FIBER 4 g
SODIUM 419 mg

EXCHANGES 3 Vegetable, 2 Meat

2 boneless pork loin chops, cut ¾ inch thick (12 ounces total)

¼ teaspoon salt

¼ teaspoon ground ginger

⅛ teaspoon black pepper

1 teaspoon cooking oil

1 teaspoon bottled minced garlic or 2 cloves garlic, minced

½ cup fresh sugar snap peas

⅓ cup sliced fresh mushrooms

⅔ cup bottled reduced-fat raspberry vinaigrette salad dressing

½ cup fresh raspberries

8 cups torn fresh spinach and/or romaine or purchased torn mixed salad greens

Pork with Berry-Dressed Greens

START TO FINISH: 20 minutes
MAKES: 4 servings

NUTRITION FACTS per serving:

CALORIES 248
TOTAL FAT 12 g total fat (2 g sat. fat)
CHOLESTEROL 46 mg
PROTEIN 21 g
CARBOHYDRATE 12 g
FIBER 7 g
SODIUM 617 mg

EXCHANGES 2 Vegetable, 2½ Meat, 1 Fat

1 Trim fat from chops. Sprinkle both sides of each chop with salt, ginger, and pepper. In a large nonstick skillet heat oil over medium heat. Add chops; cook for 8 to 12 minutes or until pork juices run clear (160°F), turning once. Remove chops from skillet, reserving drippings. Cover chops; keep warm.

2 In the same skillet cook and stir garlic in reserved drippings for 30 seconds. Add sugar snap peas and mushrooms to skillet. Pour raspberry vinaigrette dressing over all. Cover and cook for 2 to 3 minutes or until heated through. Remove from heat. Gently stir in the raspberries; set aside and keep warm.

3 Divide spinach evenly among 4 dinner plates. Thinly slice pork. Arrange pork on spinach. Pour warm raspberry mixture over all.

4   skinless, boneless chicken breast halves (about 1 pound total)

1   tablespoon olive oil

¼   teaspoon garlic-pepper blend

8   cups torn mixed salad greens

1   medium yellow or red sweet pepper, cut into bite-size strips

1   medium tomato, cut into wedges

½   cup bottled reduced-calorie salad dressing (such as a berry or roasted garlic vinaigrette or Parmesan-basil Italian)

¼   cup crumbled feta cheese

¼   cup purchased croutons

1 Brush chicken breasts with olive oil; sprinkle with garlic-pepper blend. In a medium nonstick skillet cook chicken over medium heat for 12 to 15 minutes or until no longer pink (170°F). Slice the chicken into bite-size strips. Set aside.

2 In a large serving bowl toss greens, sweet pepper, and tomato; add dressing and toss to coat. Top with chicken, feta cheese, and croutons.

Chicken Tossed Salad

START TO FINISH: 20 minutes
MAKES: 4 main-dish servings

NUTRITION FACTS per serving:
- -

CALORIES 277
TOTAL FAT 12 g total fat (2 g sat. fat)
CHOLESTEROL 74 mg
PROTEIN 29 g
CARBOHYDRATE 12 g
FIBER 3 g
SODIUM 536 mg

EXCHANGES 2 Vegetable, 3½ Meat, ½ Fat

1   10-ounce package torn mixed
      salad greens

8   ounces cooked chicken, cut into
      bite-size pieces

⅓   cup bottled Asian vinaigrette
      salad dressing

1   11-ounce can mandarin orange
      sections, drained

3   tablespoons sliced almonds,
      toasted

1 In a large bowl combine greens and chicken. Add salad dressing; toss to coat. Divide greens mixture among 4 salad plates. Top with mandarin orange sections and almonds. Serve immediately.

Asian Chicken Salad

START TO FINISH: 15 minutes
MAKES: 4 main-dish servings

NUTRITION FACTS per serving:

CALORIES 218
TOTAL FAT 9 g total fat (1 g sat. fat)
CHOLESTEROL 50 mg
PROTEIN 19 g
CARBOHYDRATE 15 g
FIBER 2 g
SODIUM 502 mg

EXCHANGES 1½ Vegetable, ½ Fruit, 2½ Meat, ½ Fat

3 skinless, boneless chicken breast halves (about 12 ounces total)

1 cup water

¼ teaspoon salt

⅔ cup low-fat mayonnaise dressing or light salad dressing

¼ cup fat-free milk

2 teaspoons curry powder

¼ teaspoon salt

2 cups chopped red apples (3 medium)

2 cups cooked wild rice, chilled

1½ cups sliced celery (3 stalks)

½ cup golden raisins

Romaine or fresh spinach leaves (optional)

1 In a medium skillet combine chicken, the water, and ¼ teaspoon salt. Bring to boiling; reduce heat. Simmer, covered, for 12 to 14 minutes or until the chicken is tender and no longer pink (170°F). Drain well; cool. Cut chicken into bite-size pieces.

2 Meanwhile, for the dressing, in a small bowl stir together mayonnaise dressing, milk, curry powder, and ¼ teaspoon salt.

3 In a large bowl stir together cooked chicken, apples, chilled wild rice, celery, and raisins; stir in the dressing. Cover and chill for at least 1 hour or up to 4 hours. If desired, serve on romaine or spinach leaves.

Curried Chicken Salad

PREP: 30 minutes   **CHILL:** 1 to 4 hours
MAKES: 6 servings

NUTRITION FACTS per serving:

CALORIES 241
TOTAL FAT 3 g total fat (1 g sat. fat)
CHOLESTEROL 38 mg
PROTEIN 17 g
CARBOHYDRATE 39 g
FIBER 4 g
SODIUM 501 mg

EXCHANGES 1½ Fruit, 1 Starch, 2 Meat

1 recipe Thyme Vinaigrette

3 skinless, boneless chicken breast halves (about 12 ounces total)

1 cup loose-pack frozen French-cut green beans

2 cups cooked brown rice, chilled

1 14-ounce can artichoke hearts, drained and quartered

1 cup shredded red cabbage

½ cup shredded carrot (1 medium)

2 tablespoons sliced green onion (1)

Lettuce leaves (optional)

Chicken and Rice Salad

START TO FINISH: 30 minutes
MAKES: 4 servings

NUTRITION FACTS per serving:

CALORIES 325
TOTAL FAT 9 g total fat (2 g sat. fat)
CHOLESTEROL 50 mg
PROTEIN 25 g
CARBOHYDRATE 32 g
FIBER 6 g
SODIUM 545 mg

EXCHANGES 2 Vegetable, 1½ Starch, 2½ Meat

1 Preheat broiler. Pour 2 tablespoons of the Thyme Vinaigrette into a small bowl; brush onto chicken. Set aside the remaining vinaigrette.

2 Place chicken on the unheated rack of a broiler pan; broil 4 to 5 inches from heat for 12 to 15 minutes or until chicken is tender and no longer pink (170°F), turning once halfway through broiling time. Cut chicken into slices.

3 Meanwhile, rinse green beans with cool water for 30 seconds; drain well. In a large bowl toss together beans, chilled rice, artichoke hearts, cabbage, carrot, and green onion. Pour the remaining vinaigrette over rice mixture; toss to gently coat.

4 If desired, arrange lettuce leaves on four dinner plates. Top with the rice mixture and chicken slices.

Thyme Vinaigrette: In a screw-top jar combine ¼ cup white wine vinegar; 2 tablespoons olive oil; 2 tablespoons water; 1 tablespoon grated Parmesan cheese; 2 teaspoons snipped fresh thyme; 1 clove garlic, minced; ¼ teaspoon salt; and ¼ teaspoon black pepper. Cover and shake well.

- ½ cup buttermilk
- 2 tablespoons low-fat mayonnaise dressing
- 1 tablespoon frozen apple juice concentrate or frozen orange juice concentrate, thawed
- 1 teaspoon Dijon-style mustard
- 6 cups torn mixed salad greens
- 2 medium pears and/or apples, sliced
- 8 ounces cooked turkey or chicken, cut into bite-size strips (1½ cups)
- ¼ cup broken walnuts, toasted (optional)

1 For dressing, in a small bowl stir together buttermilk, mayonnaise dressing, apple juice concentrate, and mustard.

2 In a salad bowl combine salad greens, pear and/or apple slices, and turkey. Drizzle with dressing; toss to coat. If desired, sprinkle with walnuts.

Turkey-Pear Salad

START TO FINISH: 25 minutes
MAKES: 4 main-dish servings

NUTRITION FACTS per serving:

CALORIES 188
TOTAL FAT 4 g total fat (1 g sat. fat)
CHOLESTEROL 46 mg
PROTEIN 19 g
CARBOHYDRATE 20 g carbo
FIBER 3 g fiber
SODIUM 179 mg

EXCHANGES 1 Vegetable, 1 Fruit, 2 Meat

Tuna Salad Niçoise

PREP: 30 minutes   **BROIL:** 8 minutes
MAKES: 4 servings

NUTRITION FACTS per serving:

CALORIES 280
TOTAL FAT 10 g total fat (1 g sat. fat)
CHOLESTEROL 51 mg
PROTEIN 30 g
CARBOHYDRATE 17 g
FIBER 4 g
SODIUM 400 mg

EXCHANGES 2 Vegetable, ½ Starch,
3½ Meat, 1 Fat

1	pound fresh or frozen tuna steaks, 1 inch thick
3	tablespoons sherry vinegar
2	tablespoons finely chopped shallots
1	tablespoon Dijon-style mustard
2	tablespoons olive oil
1	anchovy fillet, rinsed and mashed
	Salt and black pepper
8	ounces tiny new potatoes, quartered
6	ounces green beans
6	cups Bibb or Boston lettuce leaves
¾	cup thinly sliced radishes
½	cup pitted niçoise olives or ripe olives, pitted

1 Thaw fish, if frozen. Rinse fish; pat dry. For dressing, in a small mixing bowl combine vinegar and shallots. Whisk in mustard. Add oil in a thin, steady stream, whisking constantly. Stir in the anchovy. Season to taste with salt and pepper. Remove 1 tablespoon of the dressing for brushing fish; set aside remaining dressing until ready to serve.

2 Preheat broiler. Brush the 1 tablespoon dressing over both sides of fish. Place fish on the greased unheated rack of a broiler pan. Broil about 4 inches from the heat for 8 to 12 minutes or until fish flakes easily when tested with a fork, gently turning once halfway through broiling. (Or grill the fish on the rack of an uncovered grill directly over medium coals for 8 to 12 minutes or until fish flakes easily when tested with a fork, gently turning once halfway through grilling.) Cut fish into slices.

3 Meanwhile, in a medium saucepan cook potatoes in boiling water for 7 minutes. Add green beans; cook for 2 minutes more or until potatoes are tender. Drain and cool slightly.

4 To serve, arrange fish, potatoes, green beans, lettuce leaves, radishes, and olives on four dinner plates. Serve with the remaining dressing.

12 ounces fresh or frozen peeled, deveined medium shrimp or sea scallops

8 ounces dried gemelli pasta (about 2½ cups)

1 6-ounce package frozen snow peas

1 small red sweet pepper, chopped (½ cup)

4 green onions, cut into 1-inch pieces

¼ cup rice vinegar or white wine vinegar

6 teaspoons salad oil

2 tablespoons reduced-sodium soy sauce

1 tablespoon honey

¼ teaspoon crushed red pepper

Black sesame seeds or toasted sesame seeds (optional)

1 Thaw shrimp, if frozen. Cook pasta according to package directions, adding the peas to the pasta water the last 1 minute of cooking; drain and return to pan. Add sweet pepper and green onions to pasta mixture; toss to combine. Cover and set aside.

2 Meanwhile, for dressing, in a screw-top jar combine the vinegar, 4 teaspoons of the oil, the soy sauce, honey, and crushed red pepper. Cover and shake well to combine. Set aside.

3 Rinse shrimp; pat dry. Add remaining 2 teaspoons oil to a large nonstick skillet; add shrimp to hot oil. Cook and stir about 2 minutes or until opaque. Add the shrimp to the pasta mixture. Drizzle mixture with dressing and toss gently to coat. If desired, sprinkle with sesame seeds before serving.

Warm Shrimp and Pasta Salad

START TO FINISH: 30 minutes
MAKES: 4 servings

NUTRITION FACTS per serving:

- -

CALORIES 415
TOTAL FAT 9 g total fat (1 g sat. fat)
CHOLESTEROL 129 mg
PROTEIN 27 g
CARBOHYDRATE 54 g
FIBER 4 g
SODIUM 421 mg

EXCHANGES 2 Vegetable, 3 Starch, 2 Meat, 1 Fat

1 cup loose-pack frozen cut green beans or lima beans

1 15- or 16-ounce can cut wax beans, black beans, or chickpeas (garbanzo beans), rinsed and drained

½ of a 15-ounce can lower-sodium red kidney beans, rinsed and drained

½ cup chopped red or green sweet pepper

⅓ cup chopped red onion (1 small)

¼ cup cider vinegar or white vinegar

2 tablespoons sugar

2 tablespoons salad oil

½ teaspoon celery seeds

½ teaspoon dry mustard

1 clove garlic, minced

Three-Bean Salad

PREP: 15 minutes   **CHILL:** 4 to 24 hours
MAKES: 6 side-dish servings

NUTRITION FACTS per serving:

CALORIES 107
TOTAL FAT 5 g total fat (1 g sat. fat)
CHOLESTEROL 0 mg
PROTEIN 3 g
CARBOHYDRATE 16 g
FIBER 3 g
SODIUM 148 mg

EXCHANGES 1½ Vegetable, ½ Starch, 1 Fat

1 Cook frozen beans according to package directions; drain. Meanwhile, in a large bowl combine wax beans, red kidney beans, sweet pepper, and onion. Add green beans.

2 For dressing, in a screw-top jar combine the vinegar, sugar, salad oil, celery seeds, dry mustard, and garlic. Cover and shake well. Pour over vegetables; stir lightly. Cover and chill for at least 4 hours or up to 24 hours, stirring occasionally. Serve with a slotted spoon.

2 cups cubed fresh pineapple or one 15¼-ounce can pineapple chunks (juice pack), drained

1⅓ cups coarsely chopped apples and/or pears (2 medium)

½ cup thinly sliced celery

½ cup halved seedless red grapes

2 kiwifruits, peeled, halved lengthwise, and sliced

⅓ cup fat-free mayonnaise dressing or salad dressing

⅓ cup fat-free or low-fat lemon yogurt

1 tablespoon honey

2 tablespoons walnut pieces, toasted*

1 In a large bowl toss together pineapple, apples or pears, celery, grapes, and kiwifruits. In a small bowl stir together the mayonnaise dressing, yogurt, and honey; fold gently into fruit mixture. To serve, stir in walnuts.

Make-ahead directions: Prepare as above, except do not stir in walnuts. Cover and chill for up to 6 hours. To serve, stir in walnuts.

*Note: To toast walnuts, place them in a small skillet and cook over medium heat, stirring often, for 5 to 7 minutes or until golden.

Lightened Waldorf Salad

START TO FINISH: 25 minutes
MAKES: 6 to 8 side-dish servings

NUTRITION FACTS per serving:

CALORIES 147
TOTAL FAT 3 g total fat (1 g sat. fat)
CHOLESTEROL 4 mg
PROTEIN 2 g
CARBOHYDRATE 29 g
FIBER 3 g
SODIUM 142 mg

EXCHANGES 2 Fruit, ½ Fat

4   medium potatoes* (1¼ pounds total)
1   cup sliced celery (2 stalks)
¼   cup thinly sliced green onions (2)
½   cup low-fat mayonnaise dressing
½   cup light dairy sour cream
2   tablespoons fat-free milk
2   teaspoons prepared mustard
1   teaspoon snipped fresh dill or ¼ teaspoon dried dill
¼   teaspoon salt
1   hard-cooked egg, chopped
    Lettuce leaves (optional)

Creamy Potato Salad

PREP: 20 minutes   **COOK:** 20 minutes
CHILL: 4 to 24 hours
MAKES: 8 side-dish servings

NUTRITION FACTS per serving:

CALORIES 111
TOTAL FAT 3 g total fat (1 g sat. fat)
CHOLESTEROL 35 mg
PROTEIN 4 g
CARBOHYDRATE 18 g
FIBER 2 g
SODIUM 259 mg

EXCHANGES 1 Starch, ½ Fat

1 Scrub potatoes. In a large covered saucepan cook potatoes in boiling water for 20 to 25 minutes or just until tender. Drain well; cool slightly. Peel and cube potatoes. Transfer to a large bowl. Stir in celery and green onions.

2 In a small bowl stir together the mayonnaise dressing, sour cream, milk, mustard, dill, and salt. Pour over potatoes. Toss lightly to coat. Carefully fold in chopped egg.

3 Cover and chill for at least 4 hours or up to 24 hours. If desired, spoon potato mixture into a lettuce-lined bowl.

*Note: Waxy potatoes, such as long whites and round reds, have a moist, smooth texture and hold their shape after cooking. Tiny new potatoes, which are usually young round reds, also work well in salads.

- 1 cup dried elbow or medium shell macaroni or rotini
- ⅓ cup light dairy sour cream
- ¼ cup low-fat mayonnaise dressing or light salad dressing
- 2 teaspoons Dijon-style mustard
- 1 to 2 teaspoons fat-free milk
- ⅛ teaspoon black pepper
- ½ cup chopped green sweet pepper
- ¼ cup shredded carrot
- 2 tablespoons sliced green onion (1)
- ¼ cup diced cheddar cheese (1 ounce) (optional)

1 Cook macaroni according to package directions, except omit the oil and cook in lightly salted water. Drain well. Rinse with cold water; drain again.

2 For dressing, in a salad bowl stir together sour cream, mayonnaise dressing, mustard, 1 teaspoon of the milk, and the black pepper.

3 Stir the cooked macaroni, sweet pepper, carrot, and green onion into the dressing. Toss lightly to coat. If desired, gently stir in cheese. Cover and chill for at least 3 hours or up to 24 hours. Before serving, stir in the remaining milk if necessary to moisten salad.

Macaroni Salad

PREP: 20 minutes   **CHILL:** 3 to 24 hours
MAKES: 6 side-dish servings

NUTRITION FACTS per serving:

CALORIES 107
TOTAL FAT 2 g total fat (1 g sat. fat)
CHOLESTEROL 6 mg
PROTEIN 3 g
CARBOHYDRATE 18 g
FIBER 1 g
SODIUM 143 mg

EXCHANGES ½ Vegetable, 1 Starch, ½ Fat

Pear and Endive Salad

START TO FINISH: 20 minutes
MAKES: 6 side-dish servings

NUTRITION FACTS per serving:

CALORIES 129
TOTAL FAT 7 g total fat (1 g sat. fat)
CHOLESTEROL 0 mg
PROTEIN 1 g
CARBOHYDRATE 18 g
FIBER 2 g
SODIUM 48 mg

EXCHANGES 1 Vegetable, 1 Fruit, 1 Fat

3	ripe red Bartlett pears, Bosc pears, and/or apples, cored and thinly sliced
2	tablespoons water
1	tablespoon lemon juice
12	ounces Belgian endive, leaves separated (3 medium heads)
2	tablespoons coarsely chopped walnuts, toasted
	Dash salt
	Dash black pepper
2	tablespoons olive oil or salad oil
2	tablespoons sherry vinegar or white wine vinegar
1	shallot, finely chopped, or 1 tablespoon finely chopped onion
1	tablespoon honey
1	teaspoon Dijon-style mustard
	Black peppercorns (optional)

1 In a medium bowl gently toss pear and/or apple slices with 1 tablespoon of the water and the lemon juice. Arrange the endive leaves on 6 salad plates. Using a slotted spoon, spoon the sliced pears or apples onto the endive. Sprinkle with walnuts, salt, and the dash pepper.

2 For vinaigrette, in a small bowl combine oil, vinegar, the remaining 1 tablespoon water, the shallot, honey, and mustard. Whisk until thoroughly mixed.

3 Drizzle the vinaigrette over the salads. If desired, grind peppercorns over salads.

10	baby artichokes or two 8-ounce packages frozen artichoke hearts
2	tablespoons lemon juice
2	tablespoons snipped fresh mint
1	teaspoon finely shredded lemon peel
2	tablespoons lemon juice
4	teaspoons olive oil
¼	teaspoon salt
⅛	teaspoon black pepper
2	large cloves garlic, minced
1	small bulb fennel, halved and cored
½	of a small red onion
1	cup halved cherry tomatoes
	Fresh fennel leaves (optional)

1 To prepare artichokes, trim stems; cut off top one-fourth of each artichoke. Remove outer leaves until you reach the pale green parts. Halve or cut artichokes into wedges. Brush cut edges with some of the 2 tablespoons lemon juice; add remaining juice to cooking water. In a large saucepan cook artichokes in a large amount of boiling water for 12 to 15 minutes or until tender; drain. (Or cook frozen artichoke hearts according to package directions; drain.) Rinse with cold water. Drain and place in a large bowl.

2 Meanwhile, for dressing, in a small bowl combine mint, lemon peel, lemon juice, oil, salt, pepper, and garlic.

3 Thinly slice fennel and red onion. Add to artichokes along with tomatoes. Pour dressing over; toss to coat.

4 Cover and chill for at least 2 hours or up to 4 hours. Serve chilled or at room temperature. If desired, garnish with fennel leaves.

Artichoke Salad

PREP: 30 minutes   **CHILL:** 2 to 4 hours
MAKES: 6 side-dish servings

NUTRITION FACTS per serving:

CALORIES 59
TOTAL FAT 3 g total fat (0 g sat. fat)
CHOLESTEROL 0 mg
PROTEIN 2 g
CARBOHYDRATE 8 g
FIBER 6 g
SODIUM 135 mg

EXCHANGES 1 Vegetable, ½ Fat

Romaine leaves

9	cups torn mixed salad greens
1	small tart green apple, cored and cut into thin wedges
1	small red apple, cored and cut into thin wedges
3	tablespoons cider vinegar
3	tablespoons olive oil
¼	teaspoon black pepper
⅛	teaspoon salt
¼	cup mixed nuts, toasted

1 Place several romaine leaves on each salad plate. Top with the torn greens and apples.

2 In a small screw-top jar combine vinegar, oil, pepper, and salt. Cover and shake well. Drizzle dressing over salad. Sprinkle with nuts.

Nutty Apple Salad

START TO FINISH: 20 minutes
MAKES: 8 to 10 servings

NUTRITION FACTS per serving:

- -

CALORIES 106
TOTAL FAT 8 g total fat (1 g sat. fat)
CHOLESTEROL 0 mg
PROTEIN 2 g
CARBOHYDRATE 9 g
FIBER 3 g
SODIUM 73 mg

EXCHANGES 1 Vegetable, ½ Fruit, 1½ Fat

On the opener: Turkey-Ravoli Soup (*see recipe, page 104*)

BEEF

PORK & LAMB

CHICKEN & TURKEY

FISH & SEAFOOD

MEATLESS

- 6 ounces boneless beef top sirloin steak
- 1 teaspoon olive oil
- ½ cup chopped onion (1 medium)
- 2 cups water
- 1 14-ounce can beef broth
- 1 14½-ounce can low-sodium tomatoes, undrained and cut up
- ½ cup thinly sliced carrot (1 medium)
- 1 teaspoon unsweetened cocoa powder
- 1 clove garlic, minced
- 1 cup thinly sliced cabbage
- 1 ounce dried wide noodles (about ½ cup)
- 2 teaspoons paprika
- ¼ cup light dairy sour cream
  Snipped fresh parsley (optional)
  Paprika (optional)

1 Trim fat from steak. Cut steak into ½-inch cubes. In a large saucepan cook and stir steak cubes in hot oil over medium-high heat about 6 minutes or until beef is browned. Add onion; cook and stir about 3 minutes more or until tender.

2 Stir in the water, broth, undrained tomatoes, carrot, cocoa powder, and garlic. Bring to boiling; reduce heat. Simmer, uncovered, about 15 minutes or until beef is tender.

3 Stir in the cabbage, uncooked noodles, and the 2 teaspoons paprika. Simmer, uncovered, for 5 to 7 minutes more or until noodles are tender but still firm. Remove from heat. Top each serving with some of the sour cream. If desired, sprinkle with the parsley and the additional paprika.

Beef Goulash Soup

PREP: 30 minutes　　**COOK:** 20 minutes
MAKES: 4 servings (about 6 cups)

NUTRITION FACTS per serving:

CALORIES 188
TOTAL FAT 7 g total fat (3 g sat. fat)
CHOLESTEROL 36 mg
PROTEIN 14 g
CARBOHYDRATE 16 g
FIBER 3 g
SODIUM 397 mg

EXCHANGES 2 Vegetable, ½ Starch, 1½ Meat

Beef Soup with Root Vegetables

PREP: 25 minutes   **COOK:** 1½ hours
MAKES: 6 servings (about 8 cups)

NUTRITION FACTS per serving:

CALORIES 240
TOTAL FAT 9 g total fat (2 g sat. fat)
CHOLESTEROL 44 mg
PROTEIN 20 g
CARBOHYDRATE 21 g
FIBER 3 g
SODIUM 545 mg

EXCHANGES 1 Vegetable, 1 Starch,
2 Meat, ½ Fat

1	pound boneless beef round steak
2	tablespoons olive oil
2	stalks celery, sliced
1	large onion, cut into thin wedges
1	medium carrot, cut into ½-inch slices
2	cloves garlic, minced
2	14-ounce cans beef broth
1	cup water
2	sprigs fresh thyme
1	bay leaf
2	medium potatoes, peeled and cut into ¾-inch cubes
2	medium turnips, peeled and cut into ¾-inch cubes
1	large sweet potato, peeled and cut into ¾-inch cubes

1 Trim fat from steak. Cut steak into ¾-inch cubes. In a 4-quart Dutch oven cook meat, half at a time, in 1 tablespoon of the hot oil over medium heat until browned. Remove meat.

2 In the same Dutch oven heat the remaining 1 tablespoon oil over medium heat. Add celery, onion, carrot, and garlic; cook for 3 minutes, stirring frequently. Drain off fat. Return meat to Dutch oven.

3 Stir in broth, the water, thyme, and bay leaf. Bring to boiling; reduce heat. Simmer, covered, about 1¼ hours or until meat is almost tender. Discard thyme and bay leaf. Stir in potatoes, turnips, and sweet potato. Bring to boiling; reduce heat. Simmer, covered, about 15 minutes more or until meat and vegetables are tender.

Nonstick cooking spray

8 ounces boneless beef top sirloin or top round steak, cut into ¾-inch cubes

½ cup chopped onion (1 medium)

½ cup sliced celery (1 stalk)

2 cloves garlic, minced

1 cup water

1 15¼-ounce can pineapple tidbits (juice pack)

1 15- to 15¾-ounce can chili beans with chili gravy

1 14½-ounce can diced tomatoes, undrained

1 8-ounce can low-sodium tomato sauce

1 tablespoon brown sugar

2 teaspoons chili powder

¼ teaspoon salt

⅛ teaspoon cayenne pepper

Light dairy sour cream (optional)

1 Lightly coat an unheated 4-quart Dutch oven with nonstick cooking spray. Preheat over medium-high heat. Add meat, onion, celery, and garlic. Cook and stir until meat is browned and onion is tender.

2 Carefully stir in the water, undrained pineapple, undrained chili beans, undrained tomatoes, tomato sauce, brown sugar, chili powder, salt, and cayenne pepper. Bring to boiling; reduce heat. Simmer, covered, for 45 to 60 minutes or until meat is tender. If desired, serve with sour cream.

Spicy Sweet Chili

PREP: 20 minutes   **COOK:** 45 minutes
MAKES: 5 or 6 servings (about 6 cups)

NUTRITION FACTS per serving:

CALORIES 239
TOTAL FAT 2 g total fat (0 g sat. fat)
CHOLESTEROL 27 mg
PROTEIN 16 g
CARBOHYDRATE 38 g
FIBER 7 g
SODIUM 524 mg

EXCHANGES 2 Vegetable, 1 Fruit, 1 Starch, 1 Meat

2 teaspoons cooking oil

⅓ cup chopped onion (1 small)

4 cloves garlic, minced

12 ounces pork tenderloin, cut into ¾-inch cubes

2 teaspoons chili powder

2 teaspoons ground cumin

1 yellow or red sweet pepper, cut into ½-inch chunks

1 cup beer or beef broth

½ cup bottled picante sauce or salsa

1 to 2 tablespoons finely chopped canned chipotle peppers in adobo sauce

1 15-ounce can small red beans or pinto beans, rinsed and drained

1 In a large saucepan heat oil over medium-high heat. Add onion and garlic; cook about 3 minutes or until tender. In a large bowl toss pork with chili powder and cumin; add to saucepan. Cook and stir about 3 minutes or until pork is browned.

2 Stir in sweet pepper, beer or broth, picante sauce or salsa, and chipotle peppers. Bring to boiling; reduce heat. Simmer, uncovered, about 5 minutes or just until pork is tender. Add beans; heat through.

Chunky Chipotle Pork Chili

START TO FINISH: 30 minutes
MAKES: 4 servings (4 cups)

NUTRITION FACTS per serving:

CALORIES 281
TOTAL FAT 5 g total fat (1 g sat. fat)
CHOLESTEROL 50 mg
PROTEIN 27 g
CARBOHYDRATE 27 g
FIBER 7 g
SODIUM 630 mg

EXCHANGES 1 Vegetable, 1½ Starch, 3 Meat

- 1½   pounds lean boneless lamb
- 1   tablespoon cooking oil
- 1   14-ounce can reduced-sodium chicken broth
- 1¼   cups apple juice or apple cider
- 2   medium sweet potatoes, peeled and cut into bite-size pieces
- 1   cup loose-pack frozen small whole onions
- ½   teaspoon salt
- ½   teaspoon ground allspice
- ¼   teaspoon black pepper
- 2   cups loose-pack frozen cut green beans
- 1   large Jonathan, Jonagold, or Fuji apple, peeled, if desired, and cut into bite-size pieces
- ¼   cup apple juice or apple cider
- 2   tablespoons cornstarch

1 Trim fat from meat. Cut meat into 1-inch cubes. In a 4-quart Dutch oven brown meat, half at a time, in hot oil. Drain off fat. Return all meat to Dutch oven. Add broth and the 1¼ cups apple juice. Stir in sweet potatoes, onions, salt, allspice, and pepper.

2 Bake, covered, in a 350°F oven for 1 hour. Stir in green beans and apple. Cover and bake for 15 to 20 minutes more or until meat is tender. Remove Dutch oven from the oven; place on the range top.

3 In a small bowl stir together the ¼ cup apple juice and the cornstarch. Stir into meat mixture. Cook and stir over medium heat until thickened and bubbly. Cook and stir for 2 minutes more.

Sweet Potato and Lamb Stew

PREP: 30 minutes   **BAKE:** 1¼ hours
OVEN: 350°F
MAKES: 6 servings (8 cups)

NUTRITION FACTS per serving:

CALORIES 297
TOTAL FAT 6 g total fat (2 g sat. fat)
CHOLESTEROL 71 mg
PROTEIN 26 g
CARBOHYDRATE 34 g
FIBER 4 g
SODIUM 447 mg

EXCHANGES 1 Vegetable, 1 Fruit, 1 Starch, 3 Meat

1 cup chopped onion (1 large)

1 cup coarsely chopped carrots (2 medium)

1 cup sliced celery (2 stalks)

1 tablespoon cooking oil

1⅓ cups chopped tart apples

2 to 3 teaspoons curry powder

¼ teaspoon salt

3 cups reduced-sodium chicken broth

3 cups water

1 14½-ounce can low-sodium stewed tomatoes, undrained

2 cups chopped cooked chicken or turkey (about 10 ounces)

Mulligatawny Soup

PREP: 35 minutes   **COOK:** 20 minutes
MAKES: 6 servings (about 10 cups)

NUTRITION FACTS per serving:

CALORIES 173
TOTAL FAT 6 g total fat (1 g sat. fat)
CHOLESTEROL 42 mg
PROTEIN 16 g
CARBOHYDRATE 14 g
FIBER 3 g
SODIUM 498 mg

EXCHANGES 1 Vegetable, ½ Fruit, 2 Meat

1 In a Dutch oven cook and stir onion, carrots, and celery in hot oil over medium heat about 10 minutes or until crisp-tender. Reduce heat to medium-low; add apples, curry powder, and salt. Cook, covered, for 5 minutes.

2 Stir in broth, the water, and undrained tomatoes. Bring to boiling; reduce heat. Simmer, uncovered, for 10 minutes. Stir in the cooked chicken; simmer for 10 minutes more.

1 6.2-ounce package quick-cooking long grain and wild rice mix

2 14-ounce cans reduced-sodium chicken broth

1 tablespoon snipped fresh thyme or 1 teaspoon dried thyme, crushed

4 cloves garlic, minced

4 cups chopped tomatoes

1 9-ounce package frozen, chopped cooked chicken

1 cup finely chopped zucchini

¼ teaspoon freshly ground black pepper

1 tablespoon Madeira or dry sherry

1 Prepare rice mix according to package directions, except omit the seasoning packet and the margarine.

2 Meanwhile, in a Dutch oven combine chicken broth, dried thyme (if using), and garlic; bring to boiling. Stir in the tomatoes, chicken, zucchini, pepper, and fresh thyme (if using). Return to boiling; reduce heat. Simmer, covered, for 5 minutes. Stir in cooked rice and Madeira or sherry. Heat through.

Wild Rice Chicken Soup

START TO FINISH: 25 minutes
MAKES: 6 main-dish servings (about 10 cups)

NUTRITION FACTS per serving:

CALORIES 223
TOTAL FAT 4 g total fat (1 g sat. fat)
CHOLESTEROL 38 mg
PROTEIN 18 g
CARBOHYDRATE 30 g
FIBER 3 g
SODIUM 793 mg

EXCHANGES 2 Vegetable, 1 Starch, 1½ Meat

Hot and Sour Soup

START TO FINISH: 30 minutes
MAKES: 4 servings (about 5 cups)

NUTRITION FACTS per serving:

CALORIES 144
TOTAL FAT 7 g total fat (1 g sat. fat)
CHOLESTEROL 31 mg
PROTEIN 15 g
CARBOHYDRATE 6 g
FIBER 1 g
SODIUM 838 mg

EXCHANGES 1 Vegetable, 2 Meat

4   ounces fresh shiitake mushrooms, stems removed and caps thinly sliced
2   cloves garlic, minced
2   teaspoons peanut oil or cooking oil
2   14-ounce cans reduced-sodium chicken broth
2   tablespoons white vinegar or seasoned rice vinegar
2   tablespoons reduced-sodium soy sauce
½   teaspoon crushed red pepper or 1 teaspoon chile oil
1   cup shredded cooked chicken (about 5 ounces)
2   cups packaged shredded cabbage with carrot (coleslaw mix) or shredded napa cabbage
2   tablespoons cold water
1   tablespoon cornstarch
1   teaspoon toasted sesame oil
    Sliced green onions (optional)

1 In a large saucepan cook mushrooms and garlic in hot oil for 4 minutes, stirring occasionally. Stir in broth, vinegar, soy sauce, and red pepper or chile oil; bring to boiling. Stir in chicken and coleslaw mix or napa cabbage. Return to boiling; reduce heat. Simmer, uncovered, for 5 minutes.

2 In a small bowl stir together cold water and cornstarch. Stir into soup; simmer about 2 minutes or until slightly thickened. Remove from heat; stir in sesame oil. If desired, sprinkle with sliced green onions.

- ½ cup chopped celery (1 stalk)
- ½ cup sliced leek or chopped onion
- ½ cup thinly sliced carrot (1 medium)
- 1 tablespoon butter or margarine
- 1 14-ounce can reduced-sodium chicken broth
- ¼ cup all-purpose flour
- 2 cups milk
- 1 tablespoon snipped fresh thyme or basil or 1 teaspoon dried thyme or basil, crushed
- ¼ teaspoon salt
- 1½ cups chopped cooked chicken or turkey (about 8 ounces)
- ¼ cup dry white wine or reduced-sodium chicken broth

  Cracked black pepper

1 In a large saucepan cook celery, leek or onion, and carrot in hot butter until tender. In a medium bowl gradually stir the 14-ounce can of chicken broth into the flour; stir into vegetables in saucepan. Add milk, dried herb (if using), and salt. Cook and stir until slightly thickened and bubbly; cook and stir for 1 minute more.

2 Stir in chicken, wine or the ¼ cup chicken broth, and fresh herb (if using). Cook about 2 minutes more or until heated through.

3 To serve, ladle into soup bowls. Sprinkle with pepper.

Chicken-Vegetable Soup

START TO FINISH: 30 minutes
MAKES: 4 servings (about 5 cups)

NUTRITION FACTS per serving:

- -

CALORIES 254
TOTAL FAT 10 g total fat (5 g sat. fat)
CHOLESTEROL 68 mg
PROTEIN 23 g
CARBOHYDRATE 16 g
FIBER 1 g
SODIUM 560 mg

EXCHANGES ½ Milk, 1½ Vegetable, 2½ Meat, 1 Fat

6 cups reduced-sodium chicken broth

¾ cup chopped red sweet pepper (1 medium)

½ cup chopped onion (1 medium)

1½ teaspoons dried Italian seasoning, crushed

1½ cups cooked turkey cut into bite-size pieces (about 8 ounces)

1 9-ounce package refrigerated light cheese ravioli

2 cups shredded fresh spinach

Finely shredded Parmesan cheese (optional)

1 In a Dutch oven combine chicken broth, sweet pepper, onion, and Italian seasoning. Bring to boiling; reduce heat. Simmer, covered, for 5 minutes. Add turkey and ravioli. Return to boiling; reduce heat. Simmer, uncovered, about 6 minutes or just until ravioli is tender. Stir in spinach. If desired, sprinkle with Parmesan cheese.

Turkey-Ravioli Soup

START TO FINISH: 25 minutes
MAKES: 6 main-dish servings (about 8 cups)

NUTRITION FACTS per serving:

CALORIES 246
TOTAL FAT 7 g total fat (3 g sat. fat)
CHOLESTEROL 48 mg
PROTEIN 22 g
CARBOHYDRATE 24 g
FIBER 2 g
SODIUM 879 mg

EXCHANGES 1½ Vegetable, 1 Starch, 2½ Meat

12	ounces turkey breast tenderloin or skinless, boneless chicken breasts or thighs
1	tablespoon cooking oil
½	cup chopped onion (1 medium)
½	cup chopped red or green sweet pepper
1	clove garlic, minced
2	14-ounce cans reduced-sodium chicken broth
1½	cups loose-pack frozen cut green beans
1	cup loose-pack frozen whole kernel corn or one 8-ounce can whole kernel corn, drained
⅓	cup quick-cooking barley
2	tablespoons snipped fresh basil or 1½ teaspoons dried basil, crushed
¼	teaspoon salt
¼	teaspoon black pepper

1 Cut turkey or chicken into bite-size pieces or cubes. In a Dutch oven cook and stir turkey or chicken in hot oil for 5 minutes. With a slotted spoon remove from pan. In pan drippings cook onion, sweet pepper, and garlic for 3 minutes, stirring occasionally. Drain off fat.

2 Return turkey or chicken to Dutch oven. Add broth, beans, corn, barley, dried basil (if using), salt, and black pepper. Bring to boiling; reduce heat. Simmer, covered, for 10 to 15 minutes or until barley is cooked. Stir in fresh basil (if using).

Turkey Soup with Barley

PREP: 35 minutes   **COOK:** 10 minutes
MAKES: 4 servings (about 6 cups)

NUTRITION FACTS per serving:

- -

CALORIES 247
TOTAL FAT 5 g total fat (1 g sat. fat)
CHOLESTEROL 51 mg
PROTEIN 26 g
CARBOHYDRATE 25 g
FIBER 4 g
SODIUM 703 mg

EXCHANGES 1 Vegetable, 1 Starch, 2 Meat

Manhattan Clam Chowder

START TO FINISH: 40 minutes
MAKES: 4 main-dish servings (about 6½ cups)

NUTRITION FACTS per serving:
- -

CALORIES 264
TOTAL FAT 10 g total fat (2 g sat. fat)
CHOLESTEROL 43 mg
PROTEIN 18 g
CARBOHYDRATE 23 g
FIBER 3 g
SODIUM 375 mg

EXCHANGES 1 Vegetable, 1 Starch,
2 Meat, 1 Fat

1 pint shucked clams or two
6½-ounce cans minced clams

1 cup chopped celery (2 stalks)

⅓ cup chopped onion (1 small)

¼ cup chopped carrot (1 small)

2 tablespoons olive oil or cooking oil

1 8-ounce bottle clam juice or 1 cup
chicken broth

2 cups red potatoes cut into bite
size pieces

1 teaspoon dried thyme, crushed

⅛ teaspoon cayenne pepper

⅛ teaspoon black pepper

1 14½-ounce can diced tomatoes,
undrained

2 tablespoons purchased cooked
bacon pieces or cooked
crumbled bacon*

1 Chop fresh clams, if using, reserving juice; set clams aside. Strain clam juice to remove bits of shell. (Or drain canned clams, reserving juice.) If necessary, add enough water to reserved juice to equal 1½ cups liquid. Set juice aside.

2 In a large saucepan cook celery, onion, and carrot in hot oil until tender. Stir in the reserved 1½ cups clam juice and the bottled clam juice or chicken broth. Stir in potatoes, thyme, cayenne pepper, and black pepper. Bring to boiling; reduce heat. Simmer, covered, for 10 minutes. Stir in tomatoes, clams, and bacon. Return to boiling; reduce heat. Cook for 1 to 2 minutes more or until heated through.

*Note: If using bacon, cook 2 slices, reserving 2 tablespoons drippings. Omit the oil and cook the celery, onion, and carrot in the reserved drippings.

- 1 cup dried small shell macaroni or small bow ties (4 ounces)
- 4 cups hot-style vegetable juice, chilled
- 1 tablespoon lime juice or lemon juice
- 6 ounces cooked crabmeat, flaked, or chopped cooked chicken (about 1¼ cups)
- 2 medium nectarines, chopped (1⅓ cups)
- 2 roma tomatoes, chopped (about 1 cup)
- ¼ cup chopped, seeded cucumber
- 2 tablespoons snipped fresh basil
  Lime slices (optional)
  Cucumber sticks (optional)

1 Cook pasta according to package directions; drain. Rinse with cold water; drain again.

2 Meanwhile, in a large bowl stir together vegetable juice and lime juice. Stir in pasta, crabmeat, nectarines, tomatoes, cucumber, and basil. Ladle soup into glasses or bowls. If desired, garnish with lime slices and cucumber sticks.

Crab and Pasta Gazpacho

START TO FINISH: 25 minutes
MAKES: 6 servings (8 cups)

NUTRITION FACTS per serving:

- -

CALORIES 157
TOTAL FAT 1 g total fat (0 g sat. fat)
CHOLESTEROL 28 mg
PROTEIN 10 g
CARBOHYDRATE 27 g
FIBER 2 g
SODIUM 603 mg

EXCHANGES 2 Vegetable, ½ Fruit, ½ Starch, 1 Meat

1	cup chopped celery (2 stalks)
1	cup chopped onion (1 large)
2	cloves garlic
1	tablespoon olive oil
5	cups vegetable broth or chicken broth
1	cup water
½	cup Arborio rice
3	medium tomatoes
1	medium zucchini
6	cups torn fresh spinach
1	15-ounce can Great Northern beans, rinsed and drained
¼	cup snipped fresh thyme
¼	teaspoon cracked black pepper
½	cup crumbled feta cheese (2 ounces)

Hearty Bean and Rice Soup

START TO FINISH: 30 minutes
MAKES: 6 servings (about 10½ cups)

NUTRITION FACTS per serving:

- -

CALORIES 213
TOTAL FAT 6 g total fat (2 g sat. fat)
CHOLESTEROL 8 mg
PROTEIN 10 g
CARBOHYDRATE 33 g
FIBER 8 g
SODIUM 1,165 mg

EXCHANGES 2 Vegetable, 1½ Starch,
½ Meat, ½ Fat

1 In a Dutch oven cook celery, onion, and garlic in hot oil until tender. Add broth, the water, and uncooked rice. Bring to boiling; reduce heat. Simmer, covered, for 15 minutes.

2 Meanwhile, chop the tomatoes; coarsely chop the zucchini. Stir tomatoes, zucchini, torn spinach, beans, thyme, and pepper into mixture in Dutch oven. Cook and stir until heated through. Top each serving with feta cheese.

Chapter 7

Beef, Veal & Lamb

On the opener: Peppercorn Steaks *(see recipe, page 119)*

- 1 3-pound boneless beef bottom round roast
  Salt
  Black pepper
- 1 tablespoon cooking oil
- 1 14-ounce can beef broth
- ½ cup coarsely chopped onion (1 medium)
- ½ teaspoon dried marjoram, crushed
- ½ teaspoon dried thyme, crushed
- 2 cloves garlic, minced
- 4 cups cut-up vegetables (such as 2-inch pieces of peeled winter squash, carrots, parsnips, and/or green beans)
- 2 tablespoons cold water
- 1 tablespoon cornstarch

1 Trim fat from meat. Sprinkle meat lightly with salt and pepper. In a 4- to 6-quart Dutch oven brown meat on all sides in hot oil for 5 minutes, turning to brown evenly. Drain off fat. Carefully pour broth over meat. Add onion, marjoram, thyme, and garlic. Bake, covered, in a 325°F oven for 2 hours.

2 Add vegetables. Cover and bake for 30 to 40 minutes more or until tender. Transfer meat and vegetables to a serving platter; reserve cooking liquid in Dutch oven. Cover platter with foil to keep warm.

3 For gravy, strain juices into a glass measuring cup. Skim fat from juices; return 1¼ cups of the juices to Dutch oven (discard remaining juices). In a small bowl stir together the cold water and cornstarch. Stir into juices in Dutch oven. Cook and stir until thickened and bubbly. Cook and stir for 2 minutes more. Season to taste with salt and pepper. Slice meat. Spoon some of the gravy over meat and vegetables. Pass remaining gravy.

Garden Pot Roast

PREP: 25 minutes　　**BAKE:** 2½ hours
OVEN: 325°F　　**MAKES:** 8 servings

NUTRITION FACTS per serving:

CALORIES 250
TOTAL FAT 8 g total fat (2 g sat. fat)
CHOLESTEROL 83 mg
PROTEIN 33 g
CARBOHYDRATE 9 g
FIBER 2 g
SODIUM 337 mg

EXCHANGES 1½ Vegetable, 4 Meat

Nonstick cooking spray

⅓   cup sliced green onions

¼   cup finely chopped red and/or
     yellow sweet pepper

¼   cup finely chopped carrot

2   slightly beaten egg whites

½   cup finely crushed saltine crackers
     (14 crackers)

2   tablespoons fat-free milk

⅓   cup bottled chili sauce

1   tablespoon snipped fresh basil or
     oregano or ½ teaspoon dried
     basil or oregano, crushed

¼   teaspoon black pepper

1   pound extra-lean ground beef

1   tablespoon brown sugar

1   teaspoon vinegar

Fresh herb sprigs (optional)

Mom's Meat Loaf

PREP: 30 minutes   **BAKE:** 45 minutes
OVEN: 350°F   **STAND:** 10 minutes
MAKES: 6 servings

NUTRITION FACTS per serving:

CALORIES 189
TOTAL FAT 8 g total fat (3 g sat. fat)
CHOLESTEROL 48 mg
PROTEIN 16 g
CARBOHYDRATE 12 g
FIBER 1 g
SODIUM 319 mg

EXCHANGES 1 Vegetable, ½ Starch, 2 Meat

1 Coat an unheated small skillet with nonstick cooking spray. Preheat over medium heat. Add the green onions, sweet pepper, and carrot. Cook for 5 to 8 minutes or until vegetables are tender, stirring occasionally. Remove from heat; cool slightly.

2 In a large bowl stir together the egg whites, crushed crackers, milk, 2 tablespoons of the chili sauce, the basil or oregano, and black pepper. Add the cooked vegetables and the ground beef; mix well.

3 Firmly pat the meat mixture into a 7½×3½×2-inch loaf pan. Invert pan with meat mixture into a shallow baking pan; remove loaf pan. Bake the meat loaf in a 350°F oven for 30 minutes.

4 Meanwhile, in a small bowl combine remaining chili sauce, brown sugar, and vinegar; spoon over meat loaf. Bake for 15 to 20 minutes more or until internal temperature registers 160°F on an instant-read thermometer. Let stand for 10 minutes. Transfer meat loaf to a platter. To serve, cut into slices. If desired, garnish with herb sprigs.

4 small green sweet peppers
  Salt (optional)

12 ounces extra-lean ground beef

⅓ cup chopped onion (1 small)

1 cup water

⅓ cup long grain rice

1 tablespoon Worcestershire sauce

1 tablespoon snipped fresh basil or oregano or ½ teaspoon dried basil or oregano, crushed

¼ teaspoon salt

¼ teaspoon black pepper

2 medium tomatoes, peeled and chopped

¼ cup shredded cheddar or Monterey Jack cheese (1 ounce)

1 Cut tops off sweet peppers; remove seeds and membranes. Immerse sweet peppers in boiling water for 3 minutes. If desired, sprinkle insides with salt. Invert on paper towels to drain well.

2 In a large skillet cook meat and onion until meat is brown and onion is tender. Drain off fat. Stir in the water, uncooked rice, Worcestershire sauce, dried basil or oregano (if using), the ¼ teaspoon salt, and the black pepper. Bring to boiling; reduce heat. Simmer, covered, for 15 to 18 minutes or until rice is tender. Stir in tomatoes and the fresh herb (if using).

3 Spoon meat mixture into sweet peppers. Place in a 2-quart square baking dish along with any remaining meat mixture. Bake, uncovered, in a 375°F oven for 15 to 20 minutes or until heated through. Sprinkle with cheese. Let stand about 2 minutes or until cheese is melted.

Stuffed Green Peppers

PREP: 35 minutes **BAKE:** 15 minutes
OVEN: 375°F **STAND:** 2 minutes
MAKES: 4 servings

NUTRITION FACTS per serving:

CALORIES 264
TOTAL FAT 11 g total fat (5 g sat. fat)
CHOLESTEROL 61 mg
PROTEIN 19 g
CARBOHYDRATE 22 g
FIBER 3 g
SODIUM 278 mg

EXCHANGES 2 Vegetable, 1 Starch, 2½ Meat

Peppered Steak with Mushroom Sauce

START TO FINISH: 40 minutes
MAKES: 6 servings

NUTRITION FACTS per serving:

CALORIES 336
TOTAL FAT 11 g total fat (4 g sat. fat)
CHOLESTEROL 93 mg
PROTEIN 31 g
CARBOHYDRATE 26 g
FIBER 1 g
SODIUM 262 mg

EXCHANGES ½ Vegetable, 1½ Starch, 3½ Meat

6	beef tenderloin steaks or 3 beef top sirloin steaks, cut 1 inch thick (about 1½ pounds total)
1½	teaspoons dried whole green peppercorns, crushed, or ½ teaspoon coarsely ground black pepper
1½	teaspoons dried Italian seasoning, crushed
¼	teaspoon salt
	Nonstick cooking spray
⅓	cup water
½	teaspoon instant beef bouillon granules
1	3-ounce package fresh shiitake mushrooms or 3 ounces other fresh mushrooms, sliced (about 1¼ cups)
1	cup reduced-fat milk
2	tablespoons all-purpose flour
½	cup light dairy sour cream
3	cups hot cooked noodles

1 Trim fat from meat. For rub, in a small bowl combine peppercorns, 1 teaspoon of the Italian seasoning, and the salt. Sprinkle rub evenly over both sides of meat; press in with your fingers.

2 Coat an unheated large nonstick skillet with nonstick cooking spray. Preheat skillet over medium heat. Add meat; cook for 10 to 12 minutes or until medium doneness (160°F), turning once. Remove from skillet. Cover and keep warm.

3 Add the water and bouillon granules to skillet. Bring to boiling. Add mushrooms. Cook about 2 minutes or until tender. In a small bowl stir together the milk, flour, and remaining ½ teaspoon Italian seasoning. Add to skillet. Cook and stir until thickened and bubbly. Stir in sour cream; heat through but do not boil. Serve meat with noodles. Spoon the sauce over meat and noodles.

1   1¼-pound beef flank steak
½   cup beef broth
⅓   cup hoisin sauce
¼   cup reduced-sodium soy sauce
¼   cup sliced green onions (2)
3   tablespoons dry sherry or apple,
    orange, or pineapple juice
1   tablespoon sugar
1   teaspoon grated fresh ginger
4   cloves garlic, minced
    Nonstick cooking spray

1 Trim fat from steak. Place steak in a plastic bag set in a shallow dish. For marinade, in a small bowl stir together broth, hoisin sauce, soy sauce, green onions, sherry or juice, sugar, ginger, and garlic. Pour over steak; seal bag. Marinate in refrigerator for at least 4 hours or up to 24 hours, turning bag occasionally.

2 Preheat broiler. Drain steak, discarding the marinade. Lightly coat the unheated rack of a broiler pan with nonstick cooking spray. Place steak on the prepared rack. Broil 4 to 5 inches from heat for 15 to 18 minutes or until medium doneness (160°F), turning once. (Or grill steak on the rack of an uncovered grill directly over medium coals for 17 to 21 minutes or until medium doneness [160°F], turning once.) To serve, thinly slice the steak across the grain.

Asian Flank Steak

PREP: 15 minutes

BROIL: 15 minutes

MARINATE: 4 to 24 hours

MAKES: 6 servings

NUTRITION FACTS per serving:

CALORIES 167
TOTAL FAT 7 g total fat (3 g sat. fat)
CHOLESTEROL 47 mg
PROTEIN 20 g
CARBOHYDRATE 4 g
FIBER 0 g
SODIUM 344 mg

EXCHANGES 3 Meat

Pepper-Marinated Flank Steak

PREP: 10 minutes
BROIL: 15 minutes

MARINATE: 6 to 24 hours
MAKES: 6 servings

NUTRITION FACTS per serving:

CALORIES 336
TOTAL FAT 10 g total fat (4 g sat. fat)
CHOLESTEROL 40 mg
PROTEIN 34 g
CARBOHYDRATE 26 g
FIBER 4 g
SODIUM 612 mg

EXCHANGES 2 Vegetable, 1 Starch, 3½ Meat

1	1¼-pound beef flank steak
½	cup dry red wine
⅓	cup finely chopped onion (1 small)
2	tablespoons lime juice
1	tablespoon reduced-sodium soy sauce
1	tablespoon cooking oil
1	teaspoon crushed red pepper
½	teaspoon coarsely ground black pepper
½	teaspoon dried whole green peppercorns, crushed
3	cloves garlic, minced
3	pita bread rounds, halved crosswise
6	lettuce leaves
1	small red onion, sliced and separated into rings

1 Trim fat from steak. Score both sides of steak in a diamond pattern by making shallow diagonal cuts at 1-inch intervals. Place steak in a plastic bag set in a shallow dish.

2 For marinade, in a small bowl stir together wine, chopped onion, lime juice, soy sauce, oil, red pepper, black pepper, green peppercorns, and garlic. Pour over steak; seal bag. Marinate in the refrigerator for at least 6 hours or up to 24 hours, turning bag occasionally.

3 Preheat broiler. Drain steak, reserving marinade. Place steak on the unheated rack of a broiler pan. Broil 3 to 4 inches from the heat for 15 to 18 minutes or until medium doneness (160°F), turning and brushing once with reserved marinade halfway through broiling time. Discard any remaining marinade.

4 To serve, thinly slice steak diagonally across the grain. Fill pita bread halves with meat, lettuce, and onion.

- 1 cup loosely packed fresh spinach leaves
- ½ cup finely chopped water chestnuts
- ¼ cup thinly sliced green onions (2)
- ¼ cup bottled reduced-sodium teriyaki sauce
- 1 1¼-pound beef flank steak
     Salt
     Black pepper

1 Preheat broiler. Remove stems from spinach leaves. Layer leaves on top of each other; slice crosswise into thin strips. In a medium bowl combine spinach, water chestnuts, green onions, and 2 tablespoons of the teriyaki sauce.

2 Trim fat from steak. Score both sides of steak in a diamond pattern by making shallow diagonal cuts at 1-inch intervals. Place steak between 2 sheets of plastic wrap. Working from center to edges, use the flat side of a meat mallet to pound the steak into a 12×8-inch rectangle. Remove plastic wrap. Sprinkle steak lightly with salt and pepper.

3 Spread spinach mixture over steak. Starting from a long side, roll rectangle into a spiral. Starting ½ inch from 1 end, secure with wooden toothpicks at 1-inch intervals. Cut between toothpicks into 10 pinwheels. Thread 2 pinwheels onto each of 5 long skewers. Brush with some of the remaining teriyaki sauce.

4 Place skewers on the rack of an unheated broiler pan. Broil 3 to 4 inches from heat for 12 to 14 minutes or until medium doneness, turning once and brushing with teriyaki sauce halfway through broiling time. Discard any of the remaining teriyaki sauce. Remove toothpicks and skewers.

Teriyaki Beef Spirals

PREP: 20 minutes   **BROIL:** 12 minutes
MAKES: 5 servings

NUTRITION FACTS per serving:

CALORIES 175
TOTAL FAT 8 g total fat (3 g sat. fat)
CHOLESTEROL 56 mg
PROTEIN 23 g
CARBOHYDRATE 1 g
FIBER 1 g
SODIUM 139 mg

EXCHANGES 3 Meat

4   3- to 4-ounce beef tenderloin
    steaks, cut 1 inch thick

    Salt

1   tablespoon reduced-sodium soy
    sauce

1   tablespoon olive oil

1   tablespoon snipped fresh chives

2   cloves garlic, minced

½   teaspoon coriander seeds or
    cumin seeds, crushed

½   teaspoon celery seeds

½   teaspoon coarsely ground
    black pepper

1 Preheat broiler. Trim fat from steaks. Sprinkle lightly with salt. In a small bowl combine soy sauce, oil, chives, garlic, coriander seeds or cumin seeds, celery seeds, and pepper. Brush the mixture onto both sides of each steak.

2 Place steaks on the unheated rack of a broiler pan. Broil 3 to 4 inches from heat until desired doneness, turning once halfway through broiling time. (Allow 12 to 14 minutes for medium-rare doneness [145°F] or 15 to 18 minutes for medium doneness [160°F].)

Coriander-Studded Tenderloin Steak

PREP: 10 minutes   **BROIL:** 12 minutes
MAKES: 4 servings

NUTRITION FACTS per serving:

CALORIES 164
TOTAL FAT 9 g total fat (3 g sat. fat)
CHOLESTEROL 42 mg
PROTEIN 18 g
CARBOHYDRATE 1 g
FIBER 0 g
SODIUM 256 mg

EXCHANGES 2½ Meat, ½ Fat

- 2 6-ounce boneless beef ribeye steaks or beef top sirloin steaks, cut about 1 inch thick
- 1 tablespoon multicolor peppercorns, crushed
- ½ teaspoon salt
- 2 tablespoons butter or margarine, softened
- 2 teaspoons mild-flavor molasses
- ¼ teaspoon finely shredded lemon peel
- 1 teaspoon lemon juice
- 2 cups sugar snap peas
- ½ cup carrot cut into thin bite-size strips
- Lemon peel strips (optional)

1 Preheat broiler. Trim fat from steaks. Using your fingers, press the crushed peppercorns and salt onto both sides of each steak.

2 Place steaks on the unheated rack of a broiler pan. Broil 3 to 4 inches from the heat until desired doneness, turning once halfway through broiling time. (For ribeye steaks, allow 12 to 14 minutes for medium-rare doneness [145°F] or 15 to 18 minutes for medium doneness [160°F].) (For sirloin steaks, allow 15 to 17 minutes for medium-rare doneness [145°F] or 20 to 22 minutes for medium doneness [160°F].)

3 Meanwhile, in a small bowl combine softened butter, molasses, finely shredded lemon peel, and lemon juice (mixture will appear curdled). Set aside.

4 Remove strings and tips from sugar snap peas. In a covered medium saucepan cook peas and carrot in a small amount of boiling salted water for 2 to 4 minutes or until crisp-tender. Drain well. Stir in 1 tablespoon of the molasses mixture.

5 To serve, dot remaining molasses mixture evenly over steaks. Slice steaks and toss with vegetable mixture. If desired, garnish with lemon peel strips.

Peppercorn Steaks

START TO FINISH: 35 minutes
MAKES: 4 servings

NUTRITION FACTS per serving:

CALORIES 247
TOTAL FAT 12 g total fat (6 g sat. fat)
CHOLESTEROL 66 mg
PROTEIN 20 g
CARBOHYDRATE 13 g
FIBER 3 g
SODIUM 418 mg

EXCHANGES 2 Vegetable, 2½ Meat, 1 Fat

Beef Loin with Tarragon Sauce

PREP: 20 minutes **BROIL:** 12 minutes
MAKES: 4 servings

NUTRITION FACTS per serving:

CALORIES 277
TOTAL FAT 10 g total fat (4 g sat. fat)
CHOLESTEROL 89 mg
PROTEIN 34 g
CARBOHYDRATE 11 g
FIBER 1 g
SODIUM 543 mg

EXCHANGES ½ Milk, 4 Meat

2	beef top loin steaks, cut 1 inch thick (about 1¼ pounds total)
¼	teaspoon salt
¼	teaspoon black pepper
1	cup plain low-fat yogurt
¼	cup low-fat mayonnaise dressing
¼	cup very thinly sliced green onions (2)
¼	cup apple juice or apple cider
1	tablespoon snipped fresh parsley
1½	teaspoons snipped fresh tarragon or ½ teaspoon dried tarragon, crushed
¼	teaspoon salt
¼	teaspoon crushed red pepper or ⅛ teaspoon cayenne pepper

1 Preheat broiler. Trim fat from steaks. Cut steaks into 4 serving-size portions. Sprinkle steaks with ¼ teaspoon salt and the black pepper.

2 Place steaks on the unheated rack of a broiler pan. Broil 3 to 4 inches from heat until desired doneness, turning once. (Allow 12 to 14 minutes for medium-rare doneness [145°F] or 15 to 18 minutes for medium doneness [160°F].)

3 Meanwhile, for sauce, in a small bowl combine yogurt, mayonnaise dressing, green onions, juice or cider, parsley, tarragon, ¼ teaspoon salt, and the crushed or cayenne pepper. Slice steaks. Serve sauce with steak slices.

- 1   pound boneless beef round steak, cut ¾ inch thick
- 2   tablespoons all-purpose flour
- ¾   teaspoon fajita seasoning
- ⅛   teaspoon ground cumin
- ⅛   teaspoon cayenne pepper
- 2   teaspoons cooking oil
- 1½   cups bottled salsa
- ½   cup water
- 1   cup yellow and/or green sweet pepper cut into thin bite-size strips
- 2   cloves garlic, minced
- 2   cups hot cooked rice
      Snipped fresh cilantro (optional)

1 Trim fat from steak. Cut steak into 4 serving-size pieces. In a large plastic bag combine flour, fajita seasoning, cumin, and cayenne pepper; set aside. Place meat between 2 pieces of plastic wrap. Using the notched edge of a meat mallet, pound meat lightly to ½-inch thickness. Remove plastic wrap. Add meat pieces, 2 at a time, to flour mixture in bag. Seal bag; shake to coat evenly.

2 In a large nonstick skillet brown meat on both sides in hot oil. Drain off fat. Add salsa, the water, sweet pepper strips, and garlic. Bring to boiling; reduce heat. Simmer, covered, about 1¼ hours or until meat is tender. Skim off fat. Serve with hot cooked rice. If desired, sprinkle with snipped fresh cilantro.

Zesty Swiss Steak

PREP: 20 minutes   **COOK:** 1¼ hours
MAKES: 4 servings

NUTRITION FACTS per serving:

CALORIES 312
TOTAL FAT 8 g total fat (2 g sat. fat)
CHOLESTEROL 66 mg
PROTEIN 28 g
CARBOHYDRATE 31 g
FIBER 2 g
SODIUM 305 mg

EXCHANGES 2 Starch, 3 Meat

Easy Pot Roast

START TO FINISH: 25 minutes
MAKES: 4 servings

NUTRITION FACTS per serving:

CALORIES 230
TOTAL FAT 8 g total fat (3 g sat. fat)
CHOLESTEROL 72 mg
PROTEIN 23 g
CARBOHYDRATE 15 g
FIBER 2 g
SODIUM 386 mg

EXCHANGES 1 Fruit, 3 Meat

1   17-ounce package refrigerated cooked beef pot roast with juices
2   tablespoons minced shallots
1   tablespoon butter or margarine
2   tablespoons tarragon vinegar
2   cups pitted fresh fruit cut into wedges (such as apples, plums, and peaches)
    Hot cooked wide noodles (optional)
1   teaspoon snipped fresh tarragon
    Fresh tarragon sprigs (optional)

1 Remove meat from package, reserving juices. In a large skillet cook shallots in hot butter over medium heat for 1 minute. Add pot roast; reduce heat. Cover and simmer about 10 minutes or until pot roast is heated through.

2 In a small bowl stir together reserved meat juices and tarragon vinegar. Pour over meat. Spoon fruit on top. Cover; heat for 2 minutes more. If desired, serve with hot cooked noodles. Top with snipped tarragon. If desired, garnish with tarragon sprigs.

1 pound veal leg round steak or veal sirloin steak, or 4 skinless, boneless chicken breast halves (about 1 pound)

3 cups fresh mushrooms (such as cremini, porcini, baby portobello, or button), quartered, halved, or sliced

4 teaspoons olive oil or cooking oil

¼ teaspoon salt

¼ teaspoon black pepper

¾ cup dry Marsala

½ cup sliced green onions (4)

1 tablespoon snipped fresh sage or ½ teaspoon dried sage, crushed

1 tablespoon cold water

1 teaspoon cornstarch

⅛ teaspoon salt

Fresh herb sprigs (optional)

1 Cut veal into 4 serving-size pieces. Place each veal piece or chicken breast half between 2 sheets of plastic wrap. Working from center to edges, pound lightly with the flat side of a meat mallet to about ⅛-inch thickness. Remove the plastic wrap. Set meat aside.

2 In a 12-inch skillet cook the mushrooms in 2 teaspoons of the hot oil for 4 to 5 minutes or until tender. Remove from skillet. Set aside.

3 Sprinkle meat with the ¼ teaspoon salt and the pepper. In the same skillet cook veal or chicken, half at a time, in the remaining 2 teaspoons hot oil over medium-high heat for 2 to 3 minutes or until no longer pink, turning once. Transfer to dinner plates. Keep warm.

4 Add Marsala to drippings in skillet. Bring to boiling. Boil mixture gently, uncovered, for 1 minute, scraping up any browned bits. Return mushrooms to skillet; add green onions and sage. In a small bowl stir together the cold water, the cornstarch, and the ⅛ teaspoon salt; add to skillet. Cook and stir until slightly thickened and bubbly; cook and stir 1 minute more. To serve, spoon the mushroom mixture over meat. Serve immediately. If desired, garnish with herb sprigs.

Veal Marsala

START TO FINISH: 35 minutes
MAKES: 4 servings

NUTRITION FACTS per serving:

CALORIES 251
TOTAL FAT 8 g total fat (1 g sat. fat)
CHOLESTEROL 88 mg
PROTEIN 27 g
CARBOHYDRATE 7 g
FIBER 1 g
SODIUM 283 mg

EXCHANGES 1 Vegetable, 3 Meat, 1 Fat

2 medium oranges

12 ounces veal scaloppini or boneless veal leg round steak or sirloin steak, cut ¼ inch thick

¼ teaspoon salt

¼ teaspoon black pepper

2 teaspoons olive oil

⅓ cup sliced green onions

2 cloves garlic, minced

1 teaspoon grated fresh ginger

1 cup orange juice

1 tablespoon white wine vinegar

2 teaspoons cornstarch

¼ cup golden raisins

⅛ teaspoon salt

Hot cooked pasta or rice (optional)

Veal with Orange Sauce

START TO FINISH: 25 minutes
MAKES: 4 servings

NUTRITION FACTS per serving:

CALORIES 196
TOTAL FAT 4 g total fat (1 g sat. fat)
CHOLESTEROL 66 mg
PROTEIN 19 g
CARBOHYDRATE 21 g
FIBER 2 g
SODIUM 265 mg

EXCHANGES 1½ Fruit, 2½ Meat

1 Finely shred ½ teaspoon peel from 1 of the oranges; set peel aside. Peel and section oranges, discarding seeds; set aside.

2 Sprinkle meat with the ¼ teaspoon salt and the pepper. In a large nonstick skillet cook meat in hot oil over medium-high heat for 4 to 6 minutes or until browned, turning once. Remove meat from skillet, reserving drippings in skillet. Add green onions, garlic, and ginger to drippings in skillet. Cook and stir over medium heat for 1 minute.

3 In a small bowl stir together orange juice, vinegar, and cornstarch; add to skillet. Cook and stir until slightly thickened and bubbly. Add the orange peel, orange sections, raisins, and the ⅛ teaspoon salt to skillet. Toss gently to coat. Return meat to skillet; spoon sauce over meat. Heat through. If desired, serve meat over hot cooked pasta.

8   lamb rib chops, cut 1 inch thick (about 1½ pounds total)

2   tablespoons olive oil

2   teaspoons snipped fresh rosemary or ½ teaspoon dried rosemary, crushed

½   teaspoon coarsely ground black pepper

2   cloves garlic, minced

½   cup apricot preserves or peach preserves

¼   cup water

1   tablespoon Dijon-style mustard

1   teaspoon chicken bouillon granules

½   teaspoon snipped fresh rosemary or ⅛ teaspoon dried rosemary, crushed

¼   teaspoon coarsely ground black pepper

    Fresh rosemary sprigs (optional)

1 Trim fat from chops. In a small bowl combine 1 tablespoon of the oil, the 2 teaspoons snipped rosemary or ½ teaspoon dried rosemary, the ½ teaspoon pepper, and the garlic. Use your fingers or a pastry brush to rub or brush the garlic mixture onto all sides of chops.

2 For glaze, in a small saucepan combine apricot or peach preserves, the water, mustard, bouillon granules, the ½ teaspoon snipped rosemary or ⅛ teaspoon dried rosemary, and the ¼ teaspoon pepper; heat and stir until bubbly. Remove from heat; set aside.

3 In a large skillet heat the remaining 1 tablespoon oil over medium heat. Add chops; cook for 9 to 11 minutes or until medium doneness (160°F), turning once. Serve chops with glaze. If desired, garnish with rosemary sprigs.

Rosemary-Rubbed Lamb Chops

START TO FINISH: 25 minutes
MAKES: 4 servings

NUTRITION FACTS per serving:

CALORIES 289
TOTAL FAT 12 g total fat (3 g sat. fat)
CHOLESTEROL 48 mg
PROTEIN 15 g
CARBOHYDRATE 29 g
FIBER 1 g
SODIUM 361 mg

EXCHANGES 2 Fruit, 2 Meat, 1 Fat

Lamb with Herbed Mushrooms

START TO FINISH: 25 minutes
MAKES: 4 servings

NUTRITION FACTS per serving:

- -

CALORIES 165
TOTAL FAT 9 g total fat (3 g sat. fat)
CHOLESTEROL 48 mg
PROTEIN 16 g
CARBOHYDRATE 4 g
FIBER 1 g
SODIUM 280 mg

EXCHANGES 1 Vegetable, 2 Meat

8   lamb loin chops, cut 1 inch thick (about 1½ pounds total)
2   teaspoons olive oil
1   small onion, thinly sliced
2   cups sliced fresh mushrooms
1   tablespoon balsamic vinegar
¼   teaspoon salt
¼   teaspoon black pepper
2   cloves garlic, minced
1   teaspoon snipped fresh tarragon or basil or ¼ teaspoon dried tarragon or basil, crushed

1 Trim fat from chops. In a large nonstick skillet heat oil over medium heat. Add chops; cook for 9 to 11 minutes or until medium doneness (160°F), turning once. Transfer chops to a serving platter; keep warm.

2 Stir onion into drippings in skillet. Cook and stir for 2 minutes. Stir in mushrooms, balsamic vinegar, salt, pepper, and garlic. Cook and stir for 3 to 4 minutes or until mushrooms are tender. Stir in tarragon or basil. Spoon mushroom mixture over chops on platter.

On the opener: Pork Chops with Raspberries *(see recipe, page 134)*

CHOPS

HAM

ROAST

TENDERLOIN

1½ cups chopped honeydew melon

1½ cups chopped cantaloupe

1   cup strawberries, coarsely chopped

1   tablespoon snipped fresh mint

1   tablespoon lemon juice

1   tablespoon honey

4   teaspoons Jamaican jerk seasoning

2   12-ounce pork tenderloins

Fresh mint sprigs (optional)

1 For salsa, in a medium bowl combine honeydew melon, cantaloupe, strawberries, the snipped mint, lemon juice, and honey. Cover and chill for up to 1 hour.

2 Sprinkle jerk seasoning evenly over tenderloins, pressing onto surface. Place tenderloins on a rack in a shallow roasting pan. Roast in a 425°F oven for 25 to 35 minutes or until pork juices run clear (160°F).

3 To serve, slice pork and serve with salsa. If desired, garnish with mint sprigs.

Tenderloin with Melon Salsa

PREP: 25 minutes   **ROAST:** 25 minutes
OVEN: 425°F   **MAKES:** 6 servings

NUTRITION FACTS per serving:

CALORIES 187
TOTAL FAT 3 g total fat (1 g sat. fat)
CHOLESTEROL 66 mg
PROTEIN 28 g
CARBOHYDRATE 12 g
FIBER 1 g
SODIUM 254 mg

EXCHANGES 1 Fruit, 3½ Meat

Smoky-Sweet Pork

PREP: 25 minutes　　**COOK:** 1½ hours
MAKES: 8 servings

NUTRITION FACTS per serving:

CALORIES 335
TOTAL FAT 8 g total fat (2 g sat. fat)
CHOLESTEROL 50 mg
PROTEIN 23 g
CARBOHYDRATE 41 g
FIBER 3 g
SODIUM 606 mg

EXCHANGES ½ Fruit, 2 Starch, 2½ Meat

1½　pounds boneless pork top loin roast (single loin) or boneless pork blade roast

2　teaspoons cooking oil

1½　cups water

½　cup catsup

½　cup bottled barbecue sauce

1　cup chopped red onion

½　cup chopped celery

¼　cup packed brown sugar

¼　cup snipped pitted dates

2　tablespoons finely chopped canned chipotle peppers in adobo sauce

1　teaspoon dry mustard

1　teaspoon bottled minced garlic or 2 cloves garlic, minced

8　thick bread slices

8　lettuce leaves (optional)

1 Trim fat from roast. In a large saucepan brown roast on all sides in hot oil. Drain off fat. Add the water, catsup, barbecue sauce, red onion, celery, brown sugar, dates, chipotle peppers, mustard, and garlic. Bring to boiling; reduce heat. Simmer, covered, for 1½ to 2 hours or until meat is very tender, stirring sauce occasionally.

2 Remove meat from sauce. Pour sauce into large glass measure or bowl; set aside. Using 2 forks, pull meat apart into shreds. Skim fat from sauce, if necessary. Return meat to saucepan; stir in enough of the sauce to make desired consistency. Heat through.

3 To serve, top bread slices with lettuce leaves (if desired); spoon meat mixture onto lettuce.

1 2- to 2½-pound boneless pork top
   loin roast (single loin)

   Salt

   Black pepper

⅓ cup pineapple preserves

2 tablespoons coarse-grain mustard

¼ teaspoon dried mint or basil,
   crushed

1 15¼-ounce can pineapple chunks
   (juice pack), drained

1 Trim fat from roast. Place roast in a shallow
roasting pan. Season with salt and pepper.
Insert an oven-going meat thermometer into
center of roast. Roast, uncovered, in a 325°F oven
for 1 hour.

2 Meanwhile, for glaze, in a small bowl
combine preserves, mustard, and mint.

3 Spoon about half of the glaze onto the meat;
add pineapple chunks to roasting pan. Roast
for 15 to 45 minutes more or until thermometer
registers 155°F, spooning remaining glaze over
meat once.

4 Remove from oven. Cover with foil and let
stand for 15 minutes before carving. (The
temperature of the meat will rise 5°F during
standing.) Transfer roast to serving platter. Stir
together pineapple and pan drippings; serve
with meat.

Pineapple Pork Roast

PREP: 20 minutes   **ROAST:** 1¼ hours
OVEN: 325°F   **STAND:** 15 minutes
MAKES: 8 to 10 servings

NUTRITION FACTS per serving:

CALORIES 231
TOTAL FAT 6 g total fat (2 g sat. fat)
CHOLESTEROL 66 mg
PROTEIN 25 g
CARBOHYDRATE 18 g
FIBER 1 g
SODIUM 146 mg

EXCHANGES 1 Fruit, 3 Meat

Rhubarb-Sauced Pork Roast

PREP: 20 minutes
OVEN: 325°F
MAKES: 8 to 10 servings

ROAST: 1¼ hours
STAND: 15 minutes

NUTRITION FACTS per serving:

CALORIES 212
TOTAL FAT 5 g total fat (2 g sat. fat)
CHOLESTEROL 71 mg
PROTEIN 26 g
CARBOHYDRATE 12 g
FIBER 1 g
SODIUM 380 mg

EXCHANGES 1 Fruit, 3½ Meat

1	2- to 2½-pound boneless pork top loin roast (single loin)
¼	cup Dijon-style mustard
1	tablespoon snipped fresh rosemary
½	teaspoon salt
¼	teaspoon black pepper
1	to 2 tablespoons bottled minced garlic
3	cups fresh or frozen sliced rhubarb (about 1 pound)
⅓	cup orange juice
⅓	to ½ cup sugar
1	tablespoon cider vinegar
	Fresh rosemary sprig (optional)

1 Score the top and bottom of roast in a diamond pattern by making shallow diagonal cuts at 1-inch intervals. In a small bowl combine mustard, the snipped rosemary, salt, pepper, and garlic. Rub the mustard mixture evenly onto all sides of roast. Insert an oven-going meat thermometer into center of roast. Place roast on a rack in a shallow roasting pan.

2 Roast, uncovered, in a 325°F oven for 1¼ to 1¾ hours or until thermometer registers 155°F. Remove from oven.

3 Cover with foil; let stand for 15 minutes before carving. (The temperature of the meat will rise 5°F during standing.)

4 Meanwhile, for sauce, in a medium saucepan stir together rhubarb, orange juice, sugar, and vinegar. Bring to boiling; reduce heat. Simmer, covered, about 15 minutes or until rhubarb is very tender.

5 To serve, slice the roast and serve with warm sauce. If desired, garnish with rosemary sprig.

Grilling directions: Prepare as above through step 1. In a grill with a cover arrange medium coals around edge of grill. Test for medium-low heat in center of grill (not over coals). Place roast in roasting pan on grill rack in center of grill. Cover and grill for 1 to 1¼ hours or until meat thermometer registers 155°F, adding hot coals as necessary to maintain heat. Continue as above in steps 3 to 5.

- 1½ cups loose-pack frozen whole kernel corn
- 1   10-ounce can chopped tomatoes and green chile peppers
- ½   teaspoon ground cumin
- ¼   teaspoon bottled hot pepper sauce
- 2   cloves garlic, minced
- 4   boneless pork loin chops, cut ¾ inch thick (about 1½ pounds total)
- ½   teaspoon chili powder
- 2   teaspoons cooking oil
- 1   medium onion, cut into thin wedges
- 1   tablespoon snipped fresh cilantro

Fresh cilantro leaves (optional)

1 In a medium bowl combine corn, undrained tomatoes, cumin, hot pepper sauce, and garlic; set aside.

2 Trim fat from chops. Sprinkle both sides of each chop with chili powder. In a 12-inch nonstick skillet heat oil over medium-high heat. Add chops; cook chops about 4 minutes or until browned, turning once. Remove chops from skillet, reserving drippings. Reduce heat to medium. Add onion to skillet. Cook and stir for 3 minutes. Stir corn mixture into onion mixture in skillet. Place chops on corn mixture. Bring to boiling; reduce heat. Simmer, covered, for 10 to 12 minutes or until pork juices run clear (160°F).

3 To serve, remove chops from skillet. Stir snipped cilantro into corn mixture in skillet; serve corn mixture with chops. If desired, garnish with cilantro leaves.

Spicy Skillet Pork Chops

START TO FINISH: 40 minutes
MAKES: 4 servings

NUTRITION FACTS per serving:

CALORIES 330
TOTAL FAT 11 g total fat (3 g sat. fat)
CHOLESTEROL 93 mg
PROTEIN 40 g
CARBOHYDRATE 18 g
FIBER 2 g
SODIUM 360 mg

EXCHANGES 1 Vegetable, 1 Starch, 5 Meat

¾ cup reduced-sodium chicken broth

1 tablespoon white balsamic vinegar

1 tablespoon brown sugar

1½ teaspoons cornstarch

Dash ground allspice

4 pork rib chops, cut ¾ inch thick
(about 1½ pounds total)

½ teaspoon salt

¼ teaspoon black pepper

¼ teaspoon dried basil, crushed

1 tablespoon cooking oil

1 cup fresh raspberries

Pork Chops with Raspberries

START TO FINISH: 25 minutes
MAKES: 4 servings

NUTRITION FACTS per serving:

CALORIES 207
TOTAL FAT 9 g total fat (2 g sat. fat)
CHOLESTEROL 53 mg
PROTEIN 22 g
CARBOHYDRATE 8 g
FIBER 2 g
SODIUM 444 mg

EXCHANGES ½ Fruit, 3 Meat

1 In a small bowl stir together broth, balsamic vinegar, brown sugar, cornstarch, and allspice; set aside.

2 Trim fat from chops. Sprinkle both sides of each chop with salt, pepper, and basil. In a 12-inch skillet heat oil over medium heat. Add chops; cook for 8 to 12 minutes or until pork juices run clear (160°F). Transfer chops to a serving platter. Cover and keep warm. Drain fat from skillet.

3 Stir vinegar mixture. Add to skillet. Cook and stir over medium heat until slightly thickened and bubbly. Cook and stir for 2 minutes more. Gently stir in raspberries; heat through. To serve, spoon raspberry mixture over chops.

- 4 boneless pork top loin chops, cut 1 inch thick (about 1¼ pounds total)
- ¼ teaspoon salt
- ¼ teaspoon black pepper
- 2 teaspoons olive oil
- ⅓ cup water
- ¼ cup plum jam
- 1 tablespoon balsamic vinegar
- 2 teaspoons Dijon-style mustard
- ½ teaspoon chicken bouillon granules
- 1 clove garlic, minced
- 1 small plum, seeded and cut into thin wedges
- ½ cup seedless red or green grapes, halved

  Snipped fresh chives (optional)

1 Trim fat from chops. Sprinkle both sides of each chop with salt and pepper. In a large nonstick skillet heat oil over medium heat. Add chops; cook for 8 to 12 minutes or until pork juices run clear (160°F), turning once. Transfer chops to a serving platter. Cover and keep warm.

2 Add the water, jam, balsamic vinegar, mustard, chicken bouillon granules, and garlic to skillet. Whisk over medium heat until bubbly. Remove from heat. Gently stir in plum wedges and grapes. To serve, spoon plum-grape mixture over chops. If desired, sprinkle with snipped chives.

Pork Chops with Plum-Grape Sauce

START TO FINISH: 25 minutes
MAKES: 4 servings

NUTRITION FACTS per serving:

- -

CALORIES 305
TOTAL FAT 10 g total fat (3 g sat. fat)
CHOLESTEROL 83 mg
PROTEIN 31 g
CARBOHYDRATE 21 g
FIBER 1 g
SODIUM 386 mg

EXCHANGES 1½ Fruit, 4½ Meat

1   lime

1   15-ounce can Great Northern beans, rinsed and drained

1   large mango, pitted, peeled, and chopped, or 2 medium nectarines or peaches, peeled, pitted, and chopped

1   small roma tomato, seeded and chopped

¼   cup sliced green onions (2)

2   tablespoons cider vinegar

1   tablespoon fresh jalapeño chile pepper, seeded and finely chopped (see note, page 263)

1   teaspoon sugar

½   teaspoon fajita seasoning

2   cloves garlic, minced

4   boneless pork loin chops, cut ¾ inch thick (about 1½ pounds total)

1   teaspoon fajita seasoning
    Lime wedges (optional)

Fajita Pork Chops

PREP: 20 minutes   **STAND:** 30 minutes
BROIL: 9 minutes   **MAKES:** 4 servings

NUTRITION FACTS per serving:

- -

CALORIES 385
TOTAL FAT 9 g total fat (3 g sat. fat)
CHOLESTEROL 93 mg
PROTEIN 43 g
CARBOHYDRATE 32 g
FIBER 7 g
SODIUM 402 mg

EXCHANGES ½ Fruit, 1½ Starch, 5 Meat

1 Finely shred ½ teaspoon peel from lime. Squeeze juice from lime. Reserve 2 teaspoons lime juice for pork chops.

2 For salad, in a medium bowl combine finely shredded lime peel, remaining lime juice, beans, mango, tomato, green onions, vinegar, jalapeño, sugar, the ½ teaspoon fajita seasoning, and the garlic. Let stand at room temperature for 30 minutes, stirring occasionally. (Or, if desired, cover and refrigerate for up to 24 hours.)

3 Trim fat from chops. Brush the reserved 2 teaspoons lime juice onto both sides of each chop. Sprinkle chops with the 1 teaspoon fajita seasoning.

4 Preheat broiler. Place chops on the unheated rack of a broiler pan. Broil 3 to 4 inches from the heat for 9 to 11 minutes or until pork juices run clear (160°F), turning once. Slice chops and serve with salad. If desired, serve with lime wedges.

Grilling directions: Prepare as above through step 3. Place chops on the rack of an uncovered grill directly over medium coals. Grill for 12 to 15 minutes or until done (160°F), turning once. Slice chops and serve with salad.

- ¼ cup frozen orange juice concentrate, thawed
- 1 tablespoon lemon juice
- 1 tablespoon reduced-sodium soy sauce
- 1 teaspoon ground coriander
- ¼ teaspoon black pepper
- 1 clove garlic, minced
- 4 pork rib or loin chops, cut ¾ inch thick (about 1½ pounds total)

1 For marinade, in a small bowl combine orange juice concentrate, lemon juice, soy sauce, coriander, pepper, and garlic; set aside.

2 Trim fat from chops. Place chops in a plastic bag set in a bowl. Pour marinade over chops; seal bag. Marinate in the refrigerator for at least 4 hours or up to 6 hours, turning bag occasionally. Drain chops, discarding marinade.

3 Preheat broiler. Place chops on the unheated rack of a broiler pan. Broil 3 to 4 inches from heat for 9 to 12 minutes or until pork juices run clear (160°F), turning once.

Coriander Pork Chops

PREP: 10 minutes
MARINATE: 4 to 6 hours
BROIL: 9 minutes   **MAKES:** 4 servings

NUTRITION FACTS per serving:

CALORIES 263
TOTAL FAT 9 g total fat (3 g sat. fat)
CHOLESTEROL 92 mg
PROTEIN 38 g
CARBOHYDRATE 4 g
FIBER 0 g
SODIUM 141 mg

EXCHANGES ½ Fruit, 5 Meat

Barley-and-Fruit-Stuffed Chops

PREP: 30 minutes   **BROIL:** 12 minutes
MAKES: 4 servings

NUTRITION FACTS per serving:

CALORIES 216
TOTAL FAT 6 g total fat (2 g sat. fat)
CHOLESTEROL 66 mg
PROTEIN 25 g
CARBOHYDRATE 14 g
FIBER 1 g
SODIUM 236 mg

EXCHANGES ½ Fruit, ½ Starch, 3½ Meat

⅓   cup water
¼   cup chopped onion
2   tablespoons quick-cooking barley
2   tablespoons mixed dried fruit bits
½   teaspoon finely shredded orange peel or lemon peel
¼   teaspoon salt
1   tablespoon fine dry bread crumbs
¼   teaspoon dried thyme, crushed
¼   teaspoon black pepper
1   teaspoon bottled minced garlic or 2 cloves garlic, minced
4   4- to 5-ounce boneless pork loin chops, cut ¾ inch thick
2   tablespoons orange juice
1   tablespoon honey

1 For stuffing, in a small saucepan combine the water, onion, barley, fruit bits, orange peel, and salt. Bring to boiling; reduce heat. Simmer, covered, for 5 minutes. Remove from heat. Cover and let stand for 5 minutes. Stir in fine dry bread crumbs, thyme, pepper, and garlic. Set aside.

2 Meanwhile, trim fat from chops. Make a pocket in each chop by cutting horizontally from the fat side almost to the opposite side.

3 Divide stuffing among pockets in chops. If necessary, secure each opening with a wooden toothpick.

4 Preheat broiler. Place chops on the unheated rack of a broiler pan. Broil 3 to 4 inches from the heat for 12 to 15 minutes or until pork juices run clear (meat and stuffing reach 160°F), turning once.

5 Meanwhile, in a small bowl combine orange juice and honey. Brush orange juice mixture on the chops for the last 2 minutes of broiling. Before serving, discard toothpicks.

2	tablespoons golden raisins
¼	cup boiling water
1	15¼-ounce can unpeeled apricot halves in light syrup, drained
1½	teaspoons olive oil
½	teaspoon snipped fresh thyme or ⅛ teaspoon dried thyme, crushed
¼	teaspoon salt
¼	teaspoon curry powder
4	pork loin or rib chops, cut ¾ inch thick (about 1½ pounds total)
¼	teaspoon salt
¼	teaspoon black pepper
⅛	teaspoon curry powder

1 Place raisins in a small bowl; add boiling water. Cover and let stand for 15 minutes or until plump. Drain; set aside.

2 Chop ½ cup of the apricots; set aside. In a blender container or small food processor bowl combine remaining apricots, ½ teaspoon of the oil, the thyme, ¼ teaspoon salt, and the ¼ teaspoon curry powder. Blend or process until smooth. Set aside half of the mixture for glaze. For apricot chutney, gently stir raisins and reserved chopped apricots into remaining thyme mixture; set aside.

3 Brush both sides of pork chops with remaining 1 teaspoon oil. In a small bowl combine ¼ teaspoon salt, the pepper, and the ⅛ teaspoon curry powder. Rub on both sides of chops.

4 Preheat broiler. Place chops on unheated rack of a broiler pan. Broil 3 to 4 inches from the heat for 9 to 12 minutes or until pork juices run clear (160°F), turning once and brushing with the reserved apricot glaze for the last 2 to 3 minutes of broiling. Serve apricot chutney with chops.

Grilling directions: Prepare as above through step 3. Place chops on the rack of an uncovered grill directly over medium coals. Grill for 11 to 14 minutes or until pork juices run clear (160°F), turning once and brushing with the reserved apricot glaze during the last 3 minutes of grilling. Serve apricot chutney with chops.

Pork Chops with Apricot Chutney

PREP: 20 minutes **STAND:** 15 minutes
BROIL: 9 minutes **MAKES:** 4 servings

NUTRITION FACTS per serving:

CALORIES 288
TOTAL FAT 11 g total fat (3 g sat. fat)
CHOLESTEROL 76 mg
PROTEIN 26 g
CARBOHYDRATE 21 g
FIBER 2 g
SODIUM 366 mg

EXCHANGES 1½ Fruit, 3½ Meat

2 ears of corn, husked and cleaned

1 12- to 14-ounce pork tenderloin

16 baby pattypan squash (each about 1 inch in diameter) or 4 fresh tomatillos, quartered

1 small red onion, cut into ½-inch wedges

¼ cup mango chutney, finely chopped

3 tablespoons Pickapeppa Sauce*

1 tablespoon cooking oil

1 tablespoon water

Hot cooked rice (optional)

Jamaican Pork Kabobs

PREP: 15 minutes   **BROIL:** 12 minutes
MAKES: 4 servings

NUTRITION FACTS per serving:

CALORIES 259
TOTAL FAT 6 g total fat (1 g sat. fat)
CHOLESTEROL 50 mg
PROTEIN 23 g
CARBOHYDRATE 29 g
FIBER 4 g
SODIUM 150 mg

EXCHANGES 3 Vegetable, 1 Starch, 2 Meat

1 Cut corn crosswise into 1-inch pieces. In medium saucepan cook corn pieces in a small amount of boiling water for 3 minutes; drain and rinse with cold water. Meanwhile, cut tenderloin into 1-inch slices. For kabobs, on long metal skewers, alternately thread corn, tenderloin slices, squash or tomatillos, and onion wedges, leaving a ¼-inch space between pieces. In a small bowl combine chutney, Pickapeppa Sauce, oil, and the water; set aside.

2 Preheat broiler. Place kabobs on the unheated rack of a broiler pan. Broil 3 to 4 inches from the heat for 12 to 14 minutes or until pork is cooked through and the vegetables are tender, turning once and brushing with the chutney mixture for the last 5 minutes of broiling. If desired, serve with hot cooked rice.

*Note: If you can't find Pickapeppa Sauce, substitute 3 tablespoons Worcestershire sauce mixed with a dash of bottled hot pepper sauce.

Nonstick cooking spray

12	ounces lean boneless pork, cut into ½-inch cubes
1	teaspoon cooking oil
1	cup chopped onion (1 large)
1	cup chopped carrots (2 medium)
3	cloves garlic, minced
2	15-ounce cans white kidney beans (cannellini), rinsed and drained
4	roma tomatoes, chopped
⅔	cup reduced-sodium chicken broth
⅔	cup water
2	ounces smoked turkey sausage, halved lengthwise and cut into ¼-inch slices
1	teaspoon dried thyme, crushed
¼	teaspoon dried rosemary, crushed
¼	teaspoon black pepper
2	tablespoons snipped fresh thyme or flat-leaf parsley

1 Lightly coat an unheated Dutch oven with nonstick cooking spray. Preheat over medium-high heat. Add pork to Dutch oven; cook and stir until pork is browned. Remove pork from Dutch oven. Reduce heat. Carefully add oil to hot Dutch oven. Add onion, carrots, and garlic; cook until onion is tender. Stir pork, beans, tomatoes, broth, the water, turkey sausage, thyme, rosemary, and pepper into Dutch oven.

2 Bake, covered, in a 325°F oven for 40 to 45 minutes or until pork and carrots are tender. To serve, spoon into individual casseroles or bowls; sprinkle each serving with thyme.

Range top directions: Prepare as above through step 1. Simmer, covered, about 15 minutes or until the pork and carrots are tender. Serve as above.

Oven-Baked Cassoulet

PREP: 20 minutes   **BAKE:** 40 minutes
OVEN: 325°F
MAKES: 5 servings (6⅔ cups)

NUTRITION FACTS per serving:

CALORIES 263
TOTAL FAT 6 g total fat (2 g sat. fat)
CHOLESTEROL 48 mg
PROTEIN 28 g
CARBOHYDRATE 33 g
FIBER 10 g
SODIUM 500 mg

EXCHANGES 2½ Vegetable, 1½ Starch, 2½ Meat

½ cup chopped onion (1 medium)

2 cloves garlic, minced

2 tablespoons butter or margarine

3 tablespoons all-purpose flour

½ teaspoon salt

¼ teaspoon black pepper

1½ cups reduced-fat milk

2 teaspoons snipped fresh thyme or ½ teaspoon dried thyme, crushed

1½ pounds potatoes (4 to 5 medium)

5 ounces low-fat, reduced-sodium cooked ham, cut into thin strips

1 For sauce, in a medium saucepan cook onion and garlic in hot butter over medium heat until tender. Stir in flour, salt, and pepper. Add milk all at once. Cook and stir over medium heat until thickened and bubbly. Stir in thyme.

2 Scrub and thinly slice potatoes. Arrange two-thirds of the potato slices in a 2-quart casserole; cover with two-thirds of the sauce. Top with ham. Top with remaining potatoes and remaining sauce.

3 Bake, covered, in a 350°F oven for 55 minutes. Uncover and bake for 10 to 15 minutes more or until the potatoes are tender. Let potatoes stand 10 minutes before serving.

Scalloped Potatoes and Ham

PREP: 25 minutes **BAKE:** 65 minutes
OVEN: 350°F **STAND:** 10 minutes
MAKES: 8 side-dish servings

NUTRITION FACTS per serving:

CALORIES 145
TOTAL FAT 5 g total fat (3 g sat. fat)
CHOLESTEROL 19 mg
PROTEIN 7 g
CARBOHYDRATE 20 g
FIBER 2 g
SODIUM 399 mg

EXCHANGES 1½ Starch, ½ Meat

Chapter 9

Chicken & Turkey

On the opener: Spicy Chicken with Fruit *(see recipe, page 151)*

4	chicken breast halves or thighs (about 1½ pounds total)
2½	cups water
1	medium onion, sliced and separated into rings
1	teaspoon instant chicken bouillon granules
1	teaspoon snipped fresh thyme or ¼ teaspoon dried thyme, crushed
¼	teaspoon black pepper
2	cups sliced carrots (4 medium)
1	medium bulb fennel, cut into bite-size strips (1½ cups)
¼	cup cold water
2	tablespoons cornstarch
1	recipe Dumplings
	Fresh herb sprigs (optional)

1 Remove the skin from the chicken. In a large saucepan combine the chicken pieces, the 2½ cups water, the onion, bouillon granules, dried thyme (if using), and pepper. Bring to boiling; reduce heat. Simmer, covered, for 25 minutes. Add the carrots and fennel. Return to boiling and reduce heat. Simmer, covered, for 10 minutes more.

2 Remove chicken pieces from saucepan; set aside. Skim fat from broth in pan. In a small bowl stir together the ¼ cup cold water and the cornstarch; stir into broth in saucepan. Cook and stir until thickened and bubbly. Return chicken to pan; add fresh thyme (if using).

3 Drop Dumplings batter from a tablespoon into 8 mounds onto the hot chicken mixture. Cover; simmer about 10 minutes or until a wooden toothpick inserted into a dumpling comes out clean. If desired, garnish with herb sprigs.

Dumplings: In a small bowl stir together 1 cup all-purpose flour, 1½ teaspoons baking powder, ⅛ teaspoon salt, and ⅛ teaspoon coarsely ground black pepper. In another small bowl stir together 1 beaten egg, ¼ cup fat-free milk, and 1 tablespoon cooking oil. Pour into flour mixture; stir with a fork until combined.

Chicken and Dumplings

PREP: 20 minutes **COOK:** 50 minutes
MAKES: 4 servings

NUTRITION FACTS per serving:

CALORIES 327
TOTAL FAT 6 g total fat (1 g sat. fat)
CHOLESTEROL 110 mg
PROTEIN 29 g
CARBOHYDRATE 37 g
FIBER 12 g
SODIUM 558 mg

EXCHANGES 1½ Vegetable, 2 Starch, 3 Meat, ½ Fat

Chicken Tetrazzini

PREP: 30 minutes   **BAKE:** 10 minutes
OVEN: 400°F   **MAKES:** 4 servings

NUTRITION FACTS per serving:

CALORIES 394
TOTAL FAT 9 g total fat (4 g sat. fat)
CHOLESTEROL 44 mg
PROTEIN 26 g
CARBOHYDRATE 50 g
FIBER 2 g
SODIUM 492 mg

EXCHANGES 1 Vegetable, 3 Starch, 2 Meat, ½ Fat

6	ounces dried spaghetti
1½	cups sliced fresh mushrooms
¾	cup chopped red or green sweet pepper
½	cup cold water
¼	cup all-purpose flour
1	12-ounce can (1½ cups) evaporated low-fat milk
1	teaspoon instant chicken bouillon granules
¼	teaspoon black pepper
⅛	teaspoon salt
1	cup chopped cooked chicken or turkey (5 ounces)
¼	cup finely shredded Parmesan cheese (1 ounce)
2	tablespoons dry sherry or milk
	Nonstick cooking spray
1	tablespoon sliced almonds

1 Cook the spaghetti according to package directions, except omit the cooking oil and lightly salt the water. Drain well.

2 Meanwhile, in a large covered saucepan cook the mushrooms and sweet pepper in a small amount of boiling water until tender. Drain well; return to saucepan.

3 In a screw-top jar combine ½ cup cold water and flour; cover and shake well. Stir into the vegetable mixture in saucepan. Stir in the evaporated milk, bouillon granules, black pepper, and salt. Cook and stir until thickened and bubbly. Stir in the cooked spaghetti, chicken, Parmesan cheese, and dry sherry.

4 Lightly coat a 2-quart square baking dish with nonstick cooking spray. Spoon spaghetti mixture into dish. Sprinkle with almonds. Bake, uncovered, in a 400°F oven about 10 minutes or until heated through and nuts are lightly toasted.

12　skinless, boneless chicken thighs
　　(2 to 2½ pounds total)

　　Salt

　　Black pepper

2　tablespoons olive oil

1　large onion, chopped

1　medium red sweet pepper, cut
　　into thin strips

3　cloves garlic, minced

1　cup long grain rice

¼　teaspoon thread saffron, crushed,
　　or ⅛ teaspoon ground saffron

1½　cups water

½　cup pimiento-stuffed green olives,
　　halved

½　cup dry white wine, dry vermouth,
　　or chicken broth

　　Lemon wedges

　　Fresh herb sprigs (optional)

1 Sprinkle chicken with salt and black pepper. In a 12-inch skillet cook chicken in hot oil over medium-high heat about 10 minutes or until browned, turning once. Remove chicken from skillet; reserve 1 tablespoon drippings in skillet.

2 Add onion, sweet pepper, and garlic to skillet; cook and stir for 4 to 5 minutes or until vegetables are tender. Stir in uncooked rice and saffron; add the water, olives, and wine, vermouth, or chicken broth. Bring to boiling. Return chicken to skillet; reduce heat. Simmer, covered, about 25 minutes or until chicken is no longer pink (180°F) and rice is tender. Serve with lemon wedges. If desired, garnish with herb sprigs.

Chicken Thighs with Peppers

PREP: 25 minutes　　**COOK:** 25 minutes
MAKES: 6 servings

NUTRITION FACTS per serving:

CALORIES 380
TOTAL FAT 12 g total fat (2 g sat. fat)
CHOLESTEROL 121 mg
PROTEIN 33 g
CARBOHYDRATE 29 g
FIBER 1 g
SODIUM 410 mg

EXCHANGES 1 Vegetable, 1½ Starch, 3½ Meat, ½ Fat

Basque Chicken

START TO FINISH: 35 minutes
MAKES: 4 servings

NUTRITION FACTS per serving:

CALORIES 271
TOTAL FAT 7 g total fat (1 g sat. fat)
CHOLESTEROL 82 mg
PROTEIN 35 g
CARBOHYDRATE 15 g
FIBER 2 g
SODIUM 361 mg

EXCHANGES 3 Vegetable, 4 Meat

2	tablespoons all-purpose flour
4	skinless, boneless chicken breast halves (1¼ to 1½ pounds total)
1	tablespoon olive oil
2	large green and/or yellow sweet peppers, cut into thin bite-size strips
1	large onion, halved lengthwise and thinly sliced
3	cloves garlic, minced
1	teaspoon paprika
⅛	teaspoon cayenne pepper
1	14½-ounce can diced tomatoes, undrained
¼	cup reduced-sodium chicken broth
¼	cup sliced pitted ripe olives
1	tablespoon snipped fresh oregano
	Fresh oregano leaves (optional)

1 Place flour in a shallow dish. Dip chicken into flour to coat. In a large skillet cook chicken in hot oil over medium-high heat about 4 minutes or until chicken is browned, turning once. Remove chicken.

2 Add sweet peppers, onion, and garlic to skillet. Cook and stir for 3 to 4 minutes or until vegetables are nearly tender. Add paprika and cayenne pepper. Cook and stir for 1 minute more.

3 Stir in undrained tomatoes, broth, and olives. Bring to boiling. Return chicken to skillet, spooning tomato mixture over chicken. Reduce heat. Simmer, covered, about 10 minutes or until chicken is tender and no longer pink (170°F).

4 Transfer chicken to a serving platter. Stir snipped oregano into tomato mixture. Spoon the tomato mixture over chicken. If desired, garnish with oregano leaves.

- 4 skinless, boneless chicken breast halves (1¼ to 1½ pounds total)
- ⅛ teaspoon salt
  Nonstick cooking spray
- 1 cup apple juice or apple cider
- 1 red or green sweet pepper, cut into 1-inch pieces
- ¼ cup chopped onion
- 1 clove garlic, minced
- 1½ teaspoons snipped fresh sage or ½ teaspoon dried sage, crushed
- ¼ teaspoon black pepper
- 1 tablespoon cornstarch
- 1 tablespoon cold water
- 2 medium green and/or red cooking apples, sliced

1 Sprinkle chicken with salt. Coat an unheated large skillet with nonstick cooking spray. Preheat over medium-high heat. Add chicken; cook for 8 to 10 minutes or until chicken is tender and no longer pink (170°F), turning once. Remove from skillet; keep warm.

2 Add apple juice, sweet pepper, onion, garlic, dried sage (if using), and black pepper to skillet. Bring to boiling; reduce heat. Simmer, covered, for 2 minutes.

3 In a small bowl combine cornstarch and cold water; stir into mixture in skillet. Stir in apples. Cook and stir until thickened and bubbly. Cook and stir for 2 minutes more. If using, stir in the fresh sage. Return the chicken to the skillet; heat through.

Chicken with Apples and Sage

START TO FINISH: 30 minutes
MAKES: 4 servings

NUTRITION FACTS per serving:

- -

CALORIES 252
TOTAL FAT 3 g total fat (1 g sat. fat)
CHOLESTEROL 82 mg
PROTEIN 34 g
CARBOHYDRATE 23 g
FIBER 3 g
SODIUM 153 mg

EXCHANGES 1½ Fruit, 4 Meat

1 6-ounce jar marinated artichoke hearts

1 tablespoon olive oil

12 ounces skinless, boneless chicken breasts, cut into bite-size pieces

3 cloves garlic, thinly sliced

¼ cup chicken broth

¼ cup dry white wine

1 tablespoon small fresh oregano leaves or 1 teaspoon dried oregano, crushed

1 7-ounce jar roasted red sweet peppers, drained and cut into strips

¼ cup pitted kalamata olives

3 cups hot cooked campanelle or penne pasta

¼ cup crumbled feta cheese (optional)

Mediterranean Chicken and Pasta

PREP: 15 minutes   **COOK:** 10 minutes
MAKES: 4 servings

NUTRITION FACTS per serving:

CALORIES 347
TOTAL FAT 9 g total fat (1 g sat. fat)
CHOLESTEROL 49 mg
PROTEIN 26 g
CARBOHYDRATE 38 g
FIBER 3 g
SODIUM 323 mg

EXCHANGES 1 Vegetable, 2 Starch, 2½ Meat, ½ Fat

1 Drain artichokes, reserving marinade. Cut up any large pieces. Set aside. In a large skillet heat oil over medium-high heat. Add chicken and garlic. Cook and stir until chicken is browned. Add the reserved artichoke marinade, broth, wine, and, if using, dried oregano.

2 Bring to boiling; reduce heat. Simmer, covered, for 10 minutes. Stir in artichokes, roasted peppers, olives, and, if using, fresh oregano. Heat through.

3 To serve, spoon the chicken mixture over pasta. If desired, sprinkle with feta cheese.

- 2 teaspoons Jamaican jerk seasoning
- 2 fresh serrano chile peppers, seeded and finely chopped (see note, page 263)
- 4 skinless, boneless chicken breast halves (1¼ to 1½ pounds total)

  Nonstick cooking spray
- ½ cup peach nectar
- 3 green onions, bias-sliced into 1-inch pieces
- 2 cups sliced, peeled peaches
- 1 cup sliced, pitted plums
- 1 tablespoon brown sugar
- ⅛ teaspoon salt
- ½ cup pitted dark sweet cherries, halved

  Fresh serrano pepper, cut into a flower (see note, page 263) (optional)

1 In a small bowl combine jerk seasoning and 1 of the finely chopped serrano peppers. Rub mixture onto both sides of each chicken breast. Lightly coat an unheated large skillet with nonstick cooking spray. Preheat skillet over medium heat. Add chicken. Cook for 8 to 10 minutes or until tender and no longer pink (170°F), turning once. Transfer to a serving platter; keep warm.

2 Add 2 tablespoons of the peach nectar and the green onions to skillet. Cook and stir over medium heat for 4 to 5 minutes or just until green onions are tender.

3 In a medium bowl combine remaining finely chopped serrano pepper, remaining peach nectar, half of the peaches, half of the plums, the brown sugar, and salt. Add to skillet. Cook and stir over medium heat about 2 minutes or until slightly thickened and bubbly. Remove from heat. Stir in remaining peaches and plums. Stir in cherries. Spoon over chicken. If desired, garnish with pepper flower.

Spicy Chicken with Fruit

START TO FINISH: 35 minutes
MAKES: 4 servings

NUTRITION FACTS per serving:

CALORIES 271
TOTAL FAT 3 g total fat (1 g sat. fat)
CHOLESTEROL 82 mg
PROTEIN 34 g
CARBOHYDRATE 27 g
FIBER 3 g
SODIUM 323 mg

EXCHANGES 1½ Fruit, 4½ Meat

1 tablespoon reduced-sodium soy sauce

1 teaspoon grated fresh ginger

1 teaspoon chile oil

½ teaspoon sugar

½ cup all-purpose flour

4 skinless, boneless chicken breast halves (1¼ to 1½ pounds total)

1 tablespoon cooking oil

¼ cup apricot preserves

¼ cup reduced-sodium chicken broth

Hot cooked rice (optional)

Shredded orange peel (optional)

Szechwan-Fried Chicken Breasts

START TO FINISH: 30 minutes
MAKES: 4 servings

NUTRITION FACTS per serving:
- -

CALORIES 314
TOTAL FAT 7 g total fat (1 g sat. fat)
CHOLESTEROL 82 mg
PROTEIN 35 g
CARBOHYDRATE 26 g
FIBER 1 g
SODIUM 267 mg

EXCHANGES 1½ Other Carbo., 4 Meat, ½ Fat

1 In a small bowl stir together soy sauce, ginger, ½ teaspoon of the chile oil, and the sugar; set aside.

2 Place flour in a shallow bowl. Brush both sides of each chicken breast half with soy mixture; dip in flour to coat. In a large nonstick skillet cook chicken in hot cooking oil over medium-high heat for 8 to 10 minutes or until tender and no longer pink (170°F), turning once. Remove chicken from skillet; cover and keep warm.

3 For sauce, add apricot preserves, broth, and remaining ½ teaspoon chile oil to skillet. Cook and stir over medium heat until preserves melt and mixture is heated through. Spoon sauce over chicken. If desired, serve with hot cooked rice and sprinkle with orange peel.

12   ounces skinless, boneless chicken breasts, cut into bite-size strips

½   cup orange juice

¼   cup snipped fresh cilantro

1   teaspoon finely shredded lime peel

2   tablespoons lime juice

1   fresh jalapeño chile pepper, seeded and finely chopped (see note, page 263)

⅛   teaspoon salt

⅛   teaspoon black pepper

3   cloves garlic, minced

1   medium red sweet pepper, cut into thin strips

2   teaspoons cooking oil

1   cup loose-pack frozen whole kernel corn

1½   teaspoons cornstarch

8   6-inch corn tortillas

½   cup light dairy sour cream (optional)

     Fresh cilantro sprigs (optional)

1 Place chicken in a plastic bag set in a shallow dish. For marinade, in a small bowl combine orange juice, snipped cilantro, lime peel, lime juice, jalapeño pepper, salt, black pepper, and garlic. Pour over chicken; seal bag. Marinate in the refrigerator for at least 1 hour or up to 2 hours, turning bag occasionally.

2 Drain chicken, reserving marinade. In a large nonstick skillet cook and stir sweet pepper in hot oil over medium-high heat until crisp-tender. Remove sweet pepper.

3 Add chicken to skillet. Cook and stir for 3 to 4 minutes or until chicken is tender and no longer pink. Stir in corn; heat through. In a small bowl stir together the reserved marinade and the cornstarch; add to chicken mixture. Cook and stir until thickened and bubbly. Cook and stir for 2 minutes more. Return sweet pepper to skillet; stir to combine.

4 Wrap tortillas in microwave-safe paper towels. Microwave on 100% power (high) for 45 to 60 seconds or until warm. Divide the chicken mixture among tortillas. If desired, top with sour cream and garnish with cilantro sprigs.

Tex-Mex Chicken Tacos

PREP: 20 minutes   **COOK:** 15 minutes
MARINATE: 1 to 2 hours
MAKES: 4 servings

NUTRITION FACTS per serving:

CALORIES 354
TOTAL FAT 7 g total fat (1 g sat. fat)
CHOLESTEROL 49 mg
PROTEIN 26 g
CARBOHYDRATE 49 g
FIBER 4 g
SODIUM 336 mg

EXCHANGES 1 Vegetable, 1 Starch, 1 ½ Other Carbo., 2 Meat

4 chicken breast halves (about 2½ pounds total)

Nonstick cooking spray

3 tablespoons sesame seeds

3 tablespoons all-purpose flour

¼ teaspoon salt

¼ teaspoon cayenne pepper

3 tablespoons bottled reduced-sodium teriyaki sauce

1 tablespoon butter or margarine, melted

Fresh pineapple wedges (optional)

Shredded spinach (optional)

Sesame Chicken

PREP: 15 minutes **BAKE:** 45 minutes
OVEN: 400°F **MAKES:** 4 servings

NUTRITION FACTS per serving:

- -

CALORIES 293
TOTAL FAT 9 g total fat (3 g sat. fat)
CHOLESTEROL 115 mg
PROTEIN 45 g
CARBOHYDRATE 7 g
FIBER 1 g
SODIUM 460 mg

EXCHANGES 6 Meat

1 Skin chicken; set aside. Lightly coat a large baking sheet with nonstick cooking spray; set aside. In a large plastic bag combine sesame seeds, flour, salt, and cayenne pepper. Dip chicken in teriyaki sauce. Add chicken to the mixture in the plastic bag. Seal bag. Shake bag to coat the chicken.

2 Place chicken, bone sides down, on prepared baking sheet. Drizzle melted butter over chicken.

3 Bake in a 400°F oven about 45 minutes or until chicken is tender and no longer pink (170°F). If desired, garnish with pineapple wedges and spinach.

4 skinless, boneless chicken breast halves (1¼ to 1½ pounds total)

½ cup finely chopped green onions (4)

½ cup orange juice

1 tablespoon brown sugar

1 tablespoon finely chopped fresh ginger

1 tablespoon olive oil

2 cloves garlic, minced

1 teaspoon ground coriander

½ teaspoon paprika

¼ teaspoon salt

¼ teaspoon ground cinnamon

¼ teaspoon black pepper
   Nonstick cooking spray

2 cups hot cooked rice

1 Place chicken in a plastic bag set in a shallow dish. For marinade, in a small bowl combine green onions, orange juice, brown sugar, ginger, oil, garlic, coriander, paprika, salt, cinnamon, and pepper. Pour over chicken; seal bag. Marinate in the refrigerator for at least 2 hours or up to 6 hours, turning bag occasionally. Drain chicken, reserving the marinade.

2 Lightly coat a 2-quart rectangular baking dish with nonstick cooking spray. Arrange chicken in the prepared baking dish; pour marinade over chicken.

3 Bake, uncovered, in a 375°F oven about 20 minutes or until chicken is tender and no longer pink (170°F). Spoon rice onto 4 dinner plates. Transfer chicken to dinner plates. Strain the juices remaining in baking dish; spoon juices over chicken.

Ginger-Spiced Chicken

PREP: 15 minutes
MARINATE: 2 to 6 hours
BAKE: 20 minutes   **OVEN:** 375°F
MAKES: 4 servings

NUTRITION FACTS per serving:

CALORIES 332
TOTAL FAT 6 g total fat (1 g sat. fat)
CHOLESTEROL 82 mg
PROTEIN 36 g
CARBOHYDRATE 31 g
FIBER 1 g
SODIUM 228 mg

EXCHANGES ½ Starch, 1 Other Carbo., 4 Meat

Chicken-Mushroom Pasta

START TO FINISH: 30 minutes
MAKES: 6 servings

NUTRITION FACTS per serving:

CALORIES 293
TOTAL FAT 8 g total fat (2 g sat. fat)
CHOLESTEROL 35 mg
PROTEIN 22 g
CARBOHYDRATE 33 g
FIBER 2 g
SODIUM 255 mg

EXCHANGES 1 Vegetable, 1½ Starch, 2½ Meat

2⅔ cups dried penne pasta (8 ounces)

12 ounces skinless, boneless chicken breasts, cut into bite-size strips

¼ teaspoon salt

⅛ teaspoon freshly ground black pepper

2 tablespoons olive oil or cooking oil

3 large cloves garlic, minced

3 cups sliced fresh mushrooms (8 ounces)

1 medium onion, thinly sliced

½ cup chicken broth

¼ cup dry white wine

1 cup cut-up roma tomatoes

¼ cup shredded basil leaves

3 tablespoons snipped fresh oregano

¼ cup shredded Parmesan cheese

⅛ teaspoon freshly ground black pepper

1 Cook pasta in lightly salted boiling water according to package directions. Drain and return to saucepan; keep warm.

2 Meanwhile, season chicken with salt and ⅛ teaspoon pepper. In a large skillet heat 1 tablespoon of the oil over medium-high heat. Add chicken and garlic; cook and stir about 5 minutes or until chicken is tender and no longer pink. Remove from skillet; keep warm.

3 Add remaining 1 tablespoon oil to skillet. Cook mushrooms and onion in hot oil just until tender, stirring occasionally. Carefully add broth and wine. Bring to boiling; reduce heat. Boil gently, uncovered, about 2 minutes or until liquid is reduced by half. Remove skillet from the heat.

4 Add cooked pasta, chicken, tomatoes, basil, and oregano to mushroom mixture; toss to coat. Transfer to a serving dish; sprinkle with Parmesan cheese and ⅛ teaspoon pepper. Serve immediately.

- 2 tablespoons balsamic vinegar
- 2 tablespoons cooking oil
- 1 tablespoon honey
- ⅛ to ¼ teaspoon crushed red pepper
- 2 turkey breast tenderloins (about 1 pound total)

  Salt

  Black pepper
- 2 medium zucchini, halved lengthwise and cut into ¼-inch slices
- 2 cups hot cooked pasta or rice
- ½ cup chopped tomato (1 small)

  Shredded fresh basil

1 For dressing, in a small bowl stir together balsamic vinegar, 1 tablespoon of the oil, the honey, and crushed red pepper; set aside. Cut turkey tenderloins in half horizontally to make four ½-inch portions. Lightly sprinkle turkey with salt and pepper.

2 In a large nonstick skillet cook turkey in remaining 1 tablespoon hot oil over medium-high heat for 8 to 10 minutes or until tender and no longer pink (170°F), turning once. Remove from skillet; cover and keep warm.

3 Add zucchini to skillet; cook and stir about 3 minutes or until crisp-tender. Cut turkey into bite-size pieces. In a large bowl combine turkey, zucchini, and dressing. Spoon over hot cooked pasta. Sprinkle with chopped tomato and basil.

Balsamic Turkey with Zucchini

START TO FINISH: 25 minutes
MAKES: 4 servings

NUTRITION FACTS per serving:
- -

CALORIES 328
TOTAL FAT 9 g total fat (2 g sat. fat)
CHOLESTEROL 68 mg
PROTEIN 31 g
CARBOHYDRATE 30 g
FIBER 2 g
SODIUM 96 mg

EXCHANGES 1½ Vegetable, 1½ Starch, 3½ Meat, 1 Fat

Pineapple-Rum Turkey Kabobs

PREP: 15 minutes   **MARINATE:** 4 to 24 hours
BROIL: 12 minutes   **MAKES:** 4 servings

NUTRITION FACTS per serving:

- -

CALORIES 249
TOTAL FAT 4 g total fat (1 g sat. fat)
CHOLESTEROL 56 mg
PROTEIN 22 g
CARBOHYDRATE 24 g
FIBER 2 g
SODIUM 40 mg

EXCHANGES 1½ Fruit, 3 Meat

12   ounces turkey breast tenderloin steaks or boneless turkey breast, cut into 1-inch cubes

⅓   cup unsweetened pineapple juice

3   tablespoons rum or unsweetened pineapple juice

1   tablespoon brown sugar

1   tablespoon finely chopped lemongrass or 2 teaspoons finely shredded lemon peel

1   tablespoon olive oil

1   medium red onion, cut into thin wedges

2   nectarines or 3 plums, pitted and cut into thick slices

1½   cups fresh or canned pineapple chunks

Hot cooked rice (optional)

1 Place turkey in a plastic bag set in a shallow dish. For marinade, combine the ⅓ cup pineapple juice, the rum or additional pineapple juice, brown sugar, lemongrass or lemon peel, and oil. Pour over turkey. Seal bag. Marinate in refrigerator for at least 4 hours or up to 24 hours, turning bag occasionally.

2 Preheat broiler. Drain turkey, reserving marinade. In a small saucepan bring marinade to boiling. Remove from heat. On long metal skewers, alternately thread turkey and onion. Place kabobs on the unheated rack of a broiler pan; broil 3 to 4 inches from heat for 12 to 14 minutes or until turkey is tender and no longer pink, turning once and brushing occasionally with hot marinade during the first 8 minutes of broiling.

3 Meanwhile, on long metal skewers alternately thread nectarines or plums and pineapple. Brush with hot marinade. Place on broiler rack next to turkey kabobs for the last 5 minutes of broiling, turning once. Discard any remaining marinade. If desired, serve turkey and fruit kabobs with rice.

- 2 turkey breast tenderloins (about 1 pound total)
- 1 tablespoon lemon juice
- 1 tablespoon olive oil or cooking oil
- ½ teaspoon seasoned salt
- ½ teaspoon dried sage leaves, crushed
- 4 cloves garlic, minced
- 2 tablespoons apple jelly, melted
- Fresh sage leaves (optional)
- Apple slices (optional)

1 Preheat broiler. Cut turkey tenderloins in half horizontally to make four ½-inch portions. Place turkey on the unheated rack of a broiler pan. In a small bowl combine lemon juice, oil, seasoned salt, dried sage, and garlic. Brush mixture on both sides of each turkey portion.

2 Broil turkey 4 to 5 inches from the heat for 5 minutes. Turn turkey; broil for 2 minutes more. Using a clean brush, brush with apple jelly. Broil for 2 to 3 minutes more or until tender and no longer pink (170°F). Slice the turkey. If desired, garnish with sage leaves and apple slices.

Apple-Glazed Turkey

PREP: 10 minutes　　**BROIL:** 9 minutes
MAKES: 4 servings

NUTRITION FACTS per serving:

CALORIES 192
TOTAL FAT 5 g total fat (1 g sat. fat)
CHOLESTEROL 68 mg
PROTEIN 27 g
CARBOHYDRATE 8 g
FIBER 0 g
SODIUM 247 mg

EXCHANGES ½ Other Carbo., 4 Meat, ½ Fat

1/3   cup herb-seasoned stuffing mix, crushed (1/4 cup)

2   tablespoons reduced-fat milk

1   tablespoon snipped fresh sage or 1/2 teaspoon dried sage, crushed

1/4   teaspoon salt

1   pound uncooked ground turkey

1   cup torn mixed salad greens, watercress leaves, or shredded fresh spinach

4   whole wheat hamburger buns, split and toasted

1/2   cup whole cranberry sauce

1 Preheat broiler. In a large bowl combine stuffing mix, milk, sage, and salt. Add ground turkey; mix well. Shape into four 1/2-inch patties. Place patties on unheated rack of a broiler pan. Broil 4 to 5 inches from the heat for 11 to 13 minutes or until internal temperature registers 165°F on an instant-read thermometer; turn once.

2 Divide greens among buns; top with patties and cranberry sauce.

Turkey Burgers with Cranberry Sauce

PREP: 12 minutes   **BROIL:** 11 minutes
MAKES: 4 servings

NUTRITION FACTS per serving:

CALORIES 350
TOTAL FAT 11 g total fat (3 g sat. fat)
CHOLESTEROL 71 mg
PROTEIN 28 g
CARBOHYDRATE 37 g
FIBER 3 g
SODIUM 503 mg

EXCHANGES 2 Starch, 1/2 Other Carbo., 3 Meat

On the opener: Red Snapper Veracruz (*see recipe, page 170*)

1 pound fresh or frozen skinless cod, orange roughy, or catfish fillets

¼ cup reduced-fat milk

⅓ cup all-purpose flour

½ cup fine dry bread crumbs

2 tablespoons grated Parmesan cheese

¼ teaspoon lemon-pepper seasoning

2 tablespoons butter or margarine, melted

Fresh parsley sprigs (optional)

Lemon wedges (optional)

1 Thaw fish, if frozen. Rinse fish; pat dry with paper towels. If necessary, cut into 4 serving-size pieces. Measure the thickness of each piece. Place milk in a shallow dish. Place flour in another shallow dish. In a third shallow dish combine bread crumbs, Parmesan cheese, and lemon-pepper seasoning. Add melted butter to bread crumb mixture; stir until well mixed.

2 Grease a shallow baking pan; set aside. Dip fish in the milk; coat with flour. Dip again in the milk; dip in the crumb mixture, turning to coat all sides. Place fish in a single layer in prepared baking pan. Bake, uncovered, in a 450°F oven for 4 to 6 minutes per ½-inch thickness or until fish flakes easily when tested with a fork. If desired, garnish with parsley and lemon.

Oven-Fried Fish

PREP: 10 minutes
BAKE: 4 to 6 minutes per ½-inch thickness
OVEN: 450°F   **MAKES:** 4 servings

NUTRITION FACTS per serving:

CALORIES 254
TOTAL FAT 9 g total fat (5 g sat. fat)
CHOLESTEROL 75 mg
PROTEIN 26 g
CARBOHYDRATE 15 g
FIBER 1 g
SODIUM 565 mg

EXCHANGES 1 Starch, 3 Meat, 1½ Fat

Pan-Seared Salmon with Vegetables

START TO FINISH: 35 minutes
MAKES: 4 servings

NUTRITION FACTS per serving:

CALORIES 228
TOTAL FAT 9 g total fat (1 g sat. fat)
CHOLESTEROL 59 mg
PROTEIN 25 g
CARBOHYDRATE 10 g
FIBER 3 g
SODIUM 385 mg

EXCHANGES 2 Vegetable, 3 Meat

1	pound fresh or frozen skinless salmon fillets, about ¾ inch thick
3	tablespoons water
2	tablespoons dry sherry
2	tablespoons reduced-sodium soy sauce
1	teaspoon toasted sesame oil
½	teaspoon cornstarch
½	teaspoon five-spice powder
¼	teaspoon sugar
1	tablespoon cooking oil
3	medium carrots, cut lengthwise into thin ribbons*
2	teaspoons grated fresh ginger
2	cloves garlic, minced
1	medium zucchini, sliced lengthwise
6	medium green onions, bias-sliced into 1-inch lengths

1 Thaw fish, if frozen. Rinse fish; pat dry with paper towels. Cut the fish into 4 serving-size pieces. Set aside. In a small bowl combine the water, 1 tablespoon of the sherry, 1 tablespoon of the soy sauce, the sesame oil, cornstarch, ¼ teaspoon of the five-spice powder, and the sugar. Set aside.

2 In another small bowl combine the remaining 1 tablespoon sherry, 1 tablespoon soy sauce, and ¼ teaspoon five-spice powder. Brush over both sides of the salmon pieces. In a large nonstick skillet heat oil over medium heat. Add salmon; cook for 6 to 9 minutes or until fish flakes easily when tested with a fork, turning once. Remove from skillet; cover and keep warm.

3 In the same skillet stir-fry carrots, ginger, and garlic for 3 minutes. Add zucchini and green onions and stir-fry for 1 minute more or until vegetables are crisp-tender. Stir cornstarch mixture and add to skillet. Cook and stir 1 minute more.

4 To serve, spoon the vegetable mixture onto dinner plates. Top with the salmon.

*Note: Use a vegetable peeler to cut the carrots lengthwise into thin ribbons.

1   pound fresh or frozen skinless red
    snapper fillets, ½ to ¾ inch thick
    Salt and black pepper
2   tablespoons butter, melted
¾   cup soft bread crumbs (1 slice)
2   tablespoons snipped fresh flat-leaf
    parsley
1   teaspoon finely shredded orange
    peel
1   tablespoon orange juice
1   clove garlic, minced
¼   teaspoon dried oregano, crushed
¼   teaspoon black pepper
⅛   teaspoon salt
    Orange wedges (optional)

1 Thaw fish, if frozen. Preheat broiler. Rinse fish; pat dry. Cut fish into 4 serving-size portions. Place fish on the greased unheated rack of a broiler pan. Tuck under any thin edges. Sprinkle lightly with salt and pepper. Brush 2 teaspoons of the butter over the fish. Measure thickness of the fish.

2 Broil fish 4 inches from the heat for 4 to 6 minutes per ½-inch thickness or until fish flakes easily when tested with a fork.

3 Meanwhile, combine remaining butter, bread crumbs, parsley, orange peel, orange juice, garlic, oregano, the ¼ teaspoon pepper, and ⅛ teaspoon salt. Spoon mixture over broiled fish; broil 1 to 2 minutes more or until topping is light golden brown. If desired, serve with orange wedges.

Cuban Broiled Snapper with Parsley

START TO FINISH: 20 minutes
MAKES: 4 servings

NUTRITION FACTS per serving:

CALORIES 187
TOTAL FAT 8 g total fat (4 g sat. fat)
CHOLESTEROL 58 mg
PROTEIN 24 g
CARBOHYDRATE 4 g
FIBER 0 g
SODIUM 315 mg

EXCHANGES 3 Meat, 1 Fat

Sole with Caponata

START TO FINISH: 25 minutes
OVEN: 450°F   **MAKES:** 4 servings

NUTRITION FACTS per serving:
- -

CALORIES 197
TOTAL FAT 6 g total fat (1 g sat. fat)
CHOLESTEROL 52 mg
PROTEIN 21 g
CARBOHYDRATE 14 g
FIBER 2 g
SODIUM 613 mg

EXCHANGES 3 Vegetable, 3 Meat

4   4-ounce fresh or frozen skinless sole fillets

1   14½-ounce can Italian-style stewed tomatoes

2   cups chopped, peeled eggplant

1   tablespoon olive oil

1   small yellow, green, or red sweet pepper, coarsely chopped (¾ cup)

¼   cup bottled picante sauce

1   clove garlic, minced

1   tablespoon balsamic vinegar

⅛   teaspoon salt

⅛   teaspoon black pepper

2   tablespoons bottled reduced-calorie Italian salad dressing

Lime wedges (optional)

1 Thaw fish, if frozen. Rinse fish; pat dry.

2 For caponata, cut up any large tomato pieces; set aside. In a large nonstick skillet cook the eggplant in hot oil over medium-high heat about 3 minutes or until golden brown, stirring occasionally. Stir in undrained tomatoes, sweet pepper, picante sauce, and garlic. Bring to boiling; reduce heat. Simmer, uncovered, for 4 to 5 minutes or until slightly thickened. Stir in vinegar.

3 Season fish with the salt and pepper. Brush fish with the salad dressing. Roll up, securing rolls with wooden toothpicks. Place fish in a 2-quart square baking dish. Bake, uncovered, in a 450°F oven for 8 to 10 minutes or until fish flakes easily when tested with a fork. Serve caponata with fish. If desired, serve with lime wedges.

1½   pounds fresh or frozen swordfish, tuna, or shark steaks, 1 inch thick

¼   cup snipped fresh parsley

¼   cup chicken broth

1   teaspoon finely shredded lemon peel

2   tablespoons fresh lemon juice

2   tablespoons finely chopped shallot (1)

1   tablespoon snipped fresh rosemary

1   tablespoon olive oil

3   cloves garlic, minced

1½   teaspoons snipped fresh tarragon

¼   teaspoon salt

    Fresh flat-leaf parsley sprigs (optional)

    Lemon slices (optional)

1 Thaw fish, if frozen. Rinse fish; pat dry. Place fish steaks in a plastic bag set in a shallow dish. For marinade, in a bowl combine parsley, broth, lemon peel, lemon juice, shallot, rosemary, oil, garlic, tarragon, and salt. Pour marinade over fish. Seal bag. Marinate for 30 minutes in the refrigerator, turning occasionally.

2 Preheat broiler. Drain fish steaks, reserving marinade. Place fish on the greased unheated rack of a broiler pan. Broil fish 4 to 6 inches from the heat for 5 minutes, brushing once with reserved marinade. Discard any remaining marinade. Turn fish and broil for 3 to 7 minutes more or until fish flakes easily when tested with a fork. If desired, garnish with parsley sprigs and lemon slices.

Lemon-Herb Swordfish Steaks

PREP: 20 minutes   **MARINATE:** 30 minutes
BROIL: 8 minutes   **MAKES:** 4 to 6 servings

NUTRITION FACTS per serving:

CALORIES 245
TOTAL FAT 10 g total fat (2 g sat. fat)
CHOLESTEROL 64 mg
PROTEIN 34 g
CARBOHYDRATE 3 g
FIBER 0 g
SODIUM 350 mg

EXCHANGES 5 Meat

Maple-Hoisin Glazed Halibut

PREP: 10 minutes   **BROIL:** 8 minutes
MAKES: 4 servings

NUTRITION FACTS per serving:

CALORIES 210
TOTAL FAT 4 g total fat (1 g sat. fat)
CHOLESTEROL 45 mg
PROTEIN 30 g
CARBOHYDRATE 13 g
FIBER 0 g
SODIUM 285 mg

EXCHANGES 1 Starch, 4 Meat

4	5-ounce fresh or frozen halibut steaks, 1 inch thick
3	tablespoons hoisin sauce
2	tablespoons seasoned rice vinegar
2	tablespoons maple syrup
1	teaspoon grated fresh ginger
1	clove garlic, minced
¼	teaspoon crushed red pepper
¼	teaspoon coarsely ground black pepper
	Shredded napa cabbage (optional)

1 Thaw fish, if frozen. Rinse fish; pat dry. In a small bowl stir together hoisin sauce, vinegar, syrup, ginger, garlic, and crushed red pepper. Set aside.

2 Preheat broiler. Sprinkle fish with black pepper. Place fish on the greased unheated rack of a broiler pan. Broil fish 4 inches from the heat for 5 minutes. Brush with glaze; turn fish. Brush with remaining glaze. Broil for 3 to 7 minutes more or until fish flakes easily when tested with a fork. If desired, serve on a bed of napa cabbage.

1 pound fresh or frozen orange roughy fillets

3 tablespoons pineapple preserves

2 tablespoons rice vinegar

2 teaspoons snipped fresh thyme

1/8 teaspoon crushed red pepper

1 clove garlic, minced

1/4 teaspoon black pepper

1/8 teaspoon salt

Fresh thyme sprigs (optional)

Fresh pineapple wedges (optional)

1 Thaw fish, if frozen. Preheat broiler. In a small bowl stir together preserves, vinegar, snipped thyme, red pepper, and garlic; set aside.

2 Rinse fish; pat dry. Cut into 4 serving-size portions. Sprinkle fish with black pepper and salt. Place fish on the greased unheated rack of a broiler pan. Measure thickness of the fish. Broil fish 4 inches from the heat until the fish flakes easily when tested with a fork, brushing occasionally with the preserves mixture. (Allow 4 to 6 minutes per 1/2-inch thickness of fish; if fillets are 1 inch thick, turn once halfway through broiling.) If desired, garnish with thyme sprigs and pineapple wedges.

Pineapple-Glazed Orange Roughy

PREP: 10 minutes
BROIL: 4 to 6 minutes per 1/2-inch thickness
MAKES: 4 servings

NUTRITION FACTS per serving:

- -

CALORIES 125
TOTAL FAT 1 g total fat (0 g sat. fat)
CHOLESTEROL 22 mg
PROTEIN 17 g
CARBOHYDRATE 11 g
FIBER 0 g
SODIUM 150 mg

EXCHANGES 1/2 Fruit, 2 1/2 Meat

Red Snapper Veracruz

START TO FINISH: 15 minutes
MAKES: 4 servings

NUTRITION FACTS per serving:

- -

CALORIES 300
TOTAL FAT 2 g total fat (0 g sat. fat)
CHOLESTEROL 41 mg
PROTEIN 30 g
CARBOHYDRATE 38 g
FIBER 3 g
SODIUM 538 mg

EXCHANGES 1 Vegetable, 2 Starch, 3 Meat

4	4-ounce fresh or frozen skinless red snapper or orange roughy fillets, ½ to 1 inch thick
⅓	cup bottled salsa
1	clove garlic, minced
1	14-ounce can vegetable broth
1	cup quick-cooking couscous
¼	cup thinly sliced green onions (2) or coarsely chopped fresh cilantro
	Lemon wedges (optional)

1 Thaw fish, if frozen. Preheat broiler. Combine salsa and garlic; set aside. In a medium saucepan bring broth to boiling. Stir in couscous; cover and remove from heat. Let stand about 5 minutes or until liquid is absorbed. Stir in green onions.

2 Meanwhile, rinse fish; pat dry. Place fish on the greased unheated rack of a broiler pan. Measure thickness of the fish. Broil fish about 4 inches from the heat until the fish flakes easily when tested with a fork. (Allow 4 to 6 minutes per ½-inch thickness of fish; if fillets are 1 inch thick, turn once halfway through broiling.) Spoon the salsa mixture over fish; broil 1 minute more or until salsa is heated through.

3 To serve, arrange fish on couscous mixture. If desired, serve with lemon wedges.

2   8- to 10-ounce fresh or frozen
swordfish steaks, 1 inch thick

1   teaspoon garlic powder

¾   teaspoon fennel seeds, crushed

½   teaspoon lemon-pepper seasoning

¼   teaspoon salt

⅛   teaspoon crushed red pepper

1   recipe Sicilian Relish

Fresh basil sprigs (optional)

1 Thaw fish, if frozen. Preheat broiler. Rinse fish; pat dry. Cut into 4 serving-size portions. In a small bowl stir together garlic powder, crushed fennel seeds, lemon-pepper seasoning, salt, and crushed red pepper. Rub on both sides of each fish piece.

2 Place fish on the greased unheated rack of a broiler pan. Broil 4 inches from the heat for 8 to 12 minutes or until fish flakes easily when tested with a fork, turning once halfway through broiling. Serve with Sicilian Relish. If desired, garnish with basil sprigs.

Sicilian Relish: In a small bowl toss together ¾ cup chopped roma tomatoes; 3 tablespoons chopped pitted Sicilian or kalamata olives; 3 tablespoons snipped fresh basil; 2 teaspoons lemon juice; 2 cloves garlic, minced; and 2 teaspoons olive oil.

Sicilian-Style Swordfish

PREP: 20 minutes   **BROIL:** 8 minutes
MAKES: 4 servings

NUTRITION FACTS per serving:

- -

CALORIES 177
TOTAL FAT 8 g total fat (2 g sat. fat)
CHOLESTEROL 43 mg
PROTEIN 23 g
CARBOHYDRATE 4 g
FIBER 1 g
SODIUM 457 mg

EXCHANGES 3 Meat, ½ Fat

1   12-ounce fresh or frozen skinless
    salmon fillet, 1 inch thick

1½ cups apricot nectar

⅓   cup snipped dried apricots

2   tablespoons honey

2   tablespoons reduced-sodium soy
    sauce

1   tablespoon grated fresh ginger

2   cloves garlic, minced

¼   teaspoon ground cinnamon

⅛   teaspoon cayenne pepper

1 Thaw fish, if frozen. For glaze, in a medium saucepan stir together apricot nectar, apricots, honey, soy sauce, ginger, garlic, cinnamon, and cayenne pepper. Bring to boiling; reduce heat. Simmer, uncovered, about 20 minutes or until mixture is thickened and reduced by about half, stirring occasionally. Remove ¼ cup of the glaze for basting; set aside the remaining glaze until ready to serve.

2 Preheat broiler. Rinse fish; pat dry. Place fish on the greased unheated rack of a broiler pan, tucking under any thin edges.

3 Broil about 4 inches from the heat for 8 to 12 minutes or until fish flakes easily when tested with a fork, gently turning once halfway through broiling and brushing occasionally with the reserved ¼ cup glaze the last 4 minutes of broiling. Serve fish with the remaining glaze.

Sweet 'n' Heat-Glazed Salmon

PREP: 30 minutes   **BROIL:** 8 minutes
MAKES: 4 servings

NUTRITION FACTS per serving:

- -

CALORIES 239
TOTAL FAT 6 g total fat (1 g sat. fat)
CHOLESTEROL 45 mg
PROTEIN 19 g
CARBOHYDRATE 30 g
FIBER 2 g
SODIUM 350 mg

EXCHANGES 2 Fruit, 2½ Meat

4 6-ounce fresh or frozen halibut steaks, 1 inch thick

2 medium oranges

½ cup dry white wine or orange juice

2 tablespoons orange-honey spread or honey

2 teaspoons grated fresh ginger

¼ teaspoon salt

¼ teaspoon coarsely ground black pepper

4 cups torn fresh spinach and/or baby spinach

1 Thaw fish, if frozen. Peel and section oranges over a bowl to catch juices. Reserve orange sections. Measure ¼ cup orange juice (add additional orange juice, if necessary). For marinade, stir together the ¼ cup orange juice, wine, honey spread, and ginger.

2 Rinse fish; pat dry. Place fish in a plastic bag set in a shallow dish. Pour marinade over fish. Seal bag. Marinate 1 to 4 hours in the refrigerator. Drain fish, reserving the marinade.

3 Preheat broiler. Pour marinade into a small saucepan. Bring to boiling. Boil, uncovered, for 2 minutes. Keep warm. Place fish on the greased unheated rack of a broiler pan. Sprinkle with the salt and pepper. Broil fish 4 inches from the heat for 8 to 12 minutes or until fish flakes easily when tested with a fork, turning once halfway through broiling.

4 Place spinach in a medium bowl. Drizzle with ¼ cup of the hot marinade. Divide spinach among 4 dinner plates. Top with fish, reserved orange sections, and additional hot marinade.

Honey-Ginger Halibut with Oranges

PREP: 25 minutes   **MARINATE:** 1 to 4 hours
BROIL: 8 minutes   **MAKES:** 4 servings

NUTRITION FACTS per serving:

CALORIES 267
TOTAL FAT 4 g total fat (1 g sat. fat)
CHOLESTEROL 54 mg
PROTEIN 37 g
CARBOHYDRATE 14 g
FIBER 4 g
SODIUM 277 mg

EXCHANGES 1 Vegetable, ½ Fruit, 5 Meat

Tuna-Noodle Casserole

PREP: 25 minutes   **BAKE:** 20 minutes
OVEN: 375°F   **MAKES:** 6 servings

NUTRITION FACTS per serving:

CALORIES 258
TOTAL FAT 8 g total fat (4 g sat. fat)
CHOLESTEROL 52 mg
PROTEIN 18 g
CARBOHYDRATE 28 g
FIBER 3 g
SODIUM 651 mg

EXCHANGES 1½ Vegetable, 1½ Starch, 1½ Meat, 1 Fat

2   cups dried medium noodles (4 ounces)
2   cups loose-pack frozen cut green beans
⅓   cup fine dry bread crumbs
2   teaspoons butter or margarine, melted
     Nonstick cooking spray
1   cup sliced fresh mushrooms
¾   cup coarsely chopped red sweet pepper
½   cup chopped onion (1 medium)
1   10¾-ounce can reduced-fat and reduced-sodium condensed cream of mushroom or celery soup
½   cup reduced-fat milk
½   cup shredded American or process Swiss cheese (2 ounces)
1   9¼-ounce can tuna (water pack), drained and flaked

1 Cook noodles according to package directions, adding the green beans for the last 3 minutes of cooking. Drain; set aside.

2 Meanwhile, toss the bread crumbs with melted butter; set aside.

3 Lightly coat an unheated large nonstick skillet with nonstick cooking spray. Preheat over medium heat. Add mushrooms, sweet pepper, and onion. Cook and stir until vegetables are tender. Add soup, milk, and cheese, stirring until cheese is melted. Stir in cooked noodle-green bean mixture and tuna.

4 Spoon noodle mixture into a 1½-quart casserole. Sprinkle bread crumb mixture over noodle mixture. Bake, uncovered, in a 375°F oven for 20 to 25 minutes or until heated through and bread crumbs are golden.

8 ounces fresh or frozen medium shrimp in shells

Nonstick cooking spray

1 cup coarsely chopped onion (1 large)

1 clove garlic, minced

6 chicken thighs (about 1½ pounds)

1 14-ounce can reduced-sodium chicken broth

1 teaspoon snipped fresh thyme or ¼ teaspoon dried thyme, crushed

¼ teaspoon salt

¼ teaspoon ground saffron

⅛ to ¼ teaspoon cayenne pepper

1 cup long grain rice

1 medium red or green sweet pepper, coarsely chopped

1 cup loose-pack frozen peas

½ cup chopped, seeded tomato (1 medium)

1 Thaw shrimp, if frozen. Peel and devein shrimp, leaving tails intact. Rinse shrimp; pat dry with paper towels. Cover and refrigerate until needed.

2 Lightly coat an unheated Dutch oven with nonstick cooking spray. Preheat over medium heat. Add onion and garlic. Cook until onion is tender.

3 Remove skin from the chicken thighs. Add chicken thighs, broth, dried thyme (if using), salt, saffron, and cayenne pepper to Dutch oven. Bring to boiling and reduce heat. Simmer, covered, for 15 minutes.

4 Stir in uncooked rice. Return to boiling; reduce heat. Simmer, covered, about 15 minutes more or until rice is almost tender. Stir shrimp, sweet pepper, peas, tomato, and fresh thyme (if using) into the rice mixture. Simmer, covered, for 5 to 8 minutes more or until the rice and chicken are tender and the shrimp turn opaque.

Paella

PREP: 20 minutes **COOK:** 40 minutes
MAKES: 6 servings

NUTRITION FACTS per serving:

CALORIES 267
TOTAL FAT 4 g total fat (1 g sat. fat)
CHOLESTEROL 100 mg
PROTEIN 24 g
CARBOHYDRATE 33 g
FIBER 3 g
SODIUM 400 mg

EXCHANGES 1 Vegetable, 2 Starch, 2 Meat, ½ Fat

Mediterranean Shrimp Packets

PREP: 25 minutes **BAKE:** 25 minutes
OVEN: 425°F **MAKES:** 4 servings

NUTRITION FACTS per serving:

CALORIES 292
TOTAL FAT 3 g total fat (0 g sat. fat)
CHOLESTEROL 88 mg
PROTEIN 20 g
CARBOHYDRATE 46 g
FIBER 7 g
SODIUM 696 mg

EXCHANGES 2 Vegetable, 2 Starch, 1½ Meat

8	ounces fresh or frozen peeled and deveined medium shrimp
1	cup quick-cooking couscous
1	cup boiling water
2	small zucchini and/or yellow summer squash, halved lengthwise and thinly sliced
1	small red, yellow, or green sweet pepper, cut into thin bite-size strips
1	9-ounce package frozen artichoke hearts, thawed
¼	teaspoon coarsely ground black pepper
⅛	teaspoon salt
½	cup bottled reduced-calorie Italian salad dressing
¼	cup thinly sliced fresh basil or fresh spinach

1 Thaw shrimp, if frozen. Rinse shrimp; pat dry with paper towels. Set aside. Cut four 16×12-inch pieces of parchment or use precut sheets. (Or tear off four 24×18-inch pieces of heavy foil. Fold each piece in half to make four 18×12-inch pieces.)

2 In a small saucepan combine couscous and boiling water; cover and let stand for 5 minutes. Divide couscous mixture, shrimp, squash, sweet pepper, and artichokes evenly among the 4 pieces of parchment or foil. Sprinkle with black pepper and salt. Drizzle with salad dressing.

3 Bring together 2 opposite edges of parchment or foil; seal with a double fold. Fold remaining ends to completely enclose the food, allowing space for steam to build. Place the packets in a single layer on a baking pan.

4 Bake in a 425°F oven about 25 minutes or until shrimp turn opaque (carefully open a packet to check). Carefully open packets and sprinkle each with 1 tablespoon of the basil or spinach.

- 1 pound fresh or frozen swordfish or halibut steaks, 1 inch thick
- ½ teaspoon Jamaican jerk seasoning
- 4 8- to 10-inch whole wheat or flour tortillas
- 2 cups small fresh spinach leaves or shredded lettuce
- 1 recipe Mango Salsa
   Lime wedges (optional)

1 Thaw fish, if frozen. Preheat broiler. Rinse fish; pat dry. Cut fish into ¾-inch slices; sprinkle with jerk seasoning.

2 Place seasoned fish slices on the greased unheated rack of a broiler pan. Broil fish 4 inches from the heat for 5 minutes; turn fish. Broil for 3 to 7 minutes more or until fish flakes easily when tested with a fork. Meanwhile, wrap tortillas in foil. Heat package on lower rack of oven for 5 to 7 minutes.

3 Fill each warm tortilla with spinach, fish, and Mango Salsa. If desired, serve with lime wedges.

Mango Salsa: In a large bowl combine 1 large mango, peeled, seeded, and chopped; 1 large tomato, seeded and chopped; 1 small cucumber, seeded and chopped; 2 to 4 tablespoons snipped fresh cilantro; 1 fresh jalapeño chile pepper, seeded and chopped (see note, page 263); 1 thinly sliced green onion; and 1 tablespoon lime juice. Cover and chill until serving time. Serve with a slotted spoon. Makes about 3 cups.

Fish Soft Shell Tacos with Mango Salsa

PREP: 20 minutes   **BROIL:** 8 minutes
MAKES: 4 servings

NUTRITION FACTS per serving:

CALORIES 261
TOTAL FAT 5 g total fat (1 g sat. fat)
CHOLESTEROL 43 mg
PROTEIN 26 g
CARBOHYDRATE 28 g
FIBER 13 g
SODIUM 346 mg

EXCHANGES 1 Vegetable, ½ Fruit, 1 Starch, 3 Meat

Scallops with Tropical Salsa

START TO FINISH: 25 minutes
MAKES: 4 servings

NUTRITION FACTS per serving:

CALORIES 123
TOTAL FAT 3 g total fat (1 g sat. fat)
CHOLESTEROL 31 mg
PROTEIN 15 g
CARBOHYDRATE 9 g
FIBER 1 g
SODIUM 226 mg

EXCHANGES ½ Fruit, 2 Meat

1 cup finely chopped strawberry papaya or papaya
½ cup seeded and finely chopped cucumber
1 small tomato, seeded and chopped
2 tablespoons snipped fresh cilantro
1 fresh jalapeño chile pepper, seeded and finely chopped (see note, page 263)
4 teaspoons lime juice
1 teaspoon olive oil
12 ounces fresh or frozen scallops
Salt and black pepper
1 clove garlic, minced
1 teaspoon butter or margarine
Lime wedges (optional)

1 For salsa, in a small bowl stir together the papaya, cucumber, tomato, cilantro, jalapeño pepper, lime juice, and oil. Let stand at room temperature for at least 15 minutes to allow flavors to blend.

2 Meanwhile, thaw scallops, if frozen. Rinse scallops; pat dry. Halve any large scallops. Lightly sprinkle with salt and black pepper.

3 In a large nonstick skillet cook garlic in hot butter over medium heat for 30 seconds. Add scallops. Cook and stir for 2 to 3 minutes or until scallops are opaque. Use a slotted spoon to remove scallops; drain on paper towels. Serve the scallops with salsa. If desired, serve with lime wedges.

Chapter 11

Meatless

On the opener: Vegetable Curry *(see recipe, page 185)*

PASTA

VEGETABLE-BASED

GRAINS/BEANS

SOY

6	dried lasagna noodles
2½	cups zucchini and/or yellow summer squash halved lengthwise and sliced (2 medium)
2	cups sliced fresh mushrooms
⅓	cup chopped onion (1 small)
2	teaspoons olive oil
1	cup light ricotta cheese
3	tablespoons finely shredded Parmesan cheese (1 ounce)
¼	teaspoon black pepper
2	cups purchased pasta sauce
1	cup shredded part-skim mozzarella cheese (4 ounces)
½	cup chopped, seeded tomato (1 medium)

1 Cook noodles according to package directions; drain and rinse with cold water. Drain well.

2 Meanwhile, in large nonstick skillet cook and stir squash, mushrooms, and onion in hot oil over medium-high heat about 5 minutes or until tender; remove from heat and set aside. In a small bowl combine ricotta cheese, Parmesan cheese, and pepper.

3 To assemble, place 3 lasagna noodles in the bottom of a 2-quart rectangular baking dish, trimming to fit as necessary. Spoon half of the ricotta cheese mixture over the noodles. Top with half of the vegetable mixture, half of the sauce, and half of the mozzarella cheese. Layer with remaining noodles, ricotta cheese mixture, vegetable mixture, and sauce.

4 Bake, uncovered, in a 375°F oven for 30 minutes. Sprinkle with tomato and the remaining mozzarella cheese. Bake 5 minutes more or until heated through. Let stand for 10 minutes before serving.

Vegetable Lasagna

PREP: 30 minutes **BAKE:** 35 minutes
OVEN: 375°F **STAND:** 10 minutes
MAKES: 6 servings

NUTRITION FACTS per serving:

CALORIES 251
TOTAL FAT 9 g total fat (4 g sat. fat)
CHOLESTEROL 25 mg
PROTEIN 15 g
CARBOHYDRATE 30 g
FIBER 4 g
SODIUM 572 mg

EXCHANGES 1½ Vegetable, 1½ Starch, 1 Meat, ½ Fat

Broccoli and Tomato Penne

START TO FINISH: 25 minutes
MAKES: 4 servings

NUTRITION FACTS per serving:

CALORIES 275
TOTAL FAT 4 g total fat (0 g sat. fat)
CHOLESTEROL 0 mg
PROTEIN 12 g
CARBOHYDRATE 52 g
FIBER 6 g
SODIUM 63 mg

EXCHANGES 1½ Vegetable, 3 Starch

2¼ cups dried penne or cut ziti (about 8 ounces)

4 cups broccoli florets

½ cup oil-packed dried tomatoes

1 cup sliced fresh shiitake mushrooms

¼ teaspoon crushed red pepper

3 cloves garlic, minced

½ cup shredded fresh basil

Shaved Parmesan cheese (optional)

1 Cook pasta according to package directions, adding broccoli to the pasta for the last 2 minutes of cooking. Drain. Return pasta and broccoli to hot pan.

2 Meanwhile, drain the tomatoes, reserving 2 tablespoons of the oil. Cut tomatoes into strips.

3 In a medium saucepan cook mushrooms, crushed red pepper, and garlic in the hot reserved oil for 3 to 4 minutes or until the mushrooms are tender. Stir in basil. Add to pasta along with tomato strips; toss gently to combine. If desired, top with Parmesan cheese.

1½	cups quick-cooking brown rice
½	cup vegetable broth or chicken broth
¼	cup dry sherry
1	tablespoon cornstarch
1	tablespoon reduced-sodium soy sauce
1	teaspoon sugar
1	teaspoon grated fresh ginger
½	teaspoon crushed red pepper (optional)
	Nonstick cooking spray
1	cup thinly bias-sliced carrots
3	cloves garlic, minced
3	cups broccoli florets
6	ounces firm tofu (fresh bean curd), cut into ½-inch cubes

1 Prepare rice according to package directions; keep warm.

2 For sauce, in a small bowl stir together the broth, dry sherry, cornstarch, soy sauce, sugar, ginger, and, if desired, crushed red pepper. Set sauce aside.

3 Coat an unheated wok or large skillet with nonstick cooking spray. Preheat over medium-high heat. Add carrots and garlic to hot wok or skillet; stir-fry for 2 minutes. Add broccoli; stir-fry for 3 to 4 minutes more or until vegetables are crisp-tender. Push vegetables from the center of wok.

4 Stir sauce; add to center of wok. Cook and stir until thickened and bubbly. Add tofu; stir together all ingredients to coat. Cook and stir for 1 minute more.

5 To serve, spoon vegetable mixture over hot cooked rice.

Vegetable and Tofu Stir-Fry

START TO FINISH: 30 minutes
MAKES: 4 servings

NUTRITION FACTS per serving:

CALORIES 218
TOTAL FAT 3 g total fat (0 g sat. fat)
CHOLESTEROL 0 mg
PROTEIN 9 g
CARBOHYDRATE 39 g
FIBER 5 g
SODIUM 315 mg

EXCHANGES 1 Vegetable, 2 Starch, ½ Meat

3 cups mushroom broth, vegetable broth, or chicken broth

2 cups sliced fresh mushrooms (such as shiitake or button mushrooms)

½ cup chopped onion (1 medium)

2 cloves garlic, minced

2 tablespoons olive oil

1 cup Arborio rice

1 cup finely chopped zucchini

1 cup finely chopped carrots

1 15-ounce can white kidney (cannellini) beans or pinto beans, rinsed and drained

½ cup grated Parmesan cheese (2 ounces)

Risotto with Beans and Vegetables

START TO FINISH: 40 minutes
MAKES: 4 servings

NUTRITION FACTS per serving:

CALORIES 388
TOTAL FAT 11 g total fat (3 g sat. fat)
CHOLESTEROL 8 mg
PROTEIN 17 g
CARBOHYDRATE 61 g
FIBER 8 g
SODIUM 539 mg

EXCHANGES 3 Vegetable, 3 Starch, 1½ Fat

1 In a medium saucepan bring broth to boiling; reduce heat and simmer until needed. Meanwhile, in a large saucepan cook mushrooms, onion, and garlic in hot oil over medium heat about 5 minutes or until onion is tender. Add uncooked rice. Cook and stir about 5 minutes more or until rice is golden brown.

2 Slowly add 1 cup of the broth to the rice mixture, stirring constantly. Continue to cook and stir until liquid is absorbed. Add another ½ cup of the broth, the zucchini, and carrots to rice mixture, stirring constantly. Continue to cook and stir until liquid is absorbed. Add another 1 cup of the broth, ½ cup at a time, stirring constantly until the broth is absorbed. (This should take about 20 minutes.)

3 Stir the remaining ½ cup broth into rice mixture. Cook and stir until rice is slightly creamy and just tender. Stir in white kidney beans and Parmesan cheese; heat through.

- 1   large red onion, halved and cut into thin wedges
- 1   tablespoon olive oil
- 2   teaspoons curry powder
- 1   teaspoon ground cumin
- ¼   teaspoon garam masala
- ⅛   teaspoon cayenne pepper
- 3   cups cauliflower florets
- 1   14½-ounce can diced tomatoes, undrained
- 2   medium potatoes, peeled and cut into 1-inch cubes (about 1½ cups)
- 2   medium sweet potatoes, peeled and cut into 1-inch cubes (about 1½ cups)
- 1½   cups vegetable broth or water
- ¼   teaspoon salt
- ¼   teaspoon freshly ground black pepper
- 1   cup loose-pack frozen peas
- 4½   cups hot cooked couscous or brown rice

1 In a large saucepan cook onion in hot oil over medium heat about 5 minutes or until tender. Add curry powder, cumin, garam masala, and cayenne pepper. Cook and stir for 1 minute.

2 Stir in cauliflower, tomatoes, potatoes, sweet potatoes, broth, salt, and black pepper. Bring to boiling; reduce heat. Simmer, covered, for 10 to 12 minutes or until potatoes are tender. Stir in peas; heat through. Serve over couscous or brown rice.

Vegetable Curry

START TO FINISH: 35 minutes
MAKES: 6 servings

NUTRITION FACTS per serving:

CALORIES 284
TOTAL FAT 3 g total fat (0 g sat. fat)
CHOLESTEROL 0 mg
PROTEIN 9 g
CARBOHYDRATE 55 g
FIBER 7 g
SODIUM 516 mg

EXCHANGES 2 Vegetable, 3 Starch

Beans, Barley, and Tomatoes

START TO FINISH: 30 minutes
MAKES: 4 servings

NUTRITION FACTS per serving:

- -

CALORIES 171
TOTAL FAT 3 g total fat (0 g sat. fat)
CHOLESTEROL 0 mg
PROTEIN 9 g
CARBOHYDRATE 33 g
FIBER 10 g
SODIUM 484 mg

EXCHANGES 2 Vegetable, 1½ Starch

1	14-ounce can vegetable broth or chicken broth
1	teaspoon Greek seasoning or garam masala
1	cup loose-pack frozen green soybeans (shelled edamame)
¾	cup quick-cooking barley
½	cup shredded carrot
4	cups fresh spinach leaves
4	small to medium tomatoes, sliced

1 In a medium saucepan bring broth and seasoning to boiling. Add soybeans and barley. Return to boiling; reduce heat. Simmer, covered, for 12 minutes. Stir carrot into barley mixture.

2 Meanwhile, divide spinach among 4 dinner plates. Arrange tomato slices on spinach. Using a slotted spoon, spoon barley mixture over tomatoes (or drain barley mixture; spoon over tomatoes).

Make-ahead directions: Prepare as above through step 1. Cover and chill barley mixture up to 24 hours. Arrange spinach and tomatoes as above. Spoon chilled barley mixture over tomatoes.

3 cups water

1 cup cornmeal

1 cup cold water

½ teaspoon salt

Nonstick cooking spray

1 small red onion, cut into thin wedges

1 tablespoon olive oil

3 cups sliced fresh mushrooms (such as cremini, shiitake, or oyster)

1 pound fresh asparagus spears, trimmed

3 cloves garlic, thinly sliced

⅓ cup dry white wine, Marsala, vegetable broth, or chicken broth

¼ teaspoon salt

¼ cup finely shredded Asiago or Parmesan cheese (1 ounce)

2 tablespoons pine nuts, toasted

1 For polenta, in a medium saucepan bring the 3 cups water to boiling. In a small bowl combine the cornmeal, the 1 cup water, and the salt. Slowly add cornmeal mixture to the boiling water, stirring constantly. Cook and stir until mixture returns to boiling; reduce heat to low. Cook, uncovered, for 10 to 15 minutes or until thick, stirring frequently.

2 Coat an 8×8×2-inch baking pan with nonstick cooking spray. Spread hot polenta evenly into the pan; cool slightly. Cover and chill about 2 hours or until firm.

3 Bake the polenta in a 350°F oven about 20 minutes or until heated through. Meanwhile, in a large skillet cook onion in hot oil over medium heat until tender. Add mushrooms, asparagus, and garlic; cook, uncovered, about 4 minutes or until almost tender. Stir in wine and salt. Cook, uncovered, over medium-high heat for 1 minute.

4 To serve, cut polenta into 8 pieces. Divide polenta among 4 dinner plates. Spoon the mushroom mixture over polenta. Sprinkle with cheese and pine nuts.

Make-ahead directions: Prepare as above through step 2. Cover; chill up to 24 hours. Proceed as above in steps 3 and 4.

Polenta with Mushrooms and Asparagus

PREP: 30 minutes   **CHILL:** 2 hours
BAKE: 20 minutes   **OVEN:** 350°F
MAKES: 4 servings

NUTRITION FACTS per serving:

CALORIES 273
TOTAL FAT 11 g total fat (3 g sat. fat)
CHOLESTEROL 8 mg
PROTEIN 11 g
CARBOHYDRATE 33 g
FIBER 4 g
SODIUM 536 mg

EXCHANGES 2 Vegetable, 1½ Starch, ½ Meat, 1 Fat

2½ cups water

1½ cups cornmeal

1½ cups cold water

1 teaspoon salt

1 small onion, thinly sliced

1 tablespoon olive oil

4 cups fresh mushrooms, halved

¼ teaspoon salt

¼ teaspoon freshly ground black pepper

6 medium red and/or yellow sweet peppers, roasted and cut into thin bite-size strips*

1¼ cups purchased marinara sauce

1 cup shredded mozzarella cheese

Fresh basil sprigs (optional)

Vegetable Polenta Lasagna

PREP: 25 minutes **CHILL:** 1 hour
BAKE: 40 minutes **OVEN:** 350°F
MAKES: 8 servings

NUTRITION FACTS per serving:

CALORIES 210
TOTAL FAT 7 g total fat (2 g sat. fat)
CHOLESTEROL 8 mg
PROTEIN 9 g
CARBOHYDRATE 31 g
FIBER 5 g
SODIUM 581 mg

EXCHANGES 3 Vegetable, 1 Starch,
½ Meat, ½ Fat

1 For polenta, in a medium saucepan bring the 2½ cups water to boiling. In a medium bowl combine the cornmeal, the 1½ cups water, and the 1 teaspoon salt. Slowly add cornmeal mixture to boiling water, stirring constantly. Cook and stir until mixture returns to boiling; reduce heat to low. Cook about 10 minutes or until mixture is very thick, stirring occasionally. Pour the hot mixture into a 3-quart rectangular baking dish. Cool slightly. Cover and chill about 1 hour or until firm.

2 In large nonstick skillet cook onion in hot oil over medium heat for 3 to 4 minutes or until tender. Add mushrooms, the ¼ teaspoon salt, and the black pepper. Cook and stir about 5 minutes or until mushrooms are tender. Remove from heat; stir in the roasted sweet peppers.

3 Spread the marinara sauce over chilled polenta. Top with the vegetable mixture; sprinkle with cheese. Bake, covered, in a 350°F oven for 30 minutes. Uncover; bake for 10 to 15 minutes more or until edges are bubbly. If desired, garnish with basil.

*Note: To roast peppers, quarter the peppers lengthwise; remove stems, seeds, and membranes. Place peppers, cut sides down, on a foil-lined baking sheet. Roast in a 450°F oven for 15 to 20 minutes or until skins are blistered and bubbly. Seal foil around peppers to form a packet. Let stand for 20 minutes. Peel peppers.

Nonstick cooking spray

¾ cup chopped onion

3 cloves garlic, minced

1 teaspoon olive oil or cooking oil

2 10-ounce packages frozen chopped spinach, thawed and well drained

1 cup low-fat cottage cheese, drained

1 cup crumbled feta cheese (4 ounces)

½ cup refrigerated or frozen egg product, thawed

1 tablespoon snipped fresh oregano or 1 teaspoon dried oregano, crushed

¼ teaspoon coarsely ground black pepper

¼ cup finely shredded Parmesan cheese (1 ounce)

2 tablespoons fine dry bread crumbs

1 Lightly coat a 9-inch pie plate with nonstick cooking spray; set aside. In a medium saucepan cook onion and garlic in hot oil until onion is tender.

2 Stir spinach, cottage cheese, feta cheese, egg product, oregano, and black pepper into onion mixture. Spoon the mixture into the prepared pie plate.

3 In a small bowl combine Parmesan cheese and bread crumbs; sprinkle over spinach mixture. Bake, uncovered, in a 350°F oven for 30 to 35 minutes or until a knife inserted near center comes out clean. To serve, cut into wedges.

Spinach-Feta Bake

PREP: 20 minutes **BAKE:** 30 minutes
OVEN: 350°F **MAKES:** 6 servings

NUTRITION FACTS per serving:

CALORIES 156
TOTAL FAT 7 g total fat (4 g sat. fat)
CHOLESTEROL 22 mg
PROTEIN 14 g
CARBOHYDRATE 8 g
FIBER 3 g
SODIUM 666 mg

EXCHANGES 2 Vegetable, 1½ Meat

Herb-and-Bean-Stuffed Tomatoes

PREP: 25 minutes **BAKE:** 20 minutes
OVEN: 350°F **MAKES:** 4 servings

NUTRITION FACTS per serving:

CALORIES 220
TOTAL FAT 12 g total fat (3 g sat. fat)
CHOLESTEROL 8 mg
PROTEIN 9 g
CARBOHYDRATE 25 g
FIBER 5 g
SODIUM 327 mg

EXCHANGES 2 Vegetable, 1 Starch,
½ Meat, 1½ Fat

4 large red and/or yellow tomatoes

1½ cups soft bread crumbs (2 slices)

½ of a 15-ounce can white kidney (cannellini) beans, rinsed and drained

¼ cup pine nuts, toasted

2 tablespoons grated Parmesan cheese

1 tablespoon finely shredded fresh basil or ½ teaspoon dried basil, crushed

1 tablespoon olive oil

2 cloves garlic, minced

⅛ teaspoon salt

⅛ teaspoon black pepper

2 teaspoons snipped fresh thyme or ½ teaspoon dried thyme, crushed

2 teaspoons butter or margarine, melted

1 Cut off ½ inch from the top of each tomato. Finely chop enough of the tops to equal 1 cup; set aside. Remove and discard the seeds from tomatoes.

2 In a large bowl stir together the chopped tomato, ¾ cup of the bread crumbs, the beans, pine nuts, Parmesan cheese, basil, oil, garlic, salt, and pepper. Spoon the bean mixture into the tomatoes. Place the stuffed tomatoes in a 2-quart square baking dish.

3 In a small bowl combine remaining ¾ cup bread crumbs and the thyme. Sprinkle over tomatoes. Drizzle with melted butter.

4 Bake, uncovered, in a 350°F oven about 20 minutes or until crumbs are golden brown and tomatoes are heated through.

1¾ cups water

½ cup shredded carrot

¼ cup thinly sliced green onions

1 teaspoon instant vegetable bouillon granules, 1 teaspoon instant chicken bouillon granules, or ½ of a vegetable bouillon cube, crushed

3 inches stick cinnamon or dash ground cinnamon

⅛ teaspoon salt

¾ cup bulgur

⅓ cup dried cranberries or raisins

4 small or 2 large yellow or red sweet peppers*

¾ cup shredded Muenster, brick, or mozzarella cheese (3 ounces)

½ cup water

1 In a large skillet combine the 1¾ cups water, the carrot, green onions, bouillon, cinnamon, and salt. Bring to boiling; reduce heat. Simmer, covered, for 5 minutes. Stir in the bulgur and cranberries or raisins. Remove from heat. Cover and let stand for 5 minutes. If using stick cinnamon, remove from the bulgur mixture. Drain off excess liquid.

2 Meanwhile, halve the sweet peppers lengthwise; remove and discard the seeds and membranes.

3 Stir shredded cheese into bulgur mixture; spoon into sweet pepper halves. Place the sweet pepper halves in a large skillet. Add the ½ cup water. Bring to boiling; reduce heat. Simmer, covered, for 5 to 10 minutes or until sweet peppers are crisp-tender and bulgur mixture is heated through.

*Note: You may substitute 4 large poblano peppers for the sweet peppers. Prepare as above. (See chile-handling note, page 263.)

Bulgur-Stuffed Peppers

START TO FINISH: 30 minutes
MAKES: 4 servings

NUTRITION FACTS per serving:

CALORIES 246
TOTAL FAT 7 g total fat (4 g sat. fat)
CHOLESTEROL 20 mg
PROTEIN 10 g
CARBOHYDRATE 39 g
FIBER 7 g
SODIUM 348 mg

EXCHANGES 1 Vegetable, ½ Fruit, 1½ Starch, 1 Meat

2 cups dried penne pasta (6 ounces)

2 medium bulbs fennel (about 2 pounds)

1 tablespoon olive oil or cooking oil

1 tablespoon butter or margarine

3 cloves garlic, minced

¼ teaspoon crushed red pepper

2 small yellow, green, and/or red sweet peppers, cut into thin bite-size strips (about 1 cup)

1 15-ounce can Great Northern beans, rinsed and drained

1 teaspoon snipped fresh thyme or ¼ teaspoon dried thyme, crushed

Freshly ground black pepper (optional)

Penne with Fennel

START TO FINISH: 30 minutes
MAKES: 4 servings

NUTRITION FACTS per serving:

CALORIES 351
TOTAL FAT 8 g total fat (2 g sat. fat)
CHOLESTEROL 8 mg
PROTEIN 13 g
CARBOHYDRATE 59 g
FIBER 11 g
SODIUM 348 mg

EXCHANGES 2 Vegetable, 3 Starch, 1 Fat

1 In a large saucepan cook pasta according to package directions. Drain; return pasta to saucepan and keep warm.

2 Meanwhile, cut off feathery leaves and upper stalks of fennel bulbs. If desired, reserve some of the feathery leaves for garnish; discard upper stalks. Remove any wilted outer layers of stalks. Wash fennel and cut lengthwise into quarters. Remove core and discard; cut fennel into thin strips.

3 In a large skillet heat oil and butter over medium-high heat until butter is melted; add garlic and crushed red pepper. Cook for 30 seconds. Add fennel to skillet; cook and stir for 5 minutes. Add sweet pepper strips; cook for 3 minutes more. Add the beans and thyme; cook about 2 minutes or until heated through.

4 To serve, add fennel mixture to pasta; toss gently to combine. If desired, season to taste with freshly ground black pepper. If desired, garnish with reserved fennel leaves.

1 medium potato, cut into ½-inch cubes (1 cup)

1 cup coarsely chopped carrot (2 medium)

12 corn tortillas

½ cup chopped onion (1 medium)

1 clove garlic, minced

1 tablespoon olive oil or cooking oil

1 small zucchini (about 6 ounces), cut into thin bite-size strips (about 1¼ cups)

1 cup fresh or frozen whole kernel corn

1 tablespoon chili powder

½ teaspoon salt

⅛ teaspoon black pepper

8 ounces firm tofu (fresh bean curd), cut into ½-inch cubes (1½ cups)

Fresh cilantro sprigs (optional)

1 cup shredded cheddar and/or Monterey Jack cheese (4 ounces)

Bottled salsa (optional)

Sliced green onions (optional)

Dairy sour cream and/or peeled avocado slices (optional)

1 In a covered medium saucepan cook the potato and carrot in a small amount of boiling water for 7 to 8 minutes or just until tender; drain and set aside.

2 Wrap tortillas tightly in foil. Heat in a 350°F oven for 10 to 15 minutes or until heated through. Meanwhile, in a large skillet cook and stir onion and garlic in hot oil over medium-high heat for 2 minutes.

3 Add zucchini and corn; cook and stir for 3 minutes more. Add chili powder, salt, and pepper. Cook and stir for 1 minute more. Gently stir in potato-carrot mixture and tofu. Heat through.

4 Fill tortillas with vegetable mixture. If desired, garnish with cilantro sprigs. Pass cheese with tacos. If desired, serve with salsa, green onions, and sour cream and/or avocado.

Zucchini, Corn, and Potato Tacos

START TO FINISH: 40 minutes
OVEN: 350°F   **MAKES:** 6 servings

NUTRITION FACTS per serving:

CALORIES 300
TOTAL FAT 12 g total fat (5 g sat. fat)
CHOLESTEROL 20 mg
PROTEIN 13 g
CARBOHYDRATE 40 g
FIBER 5 g
SODIUM 435 mg

EXCHANGES 1 Vegetable, 2 Starch, 1 Meat, 1 Fat

6 medium red sweet peppers (8 to 10 ounces each)

4 cloves garlic, peeled

10 ounces dried pasta (such as mafalda or penne)

1 cup water

1 6-ounce can tomato paste

½ cup loosely packed fresh basil or 2 teaspoons dried basil, crushed

2 tablespoons balsamic vinegar

¼ teaspoon salt

Finely shredded Parmesan cheese (optional)

Pasta with Red Pepper Sauce

PREP: 20 minutes **BAKE:** 20 minutes
OVEN: 400°F **COOL:** 20 minutes
MAKES: 5 servings

NUTRITION FACTS per serving:

CALORIES 291
TOTAL FAT 1 g total fat (0 g sat. fat)
CHOLESTEROL 0 mg
PROTEIN 11 g
CARBOHYDRATE 60 g
FIBER 5 g
SODIUM 145 mg

EXCHANGES 3 Vegetable, 3 Starch

1 Cut peppers lengthwise into quarters; remove stems, seeds, and membranes. Place, cut sides down, on a large foil-lined baking sheet. Add garlic cloves to baking sheet. Bake in a 400°F oven about 20 minutes or until peppers are tender and lightly browned. Cool about 20 minutes or until cool enough to handle.

2 Meanwhile, cook pasta according to package directions; drain and keep warm.

3 Place half each of the sweet peppers, garlic, the water, tomato paste, basil, and vinegar in a blender container or food processor bowl. Cover and blend or process until mixture is nearly smooth. Transfer to a medium saucepan. Repeat with remaining sweet peppers, garlic, water, tomato paste, basil, and vinegar. Stir in salt. Cook and stir sauce over medium-low heat until heated through.

4 To serve, spoon sauce over hot pasta. If desired, sprinkle with Parmesan cheese.

- 1 large onion, halved and thinly sliced
- 2 cloves garlic, minced
- 1 tablespoon olive oil
- 1 14-ounce can chicken broth or vegetable broth
- ¼ cup water
- ½ teaspoon dried thyme, crushed
- ⅛ teaspoon cayenne pepper
- ¾ cup dried orzo (rosamarina)
- 2 medium carrots, cut in thin bite-size strips
- 1 15-ounce can red beans, rinsed and drained
- 1 medium turnip, cut in thin bite-size strips
- 1 medium red sweet pepper, cut into thin bite-size strips

1 In a large saucepan cook onion and garlic in hot oil just until tender. Stir in broth, the water, thyme, and cayenne pepper. Bring to boiling. Add orzo and carrots. Simmer, covered, for 10 minutes.

2 Stir in red beans, turnip, and sweet pepper. Return to boiling; reduce heat. Simmer, covered, for 2 to 3 minutes more or until orzo is tender.

Orzo with Root Vegetables

START TO FINISH: 30 minutes
MAKES: 4 servings

NUTRITION FACTS per serving:
- -
CALORIES 250
TOTAL FAT 5 g total fat (1 g sat. fat)
CHOLESTEROL 0 mg
PROTEIN 13 g
CARBOHYDRATE 43 g
FIBER 9 g
SODIUM 524 mg

EXCHANGES 2 Vegetable, 2½ Starch, ½ Fat

Wheat Berry Tabbouleh

START TO FINISH: 25 minutes
MAKES: 4 servings

NUTRITION FACTS per serving:

- -

CALORIES 277
TOTAL FAT 12 g total fat (2 g sat. fat)
CHOLESTEROL 0 mg
PROTEIN 9 g
CARBOHYDRATE 38 g
FIBER 7 g
SODIUM 594 mg

EXCHANGES 2 Starch, 1 Vegetable, 2 Fat

2 2/3 cups cooked wheat berries*
3/4 cup chopped tomato
3/4 cup chopped cucumber
1/2 cup snipped fresh parsley
1/4 cup thinly sliced green onions (2)
1 tablespoon snipped fresh mint
3 tablespoons cooking oil
3 tablespoons lemon juice
1/4 teaspoon salt
Sliced cucumber (optional)
Sliced lemon (optional)

1 In a large bowl combine cooked wheat berries, tomato, chopped cucumber, parsley, green onions, and mint.

2 For dressing, in a screw-top jar combine oil, lemon juice, and salt. Cover and shake well. Drizzle dressing over wheat berry mixture; toss to coat.

3 To serve, if desired, arrange sliced cucumber and lemon around edge of bowl.

*Note: To cook wheat berries, in a medium saucepan bring one 14-ounce can vegetable broth or chicken broth and 1/4 cup water to boiling. Add 1 cup wheat berries. Return to boiling; reduce heat. Simmer, covered, about 1 hour or until tender; drain. Cover and refrigerate up to 3 days.

Make-ahead directions: Prepare as above through step 2. Cover and chill up to 24 hours. To serve, if desired, arrange sliced cucumber and lemon around edge of bowl.

On the opener: Skinny Mashed Potatoes *(see recipe, page 200)*

1 pound dry white beans (such as Great Northern, cannellini, or navy beans) (about 2⅓ cups)

8 cups water

1 to 1½ pounds meaty smoked pork hocks

8 cups water

3 medium peaches, pitted and cut into wedges (about 3 cups)

1 cup chopped onion (1 large)

1 cup peach nectar or apple juice

¼ cup packed brown sugar

2 tablespoons snipped fresh sage or 2 teaspoons dried sage, crushed

½ teaspoon salt

½ teaspoon black pepper

1 or 2 medium peaches, peeled, pitted, and sliced

Fresh herb leaves (optional)

1 Rinse beans. In a large Dutch oven combine beans and 8 cups water. Bring to boiling; reduce heat. Simmer for 2 minutes. Remove from heat. Cover and let stand for 1 hour. (Or place beans in water in Dutch oven. Cover and let soak in a cool place overnight.)

2 Drain and rinse beans. Return beans to Dutch oven. Add pork hocks. Stir in 8 cups fresh water. Bring to boiling; reduce heat. Simmer, covered for 1 to 1½ hours or until beans are tender, stirring occasionally. Remove hocks; set aside. Drain beans. When cool enough to handle, cut meat off bones; coarsely chop meat.

3 In a 2½- to 3-quart casserole combine the beans, meat, the peach wedges, and the onion. Stir in peach nectar, brown sugar, sage, salt, and pepper.

4 Bake, covered, in a 300°F oven for 1 hour. Uncover and bake about 15 minutes more or until desired consistency, stirring occasionally. Before serving, top with the peach slices. If desired, garnish with herb leaves.

Peachy Baked Beans

PREP: 20 minutes **STAND:** 1 hour
COOK: 1 hour **BAKE:** 1¼ hours
OVEN: 300°F
MAKES: 12 side-dish servings

NUTRITION FACTS per serving:

CALORIES 200
TOTAL FAT 2 g total fat (1 g sat. fat)
CHOLESTEROL 6 mg
PROTEIN 11 g
CARBOHYDRATE 37 g
FIBER 9 g
SODIUM 252 mg

EXCHANGES 1 Fruit, 1 Starch, 1 Meat

4 medium baking potatoes (such as russet, round white, or yellow) (about 1¼ pounds)

⅓ cup light dairy sour cream ranch dip

⅛ teaspoon salt

⅛ teaspoon freshly ground black pepper

1 tablespoons snipped fresh chives or parsley

1 tablespoons butter or margarine, melted

Snipped fresh chives or parsley (optional)

Skinny Mashed Potatoes

PREP: 15 minutes **COOK:** 20 minutes
BAKE: 20 minutes **OVEN:** 350°F
MAKES: 4 side-dish servings

NUTRITION FACTS per serving:

CALORIES 138
TOTAL FAT 5 g total fat (3 g sat. fat)
CHOLESTEROL 15 mg
PROTEIN 4 g
CARBOHYDRATE 21 g
FIBER 2 g
SODIUM 216 mg

EXCHANGES 1½ Starch, ½ Fat

1 If desired, peel potatoes. Cut up potatoes. In a medium covered saucepan cook potatoes in boiling salted water for 20 to 25 minutes or until tender; drain. Transfer potatoes to a large mixing bowl. Beat potatoes with an electric mixer on low speed until mashed. Add sour cream ranch dip, salt, and pepper; beat until well mixed. Fold in the 1 tablespoon snipped chives.

2 Spoon mixture into four 8-ounce casseroles. Drizzle with melted butter. Bake, uncovered, in a 350°F oven for 20 to 25 minutes until heated through. To serve, if desired, garnish with additional snipped chives.

- ⅓ cup chopped onion (1 small)
- 1 tablespoon butter or margarine
- 3 tablespoons fine dry bread crumbs
- 1 10¾-ounce can reduced-fat and reduced-sodium condensed cream of mushroom soup
- ¼ cup fat-free plain yogurt
- 1 2-ounce jar sliced pimiento, drained
- ⅛ teaspoon black pepper
- 2 9-ounce packages frozen French-style green beans, thawed and drained*

1 In a small saucepan cook onion in hot butter over medium heat about 4 minutes or until tender. Stir in bread crumbs; set aside.

2 In a large bowl combine soup, yogurt, pimiento, and pepper. Stir in the beans. Transfer mixture to a 1-quart casserole or baking dish. Sprinkle bread crumb mixture on top.

3 Bake, uncovered, in a 350°F oven for 25 to 30 minutes or until heated through.

*Note: If you prefer thoroughly cooked beans rather than crisp-tender ones, precook them in boiling water for 5 minutes before adding to the soup mixture. Drain well.

Green Bean Casserole

PREP: 15 minutes   **BAKE:** 25 minutes
OVEN: 350°F
MAKES: 6 side-dish servings

NUTRITION FACTS per serving:

CALORIES 92
TOTAL FAT 3 g total fat (1 g sat. fat)
CHOLESTEROL 7 mg
PROTEIN 3 g
CARBOHYDRATE 12 g
FIBER 3 g
SODIUM 313 mg

EXCHANGES 1 Vegetable, ½ Starch, ½ Fat

Savory Couscous

START TO FINISH: 20 minutes
MAKES: 8 side-dish servings

NUTRITION FACTS per serving:

CALORIES 158
TOTAL FAT 2 g total fat (1 g sat. fat)
CHOLESTEROL 4 mg
PROTEIN 5 g
CARBOHYDRATE 29 g
FIBER 2 g
SODIUM 241 mg

EXCHANGES 2 Starch

2 cups water
1½ cups sliced fresh mushrooms
½ cup shredded carrot
⅓ cup thinly sliced green onions
1 tablespoon butter or margarine
2 teaspoons instant chicken bouillon granules
2 teaspoons snipped fresh basil or thyme or ½ teaspoon dried basil or thyme, crushed
1 10-ounce package quick-cooking couscous

1 In a medium saucepan heat the water, mushrooms, carrot, green onions, butter, bouillon granules, and dried herb (if using) to boiling. Stir in couscous and fresh herb (if using). Remove from heat.

2 Cover; let stand about 5 minutes or until liquid is absorbed. Fluff with fork before serving.

- 8 ounces fresh green beans, ends trimmed
- 1 small onion, cut into thin wedges
- 1 clove garlic, minced
- 1 tablespoon olive oil
  Dash salt
  Dash black pepper
- 2 medium yellow summer squash, halved lengthwise and cut into ¼-inch slices
- ⅓ cup balsamic vinegar

1 In a shallow roasting pan combine beans, onion, and garlic. Drizzle with oil; sprinkle with salt and pepper. Toss mixture until beans are evenly coated. Spread into a single layer.

2 Roast in a 450°F oven for 8 minutes. Stir in squash; roast for 5 to 7 minutes more or until vegetables are tender and slightly browned.

3 Meanwhile, in a small saucepan bring the balsamic vinegar to boiling over medium-high heat; reduce heat. Boil gently about 5 minutes or until reduced by half (vinegar will thicken slightly).

4 Drizzle the vinegar over roasted vegetables; toss until vegetables are evenly coated.

Roasted Vegetables with Balsamic Vinegar

START TO FINISH: 25 minutes
OVEN: 450°F
MAKES: 4 to 6 side-dish servings

NUTRITION FACTS per serving:

CALORIES 95
TOTAL FAT 4 g total fat (1 g sat. fat)
CHOLESTEROL 0 mg
PROTEIN 2 g
CARBOHYDRATE 14 g
FIBER 4 g
SODIUM 44 mg

EXCHANGES 3 Vegetable, ½ Fat

Nonstick cooking spray

1 pound medium sweet potatoes

1 tablespoon butter or margarine, melted

¼ teaspoon seasoned salt

Dash ground nutmeg

1 Lightly coat a 15×10×1-inch baking pan with cooking spray. Scrub potatoes; cut lengthwise into quarters. Cut each quarter into two wedges. Arrange potatoes in a single layer in the pan. Combine butter, seasoned salt, and nutmeg. Brush mixture onto potatoes.

2 Bake in a 425°F oven for 20 to 30 minutes or until brown and tender, turning once.

Baked Sweet Potato Fries

PREP: 15 minutes **BAKE:** 20 minutes
OVEN: 425°F **MAKES:** 4 servings

NUTRITION FACTS per serving:
- -

CALORIES 113
TOTAL FAT 3 g total fat (2 g sat. fat)
CHOLESTEROL 8 mg
PROTEIN 1 g
CARBOHYDRATE 20 g
FIBER 2 g
SODIUM 142 mg

EXCHANGES 1 Starch, ½ Fat

6   medium baking potatoes (2 pounds total), peeled and cut in eighths
1   cup coarsely chopped onion (1 large)
½   cup water
2   tablespoons olive oil or cooking oil
2   teaspoons snipped fresh sage or 1 teaspoon ground sage
½   teaspoon salt
¼   teaspoon black pepper
1   to 1¼ cups buttermilk
     Salt and black pepper

1 In a greased 3-quart rectangular baking dish combine potatoes and onions. In a small bowl combine water, oil, sage, the ½ teaspoon salt, and ¼ teaspoon pepper; drizzle over potatoes and onions.

2 Bake, uncovered, in a 450°F oven for 40 to 45 minutes or until the vegetables are tender and browned, stirring twice.

3 Transfer to a large mixing bowl. Mash with a potato masher or beat with an electric mixer on low speed. Gradually beat in enough buttermilk to make smooth and fluffy. Season to taste with additional salt and pepper.

Sage and Onion Mashed Potatoes

PREP: 25 minutes   **BAKE:** 40 minutes
OVEN: 450°F   **MAKES:** 8 servings

NUTRITION FACTS per serving:

CALORIES 155
TOTAL FAT 5 g total fat (1 g sat. fat)
CHOLESTEROL 1 mg
PROTEIN 4 g
CARBOHYDRATE 24 g
FIBER 2 g
SODIUM 185 mg

EXCHANGES 1½ Starch, ½ Fat

Nonstick cooking spray

- 1 cup chopped onion (1 large)
- 1 cup chopped green or red sweet pepper
- 2 tablespoons butter or margarine
- 3 tablespoons all-purpose flour
- 2 cups reduced-fat milk
- 2 slightly beaten eggs
- 2 16-ounce packages frozen whole kernel corn, thawed and drained
- 2 cups soft bread crumbs
- ¾ teaspoon salt
- ¼ teaspoon black pepper

Scalloped Corn

PREP: 25 minutes **BAKE:** 40 minutes
OVEN: 325°F **STAND:** 10 minutes
MAKES: 12 servings

NUTRITION FACTS per serving:

CALORIES 153
TOTAL FAT 5 g total fat (2 g sat. fat)
CHOLESTEROL 44 mg
PROTEIN 6 g
CARBOHYDRATE 25 g
FIBER 2 g
SODIUM 240 mg

EXCHANGES 1½ Starch, 1 Fat

1 Lightly coat a 2-quart rectangular baking dish with cooking spray; set aside. In a medium saucepan cook onion and sweet pepper in 4 teaspoons of the butter about 5 minutes or until tender. Stir in flour until vegetables are coated. Add milk all at once. Cook and stir until thickened and bubbly; remove from heat and set aside.

2 In a large bowl stir together the eggs, thawed corn, 1 cup of the bread crumbs, the salt, and pepper. Stir in the thickened mixture. Transfer mixture to the prepared baking dish. In a small saucepan melt the remaining butter. Stir in the remaining bread crumbs to coat. Sprinkle over corn mixture.

3 Bake, uncovered, in a 325°F oven for 40 to 45 minutes or just until center appears set. Let stand 10 minutes before serving.

- 1 cup peeled and thinly bias-sliced carrots (2 medium)
- 3 cups peeled, quartered, and thinly sliced rutabaga (1 small)
- ¾ cup finely shredded Swiss cheese (3 ounces)
- 2½ cups peeled and thinly sliced sweet potatoes (2 medium)
- 2 cups peeled, quartered lengthwise, and thinly sliced butternut squash (half of a small)
- 2 tablespoons water
- 2 tablespoons maple syrup or honey
- ½ teaspoon instant chicken bouillon granules
- ½ teaspoon salt
- ¼ teaspoon black pepper
- 2 tablespoons sliced almonds

1 In a 2-quart baking dish layer in order the carrots, rutabaga, ¼ cup of the cheese, sweet potatoes, and squash. Combine water, maple syrup, bouillon granules, salt, and pepper; pour over vegetables.

2 Bake, covered, in a 375°F oven about 35 minutes or just until vegetables are tender. Uncover vegetables; sprinkle with remaining ½ cup cheese and sliced almonds. Bake, uncovered, 10 to 15 minutes more or until almonds are light brown.

Golden Vegetable Gratin

PREP: 30 minutes   **BAKE:** 45 minutes
OVEN: 375°F   **MAKES:** 8 servings

NUTRITION FACTS per serving:

CALORIES 156
TOTAL FAT 5 g total fat (2 g sat. fat)
CHOLESTEROL 11 mg
PROTEIN 6 g
CARBOHYDRATE 24 g
FIBER 3 g
SODIUM 255 mg

EXCHANGES 1½ Starch, ½ Fat

2 cups 1-inch bias-sliced carrots (4 medium)

2 cups 1-inch bias-sliced parsnips (4 medium)

2 tablespoons snipped fresh parsley

2 teaspoons snipped fresh marjoram, thyme, or rosemary, or ½ teaspoon dried marjoram, thyme, or rosemary, crushed

¼ teaspoon salt

1 tablespoon olive oil or cooking oil

2 cups 1½-inch pieces peeled, seeded winter squash (about 1¼ pounds before trimming)

¼ cup packed brown sugar

Fresh thyme sprigs (optional)

Roasted Fall Vegetables

PREP: 30 minutes   **ROAST:** 65 minutes
OVEN: 375°F/450°F   **MAKES:** 8 servings

NUTRITION FACTS per serving:

CALORIES 90
TOTAL FAT 2 g total fat (0 g sat. fat)
CHOLESTEROL 0 mg
PROTEIN 1 g
CARBOHYDRATE 18 g
FIBER 3 g
SODIUM 91 mg

EXCHANGES 1 Starch

1 In a large saucepan cook carrots and parsnips in a small amount of water, covered, for 3 minutes. Drain.

2 Transfer the partially cooked carrots and parsnips to a 13×9×2-inch baking pan. Sprinkle with parsley, desired herb, and salt. Drizzle with oil. Toss gently to coat vegetables. Cover the pan with foil.

3 Bake in a 375°F oven for 30 minutes, stirring vegetables once. Stir in squash pieces. Cover and bake about 20 minutes more or just until vegetables are barely done. Remove vegetables from oven.

4 Increase oven temperature to 450°F. Stir the brown sugar into vegetables until thoroughly combined. Return vegetables to oven and bake, uncovered, for 15 to 20 minutes more or until vegetables are tender and glazed. Transfer to a serving dish. If desired, garnish with fresh thyme.

2   cloves garlic, minced

2   teaspoons olive oil

1   cup uncooked long grain white rice

2½ cups reduced-sodium chicken broth

2   teaspoons finely shredded lemon peel

1½ cups sliced fresh mushrooms

½   cup thinly sliced green onions (4)

¼   cup chopped red sweet pepper

⅛   teaspoon black pepper

2   tablespoons chopped pecans, toasted

Lemon slices (optional)

1 In a medium saucepan cook garlic in hot oil for 30 seconds. Add the rice and broth. Bring to boiling; reduce heat. Cover and simmer for 10 minutes.

2 Add the lemon peel, mushrooms, green onions, sweet pepper, and black pepper. Cover and cook 10 to 15 minutes more or until liquid is absorbed and rice is tender. Stir in toasted pecans. If desired, garnish with lemon slices.

Rice Pilaf with Toasted Pecans

START TO FINISH: 30 minutes
MAKES: 6 servings

NUTRITION FACTS per serving:

- -

CALORIES 161
TOTAL FAT 4 g total fat (0 g sat. fat)
CHOLESTEROL 0 mg
PROTEIN 5 g
CARBOHYDRATE 28 g
FIBER 1 g
SODIUM 263 mg

EXCHANGES 1 Vegetable, 1½ Starch, ½ Fat

Vegetable Kabobs

PREP: 20 minutes   **COOK:** 8 minutes
GRILL: 10 minutes   **MAKES:** 8 servings

NUTRITION FACTS per serving:
- -

CALORIES 87
TOTAL FAT 4 g total fat (1 g sat. fat)
CHOLESTEROL 0 mg
PROTEIN 2 g
CARBOHYDRATE 12 g
FIBER 2 g
SODIUM 147 mg

EXCHANGES 1 Vegetable, ½ Starch, ½ Fat

2   medium potatoes, quartered

8   red boiling onions or 2 small red onions, each cut into 8 wedges

8   baby squash, such as zucchini and/ or yellow summer squash

8   medium fresh mushrooms

4   miniature sweet peppers, halved and seeded, and/or 1 or 2 small red and/or orange sweet peppers, cut in 1-inch pieces

¼   cup bottled oil-and-vinegar salad dressing

2   teaspoons snipped fresh rosemary or ½ teaspoon dried rosemary, crushed

⅛   teaspoon salt

⅛   teaspoon black pepper

1 In a medium covered saucepan cook potatoes and onions in a small amount of lightly salted boiling water over medium heat for 8 to 10 minutes or until nearly tender, adding the squash and mushrooms for the last 1 minute. Drain well. Cool slightly.

2 On eight 10-inch skewers alternately thread the potatoes, onions, squash, mushrooms, and sweet peppers. In a small bowl combine salad dressing, rosemary, salt, and black pepper; brush over vegetables.

3 Grill kabobs on the rack of an uncovered grill directly over medium heat for 10 to 12 minutes or until vegetables are tender and lightly browned, turning and brushing occasionally with dressing mixture. (To broil kabobs, preheat broiler. Place kabobs on the greased unheated rack of a broiler pan and broil 10 to 12 minutes, brushing occasionally with dressing mixture.)

1¼ pounds broccoli, cut into spears
½ cup chopped onion (1 medium)
2 cloves garlic, minced
1 tablespoon butter
2 tablespoons all-purpose flour
¼ teaspoon salt
⅛ teaspoon black pepper
1½ cups light milk
¾ cup shredded smoked Gouda cheese (3 ounces)
¾ cup soft bread crumbs (1 slice bread)
2 teaspoons butter, melted

1 Place a steamer basket in a large saucepan. Add water to just below the bottom of the steamer basket. Bring water to boiling. Add broccoli to steamer basket. Cover and reduce heat. Steam for 6 to 8 minutes or just until broccoli is tender.

2 Meanwhile, for sauce, in a medium saucepan cook and stir the onion and garlic in the 1 tablespoon hot butter until onion is tender. Stir in flour, salt, and pepper. Stir in the milk. Cook and stir until thickened and bubbly. Gradually add cheese, stirring until melted.

3 Transfer broccoli to a 1½-quart au gratin dish or 2-quart square baking dish. Pour sauce over broccoli. Combine bread crumbs and the 2 teaspoons melted butter; sprinkle over sauce. Bake, uncovered, in 425°F oven for 15 minutes or until crumbs are lightly browned.

Smoky Gouda-Sauced Broccoli

PREP: 20 minutes   **BAKE:** 15 minutes
OVEN: 425°F   **MAKES:** 6 servings

NUTRITION FACTS per serving:

CALORIES 145
TOTAL FAT 8 g total fat (5 g sat. fat)
CHOLESTEROL 23 mg
PROTEIN 7 g
CARBOHYDRATE 13 g
FIBER 2 g
SODIUM 429 mg

EXCHANGES ½ Milk, 1 Vegetable, ½ Meat, ½ Fat

2½ cups whole red grape tomatoes, small yellow pear-shape tomatoes, and/or cherry tomatoes

Nonstick olive oil cooking spray

¼ cup finely chopped shallots

1 clove garlic, minced

1 teaspoon snipped fresh lemon thyme or thyme

¼ teaspoon salt

¼ teaspoon black pepper

4 ounces fresh mozzarella cheese, cut in ½-inch cubes (1 cup)

1 Halve about 1½ cups of the tomatoes; set aside. Lightly coat a large nonstick skillet with cooking spray. Add shallots, garlic, and thyme. Cook and stir over medium heat for 2 to 3 minutes or until shallots are tender.

2 Add all of the tomatoes, salt, and pepper. Cook and stir for 1 to 2 minutes more or until tomatoes are just warm. Remove from heat. Stir in mozzarella cubes.

Tomatoes with Fresh Mozzarella

PREP: 12 minutes   **COOK:** 3 minutes
MAKES: 4 servings

NUTRITION FACTS per serving:

CALORIES 104
TOTAL FAT 5 g total fat (3 g sat. fat)
CHOLESTEROL 16 mg
PROTEIN 8 g
CARBOHYDRATE 8 g
FIBER 1 g
SODIUM 287 mg

EXCHANGES 1 Vegetable, 1 Meat

Chapter 13

Snacks

On the opener: Fresh Mozzarella with Basil (see recipe, page 217)

SAVORY

SPREADS & DIPS

SWEET

Nonstick cooking spray

1	cup all-purpose flour
¾	cup granulated sugar
1½	teaspoons apple pie spice
½	teaspoon baking powder
½	teaspoon baking soda
⅛	teaspoon salt
1	cup finely shredded carrot
⅓	cup cooking oil
¼	cup reduced-fat milk
3	egg whites
1	teaspoon sifted powdered sugar

1 Lightly coat an 8×8×2-inch baking pan with nonstick cooking spray. Set aside.

2 In a large bowl combine the flour, granulated sugar, apple pie spice, baking powder, baking soda, and salt. Add carrot, oil, and milk. Stir to moisten. In a medium mixing bowl beat egg whites with an electric mixer on medium to high speed until stiff peaks form (tips stand straight). Fold whites into carrot mixture.

3 Pour the batter into the prepared pan. Bake in a 350°F oven for 30 to 35 minutes or until a wooden toothpick inserted near the center comes out clean. Cool completely in pan on a wire rack.

4 To serve, sprinkle with powdered sugar.

Carrot Snack Cake

PREP: 15 minutes **BAKE:** 30 minutes
OVEN: 350°F **MAKES:** 12 servings

NUTRITION FACTS per serving:
- -

CALORIES 147
TOTAL FAT 6 g total fat (1 g sat. fat)
CHOLESTEROL 0 mg
PROTEIN 2 g
CARBOHYDRATE 21 g
FIBER 1 g
SODIUM 114 mg

EXCHANGES 1½ Other Carbo., 1 Fat

16   ³/₈-inch slices baguette-style French bread

4   ounces Gorgonzola cheese or other blue cheese, crumbled

1   small ripe pear, halved, cored, and very thinly sliced

2   tablespoons flavored honey (such as French lavender honey) or regular honey

Fresh mint sprigs (optional)

1 Preheat broiler. Place bread slices on a large baking sheet. Broil 4 to 5 inches from the heat for 30 to 60 seconds or until bread is toasted. Turn bread slices over; top bread slices with Gorgonzola. Broil for 30 to 60 seconds more or until cheese is bubbly and bread is toasted.

2 Top bread slices with pear slices. Lightly drizzle pear slices with honey. Arrange bread slices on a serving platter. If desired, garnish with fresh mint sprigs. Serve immediately.

Sweet Pear and Cheese Crostini

START TO FINISH: 15 minutes
MAKES: 16 appetizers

NUTRITION FACTS per appetizer:

- -

CALORIES 72
TOTAL FAT 2 g total fat (1 g sat. fat)
CHOLESTEROL 5 mg
PROTEIN 3 g
CARBOHYDRATE 10 g
FIBER 1 g
SODIUM 175 mg

EXCHANGES 1 Starch

1   pound fresh mozzarella cheese

¼   cup roasted garlic oil or olive oil

1   to 2 teaspoons balsamic vinegar

2   tablespoons snipped fresh basil or 1 teaspoon dried basil, crushed

1   tablespoon freshly cracked black pepper

Tomato slices (optional)

Fresh basil strips (optional)

Baguette-style French bread slices, toasted (optional)

1 Cut mozzarella into ½-inch pieces. Place pieces in a medium bowl. In a small bowl combine oil, vinegar, snipped basil, and pepper. Pour over cheese; toss gently until cheese is well coated. Cover and chill for 1 hour.

2 If desired, serve with tomato, basil strips, and bread slices.

Make-ahead directions: Prepare as above through step 1. Store, covered, in the refrigerator up to 3 days. To serve, let stand at room temperature until olive oil liquefies. If desired, serve with tomato, basil strips, and bread slices.

Fresh Mozzarella with Basil

PREP: 15 minutes   **CHILL:** 1 hour
MAKES: 14 to 16 appetizers

NUTRITION FACTS per appetizer:

CALORIES 100
TOTAL FAT 8 g total fat (4 g sat. fat)
CHOLESTEROL 25 mg
PROTEIN 6 g
CARBOHYDRATE 1 g
FIBER 0 g
SODIUM 120 mg

EXCHANGES 1 Meat, ½ Fat

1   3-ounce package cream cheese, softened

¼   cup coarsely chopped macadamia nuts

2   to 3 medium heads Belgian endive, separated into individual leaves

1   large mango or papaya, cut into thin strips

1 In a small bowl combine the cream cheese and macadamia nuts. Spoon about 1 teaspoon of the cream cheese mixture onto each endive leaf.

2 Top with the mango strips. Arrange on a serving platter.

Make-ahead directions: Prepare as above through step 1. Loosely cover with plastic wrap; chill for up to 2 hours. Before serving, top with mango strips.

Endive-Mango Appetizers

START TO FINISH: 20 minutes
MAKES: about 24 appetizers

NUTRITION FACTS per appetizer:

- -

CALORIES 30
TOTAL FAT 2 g total fat (1 g sat. fat)
CHOLESTEROL 4 mg
PROTEIN 0 g
CARBOHYDRATE 2 g
FIBER 0 g
SODIUM 11 mg

EXCHANGES ½ Fat

24 large fresh mushrooms (1½ to 2 inches in diameter)

Olive oil

8 dried tomatoes (not oil-packed)

1 cup ricotta cheese

½ cup finely chopped fresh spinach

½ cup shredded Monterey Jack cheese (2 ounces)

3 tablespoons freshly grated Parmesan cheese

1 tablespoon snipped fresh basil

¼ teaspoon salt

¼ teaspoon black pepper

2 cloves garlic, minced

½ cup crumbled feta cheese (2 ounces)

Fresh basil leaves (optional)

1 Remove and discard mushroom stems. Brush mushroom caps with oil. Arrange in a shallow baking pan, stem sides down. Bake in a 350°F oven for 12 minutes. Drain off any liquid.

2 Meanwhile, cover tomatoes with boiling water; let stand for 10 minutes. Drain; coarsely chop tomatoes. In a medium bowl combine tomatoes, ricotta cheese, spinach, Monterey Jack cheese, Parmesan cheese, snipped basil, salt, pepper, and garlic. Turn mushroom caps stem sides up; fill caps with ricotta mixture. Sprinkle feta cheese over tops.

3 Bake filled caps in a 450°F oven for 8 to 10 minutes or until heated through and lightly browned. If desired, garnish with basil leaves.

Make-ahead directions: Prepare as above through step 2. Cover and chill for up to 24 hours. Bake in a 450°F oven for 8 to 10 minutes or until heated through and lightly browned. If desired, garnish with basil leaves.

Cheese-Stuffed Mushrooms

PREP: 20 minutes   **BAKE:** 8 minutes
OVEN: 350°F/450°F
MAKES: 24 appetizers

NUTRITION FACTS per appetizer:

CALORIES 43
TOTAL FAT 3 g total fat (2 g sat. fat)
CHOLESTEROL 10 mg
PROTEIN 3 g
CARBOHYDRATE 1 g
FIBER 0 g
SODIUM 98 mg

EXCHANGES ½ Meat

Smoked Salmon with Lemon-Thyme Dipping Sauce

PREP: 10 minutes   **CHILL:** 1 to 6 hours
MAKES: 8 appetizer servings

NUTRITION FACTS per serving:

CALORIES 75
TOTAL FAT 5 g total fat (1 g sat. fat)
CHOLESTEROL 11 mg
PROTEIN 5 g
CARBOHYDRATE 2 g
FIBER 0 g
SODIUM 315 mg

EXCHANGES ½ Meat, ½ Fat

⅓ cup light mayonnaise dressing or salad dressing

2 tablespoons dairy sour cream

½ teaspoon finely shredded lemon peel

1 teaspoon lemon juice

2 teaspoons snipped fresh thyme

1 8-ounce piece smoked salmon

1 lemon, halved and sliced

1 tablespoon finely chopped red onion

1 tablespoon capers, rinsed and drained

Fresh thyme sprigs (optional)

1 For sauce, in a small bowl stir together mayonnaise dressing, sour cream, lemon peel, lemon juice, and snipped thyme. Cover and chill for at least 1 hour or up to 6 hours.

2 To serve, arrange salmon and lemon on platter. Sprinkle with red onion and capers. Serve with sauce. If desired, garnish with thyme sprigs.

2 cups assorted fresh vegetables, such as baby carrots with tops; radishes; 1-inch green sweet pepper squares, halved; and/or small pattypan squash

4 ounces firm cheese, such as peppercorn cheese or smoked Gouda, cut in ½-inch chunks

4 ounces cooked smoked turkey sausage or summer sausage, cut in ¾-inch slices and quartered

2 tablespoons refrigerated basil pesto

1 tablespoon white wine vinegar

1 Place vegetables, cheese, and sausage in a plastic bag set in a bowl. For the marinade, in a small bowl stir together pesto sauce and vinegar. Pour over vegetable mixture in plastic bag. Close bag. Marinate in the refrigerator for 1 to 24 hours.

2 Remove vegetable mixture from the refrigerator. Alternately thread the vegetables, cheese, and sausage onto twelve 6-inch skewers.

Antipasto Kabobs

PREP: 30 minutes
MARINATE: 1 to 24 hours
MAKES: 12 servings

NUTRITION FACTS per serving:

CALORIES 65
TOTAL FAT 4 g total fat (2 g sat. fat)
CHOLESTEROL 15 mg
PROTEIN 4 g
CARBOHYDRATE 3 g
FIBER 1 g
SODIUM 252 mg

EXCHANGES 1 Vegetable, ½ Meat

1 cup sliced carrots (2 medium)

¼ cup chopped onion

1 clove garlic, minced

½ teaspoon curry powder

¼ teaspoon ground cumin

2 tablespoons olive oil or cooking oil

½ cup drained canned white beans (such as navy or cannellini beans)

⅛ teaspoon salt

Thinly sliced green onions or snipped fresh cilantro (optional)

Crackers, melba toast, or toasted baguette-style French bread slices

Curried Carrot Spread

START TO FINISH: 25 minutes
MAKES: 1 cup spread

NUTRITION FACTS per serving:

CALORIES 61
TOTAL FAT 3 g total fat (0 g sat. fat)
CHOLESTEROL 0 mg
PROTEIN 1 g
CARBOHYDRATE 7 g
FIBER 1 g
SODIUM 93 mg

EXCHANGES ½ Starch, ½ Fat

1 In a small covered saucepan cook carrots in a small amount of boiling water about 8 minutes or until tender. Drain.

2 Meanwhile, in a small skillet cook onion, garlic, curry powder, and cumin in oil until onion is tender. Transfer carrots and onion mixture to a food processor bowl or blender container; add beans and salt. Cover and process or blend until smooth.

3 Transfer to a bowl. If desired, garnish with green onions. Serve with crackers.

Make-ahead directions: Prepare as above through step 2. Cover and chill up to 3 days. Let stand at room temperature for 30 minutes before serving.

3 pounds (about 30) frozen plain chicken wing drummettes

½ cup packed brown sugar

1 tablespoon cornstarch

2 teaspoons grated fresh ginger

¼ to ½ teaspoon crushed red pepper

½ cup pineapple juice

½ cup reduced-sodium chicken broth or water

¼ cup finely chopped green sweet pepper

2 tablespoons soy sauce

Thinly sliced green onions (optional)

1 Place frozen chicken drummettes in a 15×10×1-inch baking pan. Bake in a 400°F oven for 50 to 60 minutes or until skins are crispy.

2 Meanwhile, in a small saucepan combine brown sugar, cornstarch, ginger, and crushed red pepper. Stir in pineapple juice, broth, sweet pepper, and soy sauce. Cook and stir over medium heat until thickened and bubbly; cook and stir 2 minutes more. Set aside.

3 Carefully drain off any juices from baking pan. Brush drummettes with some of the glaze mixture. Bake for 10 minutes more. Brush with more of the glaze mixture. Place on serving plate. If desired, sprinkle with green onions. Pass remaining glaze mixture.

Polynesian Glazed Wings

PREP: 10 minutes   **BAKE:** 1 hour
OVEN: 400°F   **MAKES:** 30 appetizers
a

NUTRITION FACTS per appetizer:

CALORIES 80
TOTAL FAT 5 g total fat (1 g sat. fat)
CHOLESTEROL 29 mg
PROTEIN 5 g
CARBOHYDRATE 5 g
FIBER 0 g
SODIUM 98 mg

EXCHANGES ½ Other Carbo., ½ Meat

Queso Dip

START TO FINISH: 20 minutes
MAKES: 2¼ cups dip

NUTRITION FACTS per serving:

CALORIES 98
TOTAL FAT 4 g total fat (2 g sat. fat)
CHOLESTEROL 10 mg
PROTEIN 4 g
CARBOHYDRATE 10 g
FIBER 1 g
SODIUM 189 mg
EXCHANGES ½ Vegetable, ½ Starch, ½ Meat

¼ cup chopped onion

2 tablespoons water

2 cloves garlic, minced

1 14½-ounce can stewed tomatoes, drained and cut up

1 4½-ounce can chopped green chile peppers, drained

½ to ¾ teaspoon chili powder

¼ teaspoon bottled hot pepper sauce

1 cup shredded reduced-fat cheddar cheese (4 ounces)

1 3-ounce package cream cheese, cubed

3 ounces fat-free cream cheese, cubed

Chopped fresh tomato (optional)

1 recipe Tortilla Crisps

1 In a medium saucepan combine onion, water, and garlic. Bring to boiling; reduce heat. Cook, uncovered, over medium heat about 2 to 3 minutes or until water has evaporated. Add stewed tomatoes, chile peppers, chili powder, and hot pepper sauce. Cook and stir until hot.

2 Add cheddar cheese and cream cheeses. Cook and stir over low heat until cheese is melted. Transfer to a serving bowl. If desired, top dip with chopped fresh tomato. Serve immediately with Tortilla Crisps.

Tortilla Crisps: Cut nine 7- or 8-inch flour tortillas into 8 wedges each. Spread one-third of the wedges in a 15×10×1-inch baking pan. Bake in a 350°F oven for 5 to 10 minutes or until wedges are dry and crisp. Repeat with remaining wedges; cool. Store in an airtight container at room temperature up to 4 days or in the freezer up to 3 weeks. Makes 72 crisps.

- 1 cup plain lowfat yogurt
- ¼ cup coarsely shredded unpeeled cucumber
- 1 tablespoon finely chopped red onion
- 1 teaspoon snipped fresh mint
- 1 8-ounce container (¾ cup) plain hummus
- ½ cup chopped, seeded tomato
- 2 ounces feta cheese, crumbled (½ cup)

  Chopped cucumber (optional)

  Sliced green onion (optional)
- 3 large white and/or wheat pita bread rounds

1 In a small bowl stir together the yogurt, shredded cucumber, chopped onion, and mint. Set aside.

2 Spread hummus in the bottom of a 10-inch quiche dish or 9-inch pie plate. Spread yogurt mixture over hummus. Sprinkle with tomato and feta cheese. If desired, top with chopped cucumber and sliced green onion.

3 Split each pita bread round in half, making 2 rounds; cut each round into 8 wedges.* Serve pita bread wedges with dip.

*Note: For crisper pita bread dippers, spread wedges in a single layer on baking sheets. Lightly sprinkle with water. Sprinkle wedges with paprika and crushed dried oregano. Bake in a 350°F oven about 10 minutes or until crisp. Cool; cover and store in a cool, dry place.

Greek Layer Dip

START TO FINISH: 20 minutes
MAKES: 10 servings

NUTRITION FACTS per serving:

CALORIES 120
TOTAL FAT 4 g total fat (1 g sat. fat)
CHOLESTEROL 6 mg
PROTEIN 5 g
CARBOHYDRATE 17 g
FIBER 2 g
SODIUM 231 mg

EXCHANGES 1 Starch, ½ Fat

2 cups small whole fresh mushrooms (about 6 ounces)

2 small zucchini and/or yellow summer squash, halved lengthwise and bias-sliced in ½-inch slices (2 cups)

1 small red sweet pepper, cut in bite-size pieces (½ cup)

1 cup cubed, peeled jicama (half of a medium)

2 tablespoons olive oil or salad oil

½ teaspoon cumin seeds

¼ teaspoon chili powder

1 clove garlic, minced

¼ cup lemon juice

1 tablespoon sugar

¼ teaspoon salt

¼ teaspoon black pepper

Marinated Zucchini and Mushrooms

PREP: 20 minutes
MARINATE: 8 to 24 hours
MAKES: about 8 servings

NUTRITION FACTS per serving:
- -

CALORIES 60
TOTAL FAT 4 g total fat (1 g sat. fat)
CHOLESTEROL 0 mg
PROTEIN 1 g
CARBOHYDRATE 6 g
FIBER 1 g
SODIUM 76 mg

EXCHANGES 1 Vegetable, ½ Fat

1 Place mushrooms, zucchini, sweet pepper, and jicama in a plastic bag set in a deep bowl.

2 For marinade, in small skillet heat oil over medium heat for 1 minute. Add cumin seeds, chili powder, and garlic; cook and stir about 1 minute or until garlic is golden and seasonings are fragrant. Remove from heat and transfer to a small bowl. Stir in lemon juice, sugar, salt, and black pepper. Mix well. Pour marinade over vegetables in bag. Seal bag. Marinate vegetables in the refrigerator for at least 8 hours or overnight, turning bag occasionally.

3 To serve, pour vegetables and marinade into serving dish. Serve with toothpicks.

- 3   7- to 8-inch spinach and/or jalapeño flour tortillas
- 1   5.2-ounce carton Boursin cheese or one 5-ounce container semisoft cheese with garlic and herb
- 12   large fresh basil leaves
- ½   of a 7-ounce jar roasted red sweet peppers, cut into ¼-inch strips
- 4   ounces thinly sliced cooked roast beef, ham, or turkey
- 1   tablespoon low-fat mayonnaise dressing
    Fresh basil leaves (optional)

1 Spread each tortilla with one-third of the Boursin cheese. Add a layer of the large basil leaves to cover cheese. Divide sweet pepper strips among the tortillas, arranging pepper strips over the basil leaves 1 to 2 inches apart. Top with meat slices. Spread 1 teaspoon mayonnaise dressing over the meat on each tortilla. Roll tortillas tightly into a spiral, enclosing the filling. Wrap each roll in plastic wrap. Chill rolls in the refrigerator for 2 to 4 hours to blend flavors.

2 To serve, remove the plastic wrap from the tortilla rolls; cut each roll into 1-inch slices, making diagonal slices, if desired. If desired, garnish with the remaining basil leaves.

Wrap and Roll Basil Pinwheels

PREP: 20 minutes   **CHILL:** 2 to 4 hours
MAKES: about 24 pinwheels

NUTRITION FACTS per pinwheel:

CALORIES 45
TOTAL FAT 3 g total fat (2 g sat. fat)
CHOLESTEROL 4 mg
PROTEIN 2 g
CARBOHYDRATE 2 g
FIBER 0 g
SODIUM 60 mg

EXCHANGES ½ Meat

6   4-inch or four 6-inch white corn
    tortillas

    Cooking oil or nonstick cooking
    spray

½   cup shredded Monterey Jack
    cheese (2 ounces)

2   to 3 medium fresh serrano chile
    peppers, halved, seeded, and
    cut into thin slices (see note,
    page 263)

1   roma tomato, chopped

2   tablespoons snipped fresh cilantro

2   tablespoons light dairy sour cream

1 Lightly brush one side of each tortilla with
cooking oil or lightly coat with cooking
spray. Divide cheese evenly among unoiled sides
of 2 larger or 3 smaller tortillas. Top with pepper
slices, chopped tomato, and cilantro. Top with
remaining tortillas, oiled sides up.

2 Heat a heavy skillet or griddle over medium
heat. Cook quesadillas, one at a time, about
1 to 2 minutes per side or until cheese melts and
tortillas are lightly browned. Cut each quesadilla
into 4 wedges. Serve warm with sour cream.

Texas-Style Quesadillas

PREP: 10 minutes   **COOK:** 4 to 6 minutes
MAKES: 6 servings

NUTRITION FACTS per serving:

CALORIES 105
TOTAL FAT 5 g total fat (2 g sat. fat)
CHOLESTEROL 10 mg
PROTEIN 4 g
CARBOHYDRATE 11 g
FIBER 1 g
SODIUM 57 mg

EXCHANGES ½ Starch, ½ Meat, ½ Fat

Desserts

1   cup all-purpose flour

¼   cup granulated sugar

1½ teaspoons baking powder

1   teaspoon finely shredded orange peel

1   teaspoon ground cinnamon

3   tablespoons butter or margarine

¼   cup cold water

4   teaspoons cornstarch

1   16-ounce package frozen unsweetened pitted tart red cherries

3   cups thinly sliced apples (1 pound)

1   egg

⅓   cup fat-free milk

1 For biscuit topping, in a medium bowl stir together flour, 2 tablespoons of the granulated sugar, the baking powder, orange peel, and ½ teaspoon of the cinnamon. Using a pastry blender, cut in butter until mixture resembles coarse crumbs. Set aside.

2 For filling, in a medium saucepan stir together the cold water, cornstarch, the remaining 2 tablespoons granulated sugar, and the remaining ½ teaspoon cinnamon; add frozen cherries. Cook and stir until thickened and bubbly. Stir in apple slices; heat through. Reduce heat; keep filling hot.

3 In a small bowl stir together egg and milk. Add to biscuit topping mixture, stirring just until moistened. Transfer hot filling to a 2-quart square baking dish. Immediately spoon topping into 9 small mounds on filling. Bake in a 400°F oven for 18 to 20 minutes or until a wooden toothpick inserted near the center of a biscuit comes out clean. Serve warm.

Cherry-Apple Cobbler

PREP: 20 minutes   **BAKE:** 18 minutes
OVEN: 400°F   **MAKES:** 9 servings

NUTRITION FACTS per serving:

CALORIES 172
TOTAL FAT 5 g total fat (3 g sat. fat)
CHOLESTEROL 35 mg
PROTEIN 3 g
CARBOHYDRATE 30 g
FIBER 3 g
SODIUM 122 mg

EXCHANGES 1 Fruit, 1 Other Carbo., 1 Fat

Tropical Fruit Pavlova

STAND: 30 minutes **PREP:** 20 minutes
BAKE: 40 minutes **OVEN:** 300°F
COOL: 1 hour **MAKES:** 6 servings

NUTRITION FACTS per serving:

CALORIES 183
TOTAL FAT 2 g total fat (1 g sat. fat)
CHOLESTEROL 8 mg
PROTEIN 4 g
CARBOHYDRATE 37 g
FIBER 1 g
SODIUM 102 mg

EXCHANGES 1 Fruit, 1½ Other Carbo.,
½ Fat

2	egg whites
¼	teaspoon cream of tartar
⅛	teaspoon salt
½	cup sugar
1	6-ounce carton piña colada, pineapple, or other tropical fruit-flavor low-fat yogurt
½	cup light dairy sour cream
4	cups cut-up, peeled fresh tropical fruit (such as pineapple, mango, papaya, star fruit [carambola], and/or kiwifruit)
2	teaspoons snipped crystallized ginger or 1 tablespoon coconut, toasted (optional)

1 Let egg whites stand at room temperature for 30 minutes. Meanwhile, line a baking sheet with parchment paper or foil. Draw a 7-inch circle on the paper or foil.

2 In a medium mixing bowl combine egg whites, cream of tartar, and salt. Beat with an electric mixer on medium speed until soft peaks form (tips curl).

3 Add the sugar, 1 tablespoon at a time, beating on high speed until very stiff peaks form (tips stand straight) and sugar is almost dissolved (about 4 minutes).

4 Gently spoon egg white mixture into a pastry bag fitted with a pastry tube. Pipe egg white mixture onto the circle on the paper or foil, building up the side to form a shell. (Or use the back of a spoon to spread the egg white mixture over circle, building up side.)

5 Bake in a 300°F oven for 40 minutes. Turn off oven. Let shell dry in oven, with door closed, for at least 1 hour. Remove from paper or foil; cool completely on a wire rack.

6 To serve, in a small bowl fold yogurt into sour cream. Spread about two-thirds of the mixture in the shell. Fill with fresh fruit. Pass remaining sour cream mixture. If desired, sprinkle with crystallized ginger or coconut.

- 1   cup canned pumpkin
- 2   slightly beaten eggs or ½ cup refrigerated or frozen egg product, thawed
- ⅓   cup packed brown sugar
- ¾   teaspoon ground cinnamon
- ⅛   teaspoon ground allspice
- 1   12-ounce can (1½ cups) evaporated milk
- ¼   cup granulated sugar

1 In a medium bowl combine pumpkin, eggs or egg product, brown sugar, cinnamon, and allspice. Stir in evaporated milk. Pour into a 9-inch quiche dish.

2 Bake in a 300°F oven for 40 to 45 minutes or until a knife inserted near the center comes out clean. Cool on a wire rack. Cover and chill for at least 2 hours or up to 24 hours.

3 Before serving, let custard stand at room temperature for 20 minutes. Meanwhile, for caramelized sugar, in a heavy 8-inch skillet heat the granulated sugar over medium-high heat until sugar begins to melt, shaking skillet occasionally to heat sugar evenly. Do not stir. Once sugar starts to melt, reduce heat to low; cook about 5 minutes more or until all of the sugar is melted and golden, stirring as needed with a wooden spoon. Quickly drizzle caramelized sugar over the custard. Serve immediately.

Cinnamon-Pumpkin Custard

PREP: 25 minutes   **BAKE:** 40 minutes
OVEN: 300°F   **CHILL:** 2 to 24 hours
STAND: 20 minutes   **MAKES:** 6 servings

NUTRITION FACTS per serving:

CALORIES 195
TOTAL FAT 6 g total fat (3 g sat. fat)
CHOLESTEROL 87 mg
PROTEIN 6 g
CARBOHYDRATE 30 g
FIBER 1 g
SODIUM 88 mg

EXCHANGES 2½ Other Carbo.

1 recipe Single-Crust Pastry
⅓ cup sugar
2 tablespoons cornstarch
1¾ cups fat-free milk
2 beaten eggs
2 tablespoons chopped crystallized ginger
1 teaspoon vanilla
⅔ cup pear nectar
1½ teaspoons cornstarch
2 small ripe pears, peeled and cored
½ cup fresh raspberries

Fresh Pear Custard Tart

PREP: 40 minutes   **COOK:** 20 minutes
BAKE: 10 minutes   **OVEN:** 450°F
CHILL: 2 hours   **MAKES:** 12 servings

NUTRITION FACTS per serving:

CALORIES 175
TOTAL FAT 6 g total fat (2 g sat. fat)
CHOLESTEROL 36 mg
PROTEIN 4 g
CARBOHYDRATE 25 g
FIBER 1 g
SODIUM 79 mg

EXCHANGES ½ Fruit, 1 Other Carbo., 1 Fat

1 Prepare Single-Crust Pastry. For vanilla cream, in a medium heavy saucepan combine sugar and 2 tablespoons cornstarch. Stir in milk. Cook and stir over medium heat until thickened and bubbly. Cook and stir 2 minutes. Remove from heat. Gradually stir about 1 cup of hot mixture into eggs. Return all of the egg mixture to saucepan. Stir in ginger. Reduce heat. Cook and stir 2 minutes more. Remove from heat. Stir in vanilla. Pour vanilla cream into baked pastry shell. Chill for 1 hour. Cover; chill until ready to assemble.

2 For glaze, in a small saucepan combine pear nectar and 1½ teaspoons cornstarch. Cook and stir until thickened and bubbly. Cook and stir for 2 minutes more. Remove from heat. Cover; cool to room temperature.

3 To assemble, thinly slice pears. Arrange in a concentric pattern over vanilla cream. Spoon glaze over pears, spreading evenly. Cover; chill 1 to 4 hours. Top with berries. Remove side of pan; transfer tart to platter.

Single-Crust Pastry: In bowl combine 1¼ cups all-purpose flour and ¼ teaspoon salt. Cut in ⅓ cup shortening until pieces are pea size. Sprinkle 1 tablespoon water over part of flour mixture; gently toss with a fork. Push moistened dough to side of bowl. Repeat, using 1 tablespoon water at a time, until all mixture is moistened (4 to 5 tablespoons total). Form into a ball. On a lightly floured surface, flatten ball of dough. Roll from center to edge, forming a circle about 13 inches in diameter. Ease pastry into an 11-inch tart pan with removable bottom; do not stretch pastry. Trim pastry to edge of tart pan. Prick bottom, sides, and corners of pastry generously with fork. Bake in a 450°F oven for 10 to 12 minutes until golden. Cool in pan on rack.

1   16-ounce can pitted tart red cherries (water pack)

½   cup sugar

2   tablespoons quick-cooking tapioca

2   egg whites

¼   teaspoon cream of tartar

⅛   teaspoon salt

2   egg yolks

⅓   cup sugar

⅓   cup all-purpose flour

1 Drain cherries, reserving ½ cup liquid. Transfer cherries to a medium saucepan. Add reserved cherry liquid, the ½ cup sugar, and the tapioca. Cook and stir over medium heat until mixture boils; reduce heat. Simmer, uncovered, for 5 minutes, stirring constantly. Keep the cherry mixture warm while preparing the batter for the topping.

2 In a medium mixing bowl beat egg whites, cream of tartar, and salt with an electric mixer on medium speed until stiff peaks form (tips stand straight); set aside. In a small mixing bowl beat egg yolks for 2 to 3 minutes or until thick and lemon colored; add the ⅓ cup sugar. Beat 1 minute more. Stir a small amount of egg white mixture into egg yolk mixture to lighten. Fold remaining egg yolk mixture into egg white mixture. Sprinkle flour over egg mixture; fold in.

3 Pour hot cherry mixture into six 6- to 8-ounce oven-safe mugs, casseroles, or custard cups or one 1½-quart casserole. Pour batter over cherry mixture. Bake in a 325°F oven about 30 minutes for the small cups or casseroles or 35 to 40 minutes for the 1½-quart casserole or until top springs back when lightly touched. Serve warm.

Cherry Puff

PREP: 25 minutes   **BAKE:** 30 minutes
OVEN: 325°F   **MAKES:** 6 servings

NUTRITION FACTS   per serving:

CALORIES 192
TOTAL FAT 2 g total fat (1 g sat. fat)
CHOLESTEROL 71 mg
PROTEIN 4 g
CARBOHYDRATE 42 g
FIBER 1 g
SODIUM 75 mg

EXCHANGES 1 Fruit, 2 Other Carbo.

½ cup sugar

2 to 3 teaspoons instant coffee crystals

2½ cups light or low-fat milk

4 beaten eggs

1 teaspoon vanilla

Fresh red raspberries (optional)

Coffee Custards

PREP: 15 minutes **BAKE:** 30 minutes
OVEN: 325°F **COOL:** 45 minutes
MAKES: 6 servings

NUTRITION FACTS per serving:

CALORIES 157
TOTAL FAT 4 g total fat (2 g sat. fat)
CHOLESTEROL 146 mg
PROTEIN 8 g
CARBOHYDRATE 21 g
FIBER 0 g
SODIUM 94 mg

EXCHANGES ½ Milk, 1 Other Carbo., ½ Fat

1 In a medium saucepan combine the sugar and coffee crystals; add milk. Cook and stir until hot and the coffee crystals are dissolved.

2 In a medium bowl gradually whisk hot milk mixture into eggs. Stir in vanilla. Place six 6-ounce custard cups or a 2-quart square baking dish in a 13×9×2-inch baking pan. Pour egg mixture into the custard cups or square baking dish. Place on the oven rack. Carefully pour boiling water into the baking pan around custard cups or square baking dish to a depth of 1 inch.

3 Bake in a 325°F oven for 30 to 40 minutes or until a knife inserted near the center comes out clean. Remove the custard cups or the square baking dish from the baking pan. Cool on a wire rack for 45 minutes.

4 If desired, garnish with fresh raspberries.

Make-ahead directions: Prepare as above through step 3. Cool completely. Cover and chill up to 24 hours. Serve as above.

6 cups fresh fruit (such as blueberries; raspberries; sliced strawberries, nectarines, peaches, pears, apricots, or bananas; and/or mango, papaya, or pineapple chunks)

1 cup vanilla low-fat yogurt

½ cup part-skim ricotta cheese

¼ cup packed brown sugar

1 Divide fruit among four 10- to 12-ounce au gratin dishes. Place dishes in a 15×10×1-inch baking pan. In a small bowl stir together yogurt and ricotta cheese. Spoon the yogurt mixture over fruit. Sprinkle with brown sugar.

2 Bake, uncovered, in a 450°F oven for 7 to 8 minutes or until brown sugar is melted. Serve immediately.

Fruited Yogurt Brûlée

PREP: 20 minutes   **BAKE:** 7 minutes
OVEN: 450°F   **MAKES:** 4 servings

NUTRITION FACTS per serving:

CALORIES 211
TOTAL FAT 4 g total fat (2 g sat. fat)
CHOLESTEROL 13 mg
PROTEIN 7 g
CARBOHYDRATE 39 g
FIBER 5 g
SODIUM 86 mg

EXCHANGES ½ Milk, 1 Fruit, 1 Other Carbo.

1⅓ cups water

⅔ cup long grain rice

½ of a 12-ounce can (¾ cup) evaporated fat-free milk

⅓ cup mixed dried fruit bits

2 teaspoons honey

¼ teaspoon pumpkin pie spice or ground cinnamon

⅛ teaspoon salt

1 cup sliced, peeled peaches or frozen sliced peaches, thawed

¼ cup vanilla fat-free yogurt

Pumpkin pie spice or ground cinnamon (optional)

Peachy Rice Pudding

START TO FINISH: 30 minutes
MAKES: 5 servings

NUTRITION FACTS per serving:

CALORIES 175
TOTAL FAT 0 g total fat (0 g sat. fat)
CHOLESTEROL 2 mg
PROTEIN 6 g
CARBOHYDRATE 47 g
FIBER 1 g
SODIUM 120 mg

EXCHANGES 1½ Fruit, 1½ Starch

1 In a medium saucepan stir together the water and uncooked rice. Bring to boiling; reduce heat. Simmer, covered, for 15 to 20 minutes or until rice is tender.

2 Stir evaporated milk, fruit bits, honey, the ¼ teaspoon pumpkin pie spice or cinnamon, and the salt into cooked rice. Bring just to boiling; reduce heat to medium-low. Cook, uncovered, about 5 minutes or until mixture is thick and creamy, stirring frequently. Serve pudding warm topped with peaches and yogurt. If desired, sprinkle with additional pumpkin pie spice or cinnamon.

½ cup port wine

1 tablespoon sugar

2 inches cinnamon stick

1 teaspoon lemon juice

2 medium pears, peeled, cored, and cut into 6 lengthwise wedges

2 cups vanilla low-fat frozen yogurt

1 In a medium skillet combine wine, sugar, cinnamon, and lemon juice. Bring to boiling, stirring to dissolve sugar. Reduce heat. Simmer, uncovered, about 7 minutes or until reduced by half. Using a slotted spoon, remove and discard cinnamon.

2 Add pears to wine mixture in skillet. Cook for 6 to 8 minutes more or until pears are tender, turning occasionally. Remove from heat and let stand about 30 minutes or until cooled to room temperature. Serve fruit with frozen yogurt, drizzling sauce over yogurt.

Port-Sauced Pears

PREP: 25 minutes
COOL: 30 minutes
MAKES: 4 servings

NUTRITION FACTS per serving:

CALORIES 218
TOTAL FAT 3 g total fat (2 g sat. fat)
CHOLESTEROL 15 mg
PROTEIN 4 g
CARBOHYDRATE 39 g
FIBER 2 g
SODIUM 86 mg

EXCHANGES ½ Fruit, 2 Other Carbo

2   egg whites

⅔   cup sugar

1   teaspoon finely shredded orange peel

¼   teaspoon cream of tartar

4   teaspoons sugar

1   tablespoon unsweetened cocoa powder

⅓   cup mascarpone cheese or reduced-fat cream cheese (Neufchâtel), softened (about 3 ounces)

½   teaspoon vanilla

2   to 3 tablespoons milk

1   cup fresh raspberries

     Fresh mint sprigs (optional)

Chocolate-Filled Orange Meringues

PREP: 35 minutes
STAND: 30 minutes + 1 hour
BAKE: 35 minutes   **OVEN:** 300°F
MAKES: 6 servings

NUTRITION FACTS per serving:

CALORIES 175
TOTAL FAT 7 g total fat (4 g sat. fat)
CHOLESTEROL 18 mg
PROTEIN 5 g
CARBOHYDRATE 27 g
FIBER 2 g
SODIUM 29 mg

EXCHANGES 1 Other Carbo., 1 Fat

1 In a large mixing bowl allow egg whites to stand at room temperature for 30 minutes. Meanwhile, cover a large baking sheet with parchment paper or foil. Draw six 3-inch circles, 3 inches apart, on paper or foil; set aside.

2 For meringues, in a small bowl stir together the ⅔ cup sugar and the orange peel. Set aside. Add cream of tartar to egg whites. Beat with an electric mixer on medium speed until soft peaks form (tips curl). Add the sugar-orange peel mixture, 1 tablespoon at a time, beating on high speed until stiff peaks form (tips stand straight). Spoon egg white mixture into the circles on the prepared baking sheet, building up sides slightly.

3 Bake in a 300°F oven for 35 minutes. Turn off oven. Let meringues dry in oven with door closed for 1 hour. Remove from oven; cool completely on baking sheet.

4 For filling, stir together the 4 teaspoons sugar and the cocoa powder. In a small bowl stir together mascarpone cheese and vanilla. Stir in the cocoa mixture and enough of the milk to make of spreading consistency. Spread cocoa mixture in cooled meringues. Top with raspberries. If desired, garnish with mint.

Make-ahead directions: Prepare as above through step 3. Transfer to an airtight storage container. Store at room temperature up to 1 week. To serve, prepare filling and serve as above.

Nonstick cooking spray

- ¾ cup sugar
- ½ cup water
- 1 tablespoon instant espresso coffee powder or 2 tablespoons instant coffee powder
- 3 ounces bittersweet or semisweet chocolate, chopped
- 2 egg yolks
- 1 teaspoon vanilla
- ½ cup unsweetened cocoa powder
- ⅓ cup all-purpose flour
- 5 egg whites
- ½ of an 8-ounce container frozen light whipped dessert topping, thawed
- 1½ cups fresh raspberries or sliced strawberries

1 Lightly coat a 9-inch springform pan with nonstick cooking spray; set aside. In a medium saucepan stir together sugar, the water, and espresso powder. Cook and stir over medium-low heat until the sugar dissolves. Stir in the chocolate until melted. Remove from heat. Place egg yolks in a small bowl. Gradually stir the chocolate mixture into egg yolks; stir in vanilla (mixture may appear slightly grainy). Set aside.

2 In a medium bowl stir together the cocoa powder and flour. Stir in the melted chocolate mixture until smooth. In a large mixing bowl beat egg whites with an electric mixer on medium speed until stiff peaks form (tips stand straight). Stir a small amount of the stiffly beaten egg whites into the chocolate mixture to lighten. Fold chocolate mixture into remaining egg whites. Pour into the prepared pan.

3 Bake in a 350°F oven about 30 minutes or until the top springs back when lightly touched. Cool in pan on a wire rack for 10 minutes. Loosen and remove side of pan. Cool cake completely.

4 To serve, cut cake into wedges. Top with whipped topping and berries.

Mocha Cake

PREP: 25 minutes **BAKE:** 30 minutes
OVEN: 350°F **MAKES:** 12 servings

NUTRITION FACTS per serving:

CALORIES 156
TOTAL FAT 5 g total fat (3 g sat. fat)
CHOLESTEROL 35 mg
PROTEIN 4 g
CARBOHYDRATE 25 g
FIBER 2 g
SODIUM 25 mg

EXCHANGES 1½ Other Carbo., ½ Fat

1 cup all-purpose flour
¼ teaspoon baking soda
¼ cup butter
⅔ cup granulated sugar
⅓ cup unsweetened cocoa powder
¼ cup packed brown sugar
¼ cup buttermilk or sour milk*
1 teaspoon vanilla
 Nonstick cooking spray
1 tablespoon sifted powdered sugar

Brownie Cookies

PREP: 20 minutes   **CHILL:** 1 hour
BAKE: 8 minutes per batch
OVEN: 350°F   **COOL:** 1 minute
MAKES: 24 cookies

NUTRITION FACTS per cookie:

CALORIES 73
TOTAL FAT 2 g total fat (1 g sat. fat)
CHOLESTEROL 6 mg
PROTEIN 1 g
CARBOHYDRATE 12 g
FIBER 0 g
SODIUM 38 mg

EXCHANGES 1 Other Carbo.

1 In a small bowl stir together flour and baking soda; set aside. In a medium saucepan melt butter; remove from heat. Stir in granulated sugar, cocoa powder, and brown sugar. Stir in buttermilk and vanilla. Stir in flour mixture just until combined. Cover and chill dough for 1 hour. (Dough will be stiff.)

2 Lightly coat cookie sheets with nonstick cooking spray. Drop chilled dough by rounded teaspoons onto prepared cookie sheets.

3 Bake in a 350°F oven for 8 to 10 minutes or until edges are set. Cool on cookie sheet for 1 minute. Transfer to a wire rack and let cool. Sprinkle with powdered sugar.

*Note: To make ¼ cup sour milk, place ¾ teaspoon lemon juice or vinegar in a glass measuring cup. Add enough milk to equal ¼ cup total liquid; stir. Let mixture stand for 5 minutes before using.

- 1½ cups egg whites (10 to 12 large)
- 1½ cups sifted powdered sugar
- 1 cup sifted cake flour or sifted all-purpose flour
- 1½ teaspoons cream of tartar
- 1 teaspoon vanilla
- 1 cup granulated sugar
- 1½ cups freeze-dried blueberries*
- 1 tablespoon finely shredded orange peel
- 1 cup sifted powdered sugar
- 3 to 5 teaspoons frozen orange juice concentrate, thawed

1 In a very large mixing bowl allow egg whites to stand at room temperature for 30 minutes. Meanwhile, sift the 1½ cups powdered sugar and the flour together 3 times. Set aside.

2 Add cream of tartar and vanilla to egg whites. Beat with an electric mixer on medium speed until soft peaks form (tips curl). Gradually add granulated sugar, about 2 tablespoons at a time, beating until stiff peaks form (tips stand straight).

3 Sift one-fourth of the powdered sugar mixture over beaten egg whites; fold in gently. Repeat, folding in the remaining powdered sugar mixture by fourths. Gently fold in freeze-dried blueberries and orange peel. Pour into an ungreased 10-inch tube pan. Gently cut through batter to remove air pockets.

4 Bake cake on the lowest rack in a 350°F oven for 40 to 45 minutes or until top springs back when lightly touched. Immediately invert cake in pan; cool completely in pan. Loosen cake from pan; remove cake.

5 In a small bowl combine the 1 cup powdered sugar and 3 teaspoons of the orange juice concentrate. Stir in enough of the remaining orange juice concentrate, 1 teaspoon at a time, to reach a drizzling consistency. Drizzle over cooled cake.

*Note: Look for freeze-dried blueberries in the produce section of the supermarket. Do not substitute dried blueberries.

Orange-Blueberry Angel Food Cake

STAND: 30 minutes **PREP:** 20 minutes
BAKE: 40 minutes **OVEN:** 350°F
MAKES: 12 servings

NUTRITION FACTS per serving:

- -

CALORIES 208
TOTAL FAT 0 g total fat (0 g sat. fat)
CHOLESTEROL 0 mg
PROTEIN 4 g
CARBOHYDRATE 48 g
FIBER 0 g
SODIUM 48 mg

EXCHANGES 3 Other Carbo.

Maple-Glazed Pears and Cereal

PREP: 15 minutes **BAKE:** 20 minutes
OVEN: 350°F **MAKES:** 8 servings

NUTRITION FACTS per serving:

CALORIES 213
TOTAL FAT 3 g total fat (0 g sat. fat)
CHOLESTEROL 0 mg
PROTEIN 3 g
CARBOHYDRATE 46 g
FIBER 4 g
SODIUM 286 mg

EXCHANGES 1 Fruit, 1 Other Carbo., 1 Starch

4	medium, ripe pears, peeled, if desired
¾	cup desired dried fruit, such as dried cranberries, cherries, apricots, or raisins
3	tablespoons chopped walnuts, toasted
3	tablespoons maple syrup
¾	cup pear nectar or apple juice
3	cups cooked multigrain cereal

1 Cut pears into halves, leaving stems intact on 4 of the halves. Remove cores. Arrange pears, cut sides up, in a 3-quart baking dish. Top pears with desired dried fruit and walnuts. Drizzle pears with maple syrup. Add the pear nectar to the baking dish.

2 Bake, uncovered, in a 350°F oven for 20 to 25 minutes or until pears are tender, basting occasionally with the cooking liquid. Serve warm pear halves with hot cereal. Drizzle with any remaining cooking liquid.

Nonstick cooking spray

- 2 tablespoons granulated sugar
- 1 teaspoon instant espresso coffee powder or 1 teaspoon instant coffee powder
- ¾ cup granulated sugar
- ½ cup unsweetened cocoa powder
- 1 tablespoon all-purpose flour
- ⅛ teaspoon salt
- ½ cup milk
- 2 egg yolks
- 4 egg whites
- 1 teaspoon vanilla
- ⅛ teaspoon cream of tartar

Sifted powdered sugar (optional)

1 Lightly coat eight 4- to 6-ounce ramekins with nonstick cooking spray. In a small bowl stir together the 2 tablespoons granulated sugar and the espresso powder. Sprinkle on the side and bottom of each dish. Place in a shallow baking pan; set aside.

2 In a medium saucepan stir together ½ cup of the granulated sugar, the cocoa powder, flour, and salt. Gradually stir in milk. Cook and stir over medium-high heat until thickened and bubbly. Reduce heat; cook and stir for 1 minute more. Remove from heat. Slightly beat egg yolks. Slowly add chocolate mixture to egg yolks, stirring constantly.

3 In a large mixing bowl combine egg whites, vanilla, and cream of tartar. Beat with an electric mixer on high speed until soft peaks form (tips curl). Gradually add remaining ¼ cup granulated sugar, beating on high speed until stiff peaks form (tips stand straight). Gently fold chocolate mixture into egg whites. Spoon into prepared dishes.

4 Bake in a 350°F oven about 25 minutes or until a knife inserted near centers comes out clean. If desired, sprinkle with powdered sugar. Serve immediately.

Dark Chocolate Soufflés

PREP: 25 minutes **BAKE:** 25 minutes
OVEN: 350°F **MAKES:** 8 servings

NUTRITION FACTS per serving:

CALORIES 140
TOTAL FAT 2 g total fat (1 g sat. fat)
CHOLESTEROL 54 mg
PROTEIN 4 g
CARBOHYDRATE 25 g
FIBER 0 g
SODIUM 74 mg

EXCHANGES 2 Other Carbo.

½ cup dried tart cherries

3 tablespoons frozen apple juice concentrate, thawed

¼ teaspoon ground cinnamon

¼ of an 8-ounce package reduced-fat cream cheese (Neufchâtel)

¼ cup granulated sugar

2 tablespoons refrigerated or frozen egg product, thawed

6 sheets frozen phyllo dough (17×12-inch sheets), thawed

Nonstick cooking spray

¼ cup graham cracker crumbs

Sifted powdered sugar

Cherry Cheese Turnovers

PREP: 30 minutes **BAKE:** 12 minutes
OVEN: 350°F **MAKES:** 12 servings

NUTRITION FACTS per serving:

- -

CALORIES 92
TOTAL FAT 2 g total fat (1 g sat. fat)
CHOLESTEROL 4 mg
PROTEIN 2 g
CARBOHYDRATE 17 g
FIBER 0 g
SODIUM 86 mg

EXCHANGES 1 Other Carbo., ½ Fat

1 For filling, in a small saucepan combine cherries, apple juice concentrate, and cinnamon. Bring to boiling; reduce heat. Simmer, covered, about 5 minutes or until liquid is absorbed. Remove from heat. In a small mixing bowl beat cream cheese and 2 tablespoons of the granulated sugar with an electric mixer on medium speed until fluffy. Beat in egg product. Gently stir in cherry mixture. Set aside.

2 Lightly coat both sides of 1 sheet of the phyllo dough with nonstick cooking spray. (To keep remaining sheets of phyllo dough from drying out, place them on a sheet of waxed paper. Cover with a dry kitchen towel; place a damp kitchen towel on top.) Sprinkle with 2 teaspoons of the graham cracker crumbs and 1 teaspoon of the remaining granulated sugar. Repeat layers 2 more times, coating just the top side of each phyllo sheet. Cut phyllo stack crosswise into 6 strips. Place 1 well-rounded teaspoon of the filling about 1 inch from the end of each strip. Bring a corner of the phyllo over the filling so the short edge lines up with the long edge. Continue folding the triangular shape along the strip until the end is reached. Repeat with remaining strips.

3 Repeat with the remaining phyllo dough, graham cracker crumbs, granulated sugar, and filling. Place on baking sheet. Bake in a 350°F oven for 12 to 15 minutes or until lightly browned and crisp. Transfer to a wire rack and let cool. Sprinkle with powdered sugar.

2   6- to 7-inch flour tortillas

Butter-flavor nonstick cooking spray or nonstick cooking spray

1   teaspoon granulated sugar

⅛   teaspoon pumpkin pie spice

2   apples or pears, peeled, cored, and sliced

1   tablespoon brown sugar

½   teaspoon pumpkin pie spice

1   5½-ounce can apple juice

1   tablespoon dried currants

Sifted powdered sugar (optional)

1 Place tortillas on a baking sheet. Lightly coat tortillas with nonstick cooking spray. In a small bowl stir together granulated sugar and the ⅛ teaspoon pumpkin pie spice. Sprinkle over tortillas. Bake in a 400°F oven about 10 minutes or until crisp. Cool completely on a wire rack.

2 Meanwhile, lightly coat a medium nonstick skillet with nonstick cooking spray. Preheat over medium heat. Add apples or pears, brown sugar, and the ½ teaspoon pumpkin pie spice; cook and stir about 10 minutes or until golden. Add apple juice and currants. Continue cooking, stirring occasionally, about 20 minutes or until the apples caramelize and the liquid evaporates.

3 Spoon apple mixture over tortillas. If desired, sprinkle with powdered sugar. Serve immediately.

Caramelized Apple Tostadas

PREP: 10 minutes   **BAKE:** 10 minutes
OVEN: 400°F   **COOK:** 30 minutes
MAKES: 2 servings

NUTRITION FACTS per serving:

CALORIES 222
TOTAL FAT 2 g total fat (0 g sat. fat)
CHOLESTEROL 0 mg
PROTEIN 2 g
CARBOHYDRATE 52 g
FIBER 5 g
SODIUM 74 mg

EXCHANGES 1 Fruit, 1½ Other Carbo.

¾ cup seeded watermelon balls, chilled

¾ cup seeded cantaloupe balls, chilled

¾ cup seeded honeydew melon balls, chilled

1 cup lemon sorbet or mango sorbet

½ cup sweet sparkling wine, chilled

Fresh mint sprigs (optional)

1 Divide melon balls among 4 wineglasses or goblets. Scoop about ¼ cup sorbet on top of melon in each glass or goblet. Pour about 2 tablespoons sparkling wine over sorbet and melon in each glass or goblet. If desired, garnish with mint. Serve immediately.

Sorbet Melon Parfaits

START TO FINISH: 15 minutes
MAKES: 4 servings

NUTRITION FACTS per serving:
- -

CALORIES 112
TOTAL FAT 0 g total fat (0 g sat. fat)
CHOLESTEROL 0 mg
PROTEIN 1 g
CARBOHYDRATE 24 g
FIBER 1 g
SODIUM 7 mg

EXCHANGES 1 Fruit, ½ Other Carbo.

1   stalk lemongrass, cut up

¾   cup cold water

1   teaspoon green tea leaves or
     1 green tea bag

2   cups tangerine juice

¼   cup light-colored corn syrup

    Tangerine slices, halved (optional)

    Snipped fresh mint (optional)

1 Using the flat side of a meat mallet, lightly pound lemongrass to slightly crush. Place in a small saucepan; add the cold water. Bring just to boiling over medium heat. Remove from heat. Add tea leaves to hot liquid. Steep for 2 minutes.

2 Strain the hot liquid into a medium bowl; discard solids. Let liquid stand about 30 minutes or until cool.

3 Stir tangerine juice and corn syrup into liquid. Pour into a nonmetal freezer container.* Cover and freeze about 4 hours or until nearly firm.

4 Break the mixture into chunks. Transfer to a chilled medium mixing bowl. Beat with an electric mixer on medium speed until smooth. Return to freezer container. Cover and freeze about 2 hours or until firm.

5 To serve, scoop into chilled serving dishes. If desired, garnish with tangerine slices and mint.

*Note: If you prefer, freeze the green tea mixture in a no-ice, no-salt electric ice cream maker according to the manufacturer's directions.

Green Tea and Tangerine Sorbet

PREP: 10 minutes   **STAND:** 30 minutes
FREEZE: 4 hours + 2 hours
MAKES: 6 servings

NUTRITION FACTS per serving:
- -

CALORIES 74
TOTAL FAT 0 g total fat (0 g sat. fat)
CHOLESTEROL 0 mg
PROTEIN 0 g
CARBOHYDRATE 19 g
FIBER 0 g
SODIUM 18 mg

EXCHANGES 1 Other Carbo.

4 cups sliced, peeled fresh peaches or one 16-ounce package frozen unsweetened peach slices, thawed

⅓ cup sugar

2 teaspoons finely shredded lemon peel

3 tablespoons lemon juice

½ of an 8-ounce container frozen fat-free whipped dessert topping, thawed

½ cup light dairy sour cream

   Fresh raspberries (optional)

   Purchased sugar cookies (optional)

1 In a large food processor bowl combine peaches, sugar, lemon peel, and lemon juice. Cover and process until smooth. Transfer to a large bowl. Fold in whipped topping and sour cream.

2 Transfer to a freezer container. Cover and freeze for at least 4 hours or up to 24 hours. Before serving, let stand at room temperature for 15 to 20 minutes to soften slightly. If desired, garnish with raspberries and serve with cookies.

Peach Freeze

PREP: 20 minutes **FREEZE:** 4 to 24 hours
STAND: 15 minutes **MAKES:** 6 servings

NUTRITION FACTS per serving:

CALORIES 200
TOTAL FAT 2 g total fat (1 g sat. fat)
CHOLESTEROL 7 mg
PROTEIN 3 g
CARBOHYDRATE 44 g
FIBER 5 g
SODIUM 24 mg

EXCHANGES 1 Fruit, 2 Other Carbo., ½ Fat

On the opener: Grilled Chicken with Pineapple Relish (*see recipe, page 263*)

8 ounces beef top round steak

½ cup reduced-sodium beef broth

3 tablespoons reduced-sodium soy sauce

2½ teaspoons cornstarch

1 teaspoon sugar

1 teaspoon grated fresh ginger

Nonstick cooking spray

1¼ pounds fresh asparagus spears, trimmed and cut in 2-inch pieces (3 cups), or 3 cups small broccoli florets

1½ cups sliced fresh mushrooms

4 green onions, bias-sliced into 2-inch lengths (½ cup)

1 tablespoon cooking oil

2 cups hot cooked rice

1 If desired, partially freeze beef for easier slicing. Trim fat from beef. Thinly slice beef across the grain into bite-size strips. Set aside. For the sauce, in a small bowl stir together the beef broth, soy sauce, cornstarch, sugar, and ginger; set aside.

2 Lightly coat an unheated wok or large skillet with nonstick cooking spray. Preheat over medium-high heat. Add asparagus or broccoli, mushrooms, and green onions. Stir-fry for 3 to 4 minutes or until vegetables are crisp-tender. Remove from wok or skillet.

3 Carefully add the oil to wok or skillet. Add beef; stir-fry for 2 to 3 minutes or until brown. Push the beef from center of the wok or skillet. Stir sauce. Add sauce to center of wok or skillet. Cook and stir until thickened and bubbly.

4 Return vegetables to wok or skillet. Stir all ingredients together to coat with sauce; heat through. Serve immediately over hot cooked rice.

Ginger Beef Stir-Fry

START TO FINISH: 30 minutes
MAKES: 4 servings

NUTRITION FACTS per serving:

CALORIES 258
TOTAL FAT 7 g total fat (2 g sat. fat)
CHOLESTEROL 25 mg
PROTEIN 19 g
CARBOHYDRATE 31 g
FIBER 3 g
SODIUM 523 mg

EXCHANGES 1½ Vegetable, 1½ Starch, 1½ Meat, ½ Fat

Quick Honey-Garlic Pot Roast

PREP: 10 minutes **COOK:** 20 minutes
MAKES: 4 servings

NUTRITION FACTS per serving:

CALORIES 305
TOTAL FAT 9 g total fat (4 g sat. fat)
CHOLESTEROL 64 mg
PROTEIN 26 g
CARBOHYDRATE 35 g
FIBER 4 g
SODIUM 502 mg

EXCHANGES 1 Vegetable, 2 Starch, 3 Meat

1	17-ounce package refrigerated cooked beef roast au jus or beef pot roast with juices
2	tablespoons honey
1	tablespoon Worcestershire sauce
1	to 1½ teaspoons bottled roasted minced garlic
¼	teaspoon black pepper
2	cups packaged peeled baby carrots, halved lengthwise
12	ounces tiny new potatoes, halved
1	medium red onion, cut in thin wedges

1 Remove meat from package, reserving juices. In a medium bowl combine reserved juices, honey, Worcestershire sauce, roasted garlic, and pepper. Place meat in a large nonstick skillet. Arrange carrots, potatoes, and onion around meat. Pour honey mixture over meat and vegetables.

2 Bring mixture to boiling; reduce heat. Cover and simmer for 20 to 25 minutes or until vegetables are tender and meat is heated through. Transfer meat and vegetables to a serving platter. Spoon sauce over meat and vegetables.

- 8 ounces boneless beef top sirloin steak
- 1 pound fresh asparagus
- 8 ounces dried bow tie pasta
- 1 8-ounce carton light dairy sour cream
- 2 tablespoons all-purpose flour
- 2/3 cup water
- 1 tablespoon honey
- 1/2 teaspoon salt
- 1/4 teaspoon black pepper
- 2 tablespoons finely chopped shallot
- 1 teaspoon cooking oil
- 2 teaspoons snipped fresh tarragon

  Fresh tarragon sprigs (optional)

1 If desired, partially freeze steak before slicing. Cut off and discard woody bases from fresh asparagus. If desired, scrape off scales. Bias-slice asparagus into 1-inch pieces; set aside. Cook pasta according to package directions, adding asparagus for the last 3 minutes of cooking. Drain well; keep warm.

2 Meanwhile, trim fat from steak. Thinly slice steak across the grain into bite-size strips. In a medium bowl stir together sour cream and flour. Stir in the water, honey, salt, and pepper. Set aside.

3 In a large nonstick skillet cook and stir the meat and shallot in hot oil over medium-high heat about 5 minutes or until meat is browned. Drain off fat.

4 Stir sour cream mixture into meat mixture in skillet. Cook and stir until thickened and bubbly. Cook and stir for 1 minute more. Stir in drained pasta, asparagus, and snipped tarragon. Heat through. If desired, garnish with tarragon sprigs.

Pasta with Beef and Asparagus

START TO FINISH: 30 minutes
MAKES: 4 servings

NUTRITION FACTS per serving:

CALORIES 421
TOTAL FAT 11 g total fat (4 g sat. fat)
CHOLESTEROL 107 mg
PROTEIN 26 g
CARBOHYDRATE 54 g
FIBER 3 g
SODIUM 373 mg

EXCHANGES 2 Vegetable, 3 Starch, 2 Meat, 1/2 Fat

1   15-ounce can black beans, rinsed and drained

1   14-ounce can beef broth

1¾   cups water

12   ounces cooked pork, cut into bite-size strips

3   plantains, peeled and sliced

1   cup chopped tomatoes

½   of a 16-ounce package (2 cups) frozen pepper stir-fry vegetables (yellow, green, and red sweet peppers and onion)

1   tablespoon grated fresh ginger

1   teaspoon ground cumin

¼   teaspoon salt

¼   teaspoon crushed red pepper

3   cups hot cooked rice

     Dried chile peppers (optional)

1 In a Dutch oven combine the beans, broth, and the water; heat to boiling.

2 Add the pork, plantains, and tomatoes to the bean mixture. Stir in the frozen vegetables, ginger, cumin, salt, and crushed red pepper. Return mixture to boiling; reduce heat. Simmer, covered, about 10 minutes or until plantains are tender. Serve with hot cooked rice. If desired, garnish with chile peppers.

Caribbean-Style Pork Stew

START TO FINISH: 30 minutes
MAKES: 6 servings (8½ cups)

NUTRITION FACTS per serving:

CALORIES 401
TOTAL FAT 7 g total fat (2 g sat. fat)
CHOLESTEROL 46 mg
PROTEIN 25 g
CARBOHYDRATE 64 g
FIBER 7 g
SODIUM 543 mg

EXCHANGES 1 Vegetable, 2 Fruit, 2 Starch, 2½ Meat

- 1 tablespoon olive oil
- 1 1-pound tube refrigerated cooked polenta, cut into 12 slices and quartered
- 8 ounces light smoked turkey sausage, halved lengthwise and cut into ½-inch slices
- 2 medium red, green, and/or yellow sweet peppers, cut into bite-size pieces
- 1 medium onion, cut into bite-size pieces
- 1 cup sliced fresh mushrooms
- ½ cup purchased pasta sauce

1 In a 12-inch nonstick skillet heat the oil over medium heat. Add polenta in a single layer; cook for 10 to 12 minutes or until lightly browned, stirring occasionally. Remove polenta from skillet; keep warm.

2 Add sausage, sweet peppers, onion, and mushrooms to skillet. Cook and stir until sausage is brown and vegetables are crisp-tender. Stir in pasta sauce. Add polenta; gently toss ingredients to combine. Heat through.

Sausage and Vegetables with Polenta

START TO FINISH: 35 minutes
MAKES: 4 servings

NUTRITION FACTS per serving:

CALORIES 260
TOTAL FAT 9 g total fat (2 g sat. fat)
CHOLESTEROL 38 mg
PROTEIN 14 g
CARBOHYDRATE 32 g
FIBER 5 g
SODIUM 1,088 mg

EXCHANGES 2 Vegetable, 1½ Starch, 1 Meat, 1 Fat

8 ounces boneless pork loin

2 teaspoons cooking oil

¼ cup light dairy sour cream

¼ teaspoon chipotle chili powder, crushed dried chipotle chile pepper, or chili powder

4 6-inch flour tortillas, warmed, if desired*

½ cup shredded lettuce

½ cup diced tomato

½ cup shredded reduced-fat cheddar cheese (2 ounces)

Bottled salsa

Pork Soft Shell Tacos

START TO FINISH: 25 minutes
MAKES: 4 servings

NUTRITION FACTS per serving:

CALORIES 240
TOTAL FAT 11 g total fat (4 g sat. fat)
CHOLESTEROL 48 mg
PROTEIN 19 g
CARBOHYDRATE 14 g
FIBER 1 g
SODIUM 263 mg

EXCHANGES ½ Vegetable, 1 Starch, 2 Meat, 1½ Fat

1 If desired, partially freeze pork for easier slicing. Trim fat from pork. Thinly slice pork across the grain into bite-size strips. In a large skillet cook pork strips in hot oil over medium-high heat until cooked through; set aside.

2 In a small bowl combine sour cream and chipotle chili powder, chipotle pepper, or chili powder; set aside.

3 Spoon one-fourth of the pork onto each tortilla just below the center. Top pork with lettuce, tomato, and cheese. Fold top half of each tortilla over filling. Serve with sour cream mixture and salsa.

*Note: To warm tortillas, wrap them in foil. Place in a 350°F oven for 10 to 15 minutes or until warmed.

- ½ teaspoon black pepper
- ¼ teaspoon celery salt
- 4 boneless pork rib chops (about 1 pound total)
- 1 large onion, thinly sliced and separated into rings
- 2 teaspoons cooking oil
- 2 tablespoons water
- ¾ cup fresh cranberries
- ¼ cup sugar
- 3 tablespoons water
- 2 tablespoons frozen orange juice concentrate, thawed
- 2 teaspoons finely shredded orange peel
- ½ teaspoon ground sage
- ¼ teaspoon salt

1 For rub, in a small bowl stir together pepper and celery salt. Sprinkle rub evenly onto both sides of chops; rub in with your fingers. In a medium skillet cook chops and onion rings in hot oil until chops are brown, turning once. Carefully add the 2 tablespoons water to skillet. Cover and cook over medium heat for 15 to 20 minutes more or until pork is done and juices run clear (160°F). Transfer chops to serving plates; keep warm. Using a slotted spoon, remove onions from juices; set aside.

2 Meanwhile, for the sauce, in a medium saucepan combine the cranberries, sugar, the 3 tablespoons water, the orange juice concentrate, orange peel, sage, and salt. Cook and stir over medium heat about 10 minutes or until the cranberry skins pop and mixture thickens. Remove from heat.

3 To serve, spoon sauce and onions over pork chops.

Cranberry-Onion Pork Chops

START TO FINISH: 30 minutes
MAKES: 4 servings

NUTRITION FACTS per serving:

CALORIES 277
TOTAL FAT 9 g total fat (3 g sat. fat)
CHOLESTEROL 62 mg
PROTEIN 26 g
CARBOHYDRATE 22 g
FIBER 2 g
SODIUM 288 mg

EXCHANGES 1 Vegetable, 1 Fruit, 3 Meat

Spicy Chicken Pizza

PREP: 25 minutes **BAKE:** 13 minutes
OVEN: 400°F **MAKES:** 6 servings

NUTRITION FACTS per serving:

CALORIES 305
TOTAL FAT 9 g total fat (3 g sat. fat)
CHOLESTEROL 43 mg
PROTEIN 21 g
CARBOHYDRATE 34 g
FIBER 2 g
SODIUM 527 mg

EXCHANGES ½ Vegetable, 2 Starch,
2 Meat, ½ Fat

12 ounces skinless, boneless chicken breasts, cut into thin strips

2 teaspoons cooking oil

1 medium red sweet pepper, cut into thin strips

½ of a medium red onion, thinly sliced

Nonstick cooking spray

1 10-ounce package refrigerated pizza dough

½ cup bottled mild picante sauce

½ cup shredded sharp cheddar cheese (2 ounces)

1 In a large nonstick skillet cook chicken strips in hot oil over medium-high heat about 5 minutes or until no longer pink. Remove from skillet. Add sweet pepper and onion to skillet; cook about 5 minutes or until tender. Remove from skillet; set aside.

2 Coat a 15×10×1-inch baking pan with nonstick cooking spray. Unroll pizza dough into pan; press with fingers to form a 12×8-inch rectangle. Pinch edges of dough to form a crust.

3 Spread crust with picante sauce. Top with chicken and vegetables; sprinkle with cheddar cheese. Bake in a 400°F oven for 13 to 18 minutes or until crust is brown and cheese is melted.

- 6 ounces dried fettuccine or linguine
- 2 cups broccoli or cauliflower florets
- ½ cup reduced-sodium chicken broth
- 3 tablespoons lemon juice
- 1 tablespoon honey
- 2 teaspoons cornstarch
- ¼ teaspoon ground white pepper
- 12 ounces skinless, boneless chicken breasts, cut into bite-size strips
- 2 teaspoons olive oil or cooking oil
- ½ cup shredded carrot
- 1 tablespoon snipped fresh tarragon or ½ teaspoon dried tarragon, crushed

Lemon slices, halved (optional)

1 Cook pasta according to package directions, adding the broccoli or cauliflower for the last 4 minutes of cooking. Drain.

2 Meanwhile, in a small bowl combine broth, lemon juice, honey, cornstarch, and white pepper; set aside.

3 In a large nonstick skillet stir-fry chicken in hot oil for 3 to 4 minutes or until no longer pink. Stir cornstarch mixture; add to skillet. Cook and stir until thickened and bubbly. Add carrot and tarragon; cook 1 minute more.

4 To serve, spoon chicken mixture over pasta. If desired, garnish with lemon slices. Serve immediately.

Lemon-Tarragon Chicken Toss

START TO FINISH: 20 minutes
MAKES: 4 servings

NUTRITION FACTS per serving:

CALORIES 320
TOTAL FAT 4 g total fat (1 g sat. fat)
CHOLESTEROL 49 mg
PROTEIN 27 g
CARBOHYDRATE 43 g
FIBER 3 g
SODIUM 143 mg

EXCHANGES 1 Vegetable, 2½ Starch, 2½ Meat

¼ cup crumbled basil-and-tomato feta cheese (1 ounce)*

2 tablespoons fat-free cream cheese (1 ounce)

4 skinless, boneless chicken breast halves (about 1¼ pounds total)

¼ to ½ teaspoon black pepper
Dash salt

1 teaspoon olive oil or cooking oil

¼ cup chicken broth

1 10-ounce package prewashed fresh spinach, trimmed (8 cups)

2 tablespoons walnut or pecan pieces, toasted

1 tablespoon lemon juice
Lemon slices, halved (optional)

Feta-Stuffed Chicken

START TO FINISH: 30 minutes
MAKES: 4 servings

NUTRITION FACTS per serving:

CALORIES 231
TOTAL FAT 8 g total fat (2 g sat. fat)
CHOLESTEROL 90 mg
PROTEIN 38 g
CARBOHYDRATE 2 g
FIBER 6 g
SODIUM 334 mg

EXCHANGES 1 Vegetable, 4½ Meat

1 In a small bowl combine feta cheese and cream cheese; set aside. Using a sharp knife, cut a horizontal slit through the thickest portion of each chicken breast half to form a pocket. Stuff pockets with the cheese mixture. If necessary, secure openings with wooden toothpicks. Sprinkle chicken with pepper and salt.

2 In a large nonstick skillet cook chicken in hot oil over medium-high heat about 12 minutes or until tender and no longer pink, turning once (reduce heat to medium if chicken browns too quickly). Remove chicken from skillet. Cover and keep warm.

3 Carefully add chicken broth to skillet. Bring to boiling; add half of the spinach. Cover and cook about 3 minutes or just until spinach is wilted. Remove spinach from skillet, reserving liquid in pan. Repeat with remaining spinach. Return all spinach to skillet. Stir in the nuts and lemon juice.

4 To serve, divide spinach mixture among 4 dinner plates. Top with chicken breasts. If desired, garnish with lemon slices.

*Note: If basil-and-tomato feta cheese is not available, stir 1 teaspoon finely snipped fresh basil and 1 teaspoon snipped oil-packed dried tomatoes, drained, into ¼ cup plain feta cheese.

- ¾ teaspoon ground cardamom
- ½ teaspoon salt
- ½ to 1 teaspoon coarsely ground black pepper
- 4 skinless, boneless chicken breast halves (about 1¼ pounds total)
- 2 teaspoons olive oil
- ½ of a medium fresh pineapple, peeled, cored, and coarsely chopped (about 1⅔ cups)
- ½ of a medium red sweet pepper, finely chopped
- 2 tablespoons snipped fresh cilantro or fresh parsley
- 2 tablespoons lime juice
- 2 tablespoons thinly sliced green onion (1)
- 1 fresh jalapeño chile pepper, seeded and finely chopped*
  Fresh herb sprigs (optional)

1 In a small bowl combine ½ teaspoon of the cardamom, the salt, and black pepper. Rub both sides of chicken with oil; sprinkle evenly with spice mixture.

2 Grill chicken on the rack of an uncovered grill directly over medium coals for 12 to 15 minutes or until chicken is no longer pink (170°F), turning once.

3 For relish, in a medium bowl combine pineapple, sweet pepper, cilantro, lime juice, green onion, jalapeño pepper, and the remaining ¼ teaspoon cardamom. Serve chicken with relish. If desired, garnish with herb sprigs.

*Note: Because chile peppers contain volatile oils that can burn your skin and eyes, avoid direct contact with them as much as possible. When working with chile peppers, wear plastic or rubber gloves. If your bare hands do touch the peppers, wash your hands and nails well with soap and warm water.

Grilled Chicken with Pineapple Relish

PREP: 20 minutes   **GRILL:** 12 minutes
MAKES: 4 servings

NUTRITION FACTS per serving:

CALORIES 228
TOTAL FAT 5 g total fat (1 g sat. fat)
CHOLESTEROL 82 mg
PROTEIN 34 g
CARBOHYDRATE 12 g
FIBER 2 g
SODIUM 373 mg

EXCHANGES 1 Fruit, 4½ Meat

8 ounces uncooked bulk turkey sausage

½ cup chopped onion (1 medium)

2 cups purchased spaghetti sauce

1 cup water

2 cups dried wide noodles

1½ cups coarsely chopped zucchini

½ cup fat-free ricotta cheese

2 tablespoons grated Parmesan or Romano cheese

1 tablespoon snipped fresh parsley

½ cup shredded reduced-fat mozzarella cheese (2 ounces)

Slimmed Skillet Lasagna

PREP: 20 minutes **COOK:** 16 minutes
STAND: 10 minutes **MAKES:** 6 servings

NUTRITION FACTS per serving:

CALORIES 221
TOTAL FAT 8 g total fat (3 g sat. fat)
CHOLESTEROL 35 mg
PROTEIN 17 g
CARBOHYDRATE 22 g
FIBER 3 g
SODIUM 805 mg

EXCHANGES 1 Vegetable, 1 Starch, 2 Meat

1 In a large skillet cook sausage and onion until meat is brown and onion is tender, breaking up the meat during cooking. Drain off fat. Stir in spaghetti sauce and the water. Bring to boiling. Stir in uncooked noodles and zucchini. Return to boiling; reduce heat. Simmer, covered, about 12 minutes or until noodles are tender, stirring occasionally.

2 Meanwhile, in a small bowl stir together ricotta cheese, Parmesan cheese, and parsley. Drop cheese mixture by spoonfuls into 6 mounds over the sausage-noodle mixture in the skillet. Sprinkle each mound with mozzarella. Cover and cook on low heat for 4 to 5 minutes or until cheese mixture is heated through. Let stand for 10 minutes before serving.

3 cups dried mini lasagna pasta, broken mafalda, or medium noodles

2 cups chopped broccoli rabe or broccoli (6 ounces)

1 medium red sweet pepper, chopped

1 tablespoon butter or margarine

1 10-ounce container refrigerated light Alfredo sauce

2 teaspoons snipped fresh dill

1 to 2 tablespoons milk (optional)

8 ounces flaked, cooked tuna* or one 9½-ounce can tuna (water pack), drained and broken into chunks

½ cup sliced almonds, toasted (optional)

   Fresh dill sprigs (optional)

1 Cook pasta according to package directions; drain. Meanwhile, in a large saucepan cook the broccoli rabe or broccoli and sweet pepper in hot butter until tender. Stir in Alfredo sauce and snipped dill. If necessary, add milk until desired consistency.

2 Gently stir in cooked pasta and tuna. Heat through. To serve, transfer pasta to a warm serving dish. If desired, sprinkle with almonds and garnish with dill sprigs.

*Note: To broil fresh tuna, place on the greased unheated rack of a broiler pan. Broil 4 inches from the heat for 4 to 6 minutes per ½-inch thickness or until fish flakes easily when tested with a fork. If fish is more than 1 inch thick, turn it over halfway through cooking. To poach tuna, add 1½ cups water to a large skillet. Bring to boiling; add fish. Simmer, uncovered, for 4 to 6 minutes per ½-inch thickness or until fish flakes easily when tested with a fork.

Tuna and Pasta Alfredo

START TO FINISH: 25 minutes
MAKES: 6 servings

NUTRITION FACTS per serving:
- -

CALORIES 370
TOTAL FAT 10 g total fat (5 g sat. fat)
CHOLESTEROL 40 mg
PROTEIN 20 g
CARBOHYDRATE 46 g
FIBER 3 g
SODIUM 266 mg

EXCHANGES 1 Vegetable, 2½ Starch, 1½ Meat, ½ Fat

1 pound fresh or frozen sea scallops

8 ounces dried angel hair pasta, linguine, or spaghetti

½ teaspoon finely shredded lemon peel

¼ teaspoon crushed red pepper

3 cloves garlic, minced

2 tablespoons butter or margarine

2 tablespoons lemon juice

2 cups fresh baby spinach

1 cup coarsely shredded carrot

Lemon slices (optional)

1 Thaw scallops, if frozen. Rinse scallops; pat dry with paper towels. Halve any large scallops. Cook pasta in lightly salted water according to package directions. Drain and return pasta to hot pan.

2 Meanwhile, in a large skillet cook scallops, lemon peel, red pepper, and garlic in hot butter over medium heat for 3 to 4 minutes or until scallops turn opaque. Add lemon juice, tossing to coat. Add scallop mixture, spinach, and carrot to cooked pasta, tossing lightly to combine. If desired, garnish with lemon slices.

Lemony Scallop and Spinach Pasta

START TO FINISH: 25 minutes
MAKES: 4 servings

NUTRITION FACTS per serving:

CALORIES 385
TOTAL FAT 8 g total fat (4 g sat. fat)
CHOLESTEROL 54 mg
PROTEIN 27 g
CARBOHYDRATE 50 g
FIBER 4 g
SODIUM 277 mg

EXCHANGES 1 Vegetable, 3 Starch, 2 Meat

On the opener: Ginger Noodle Bowl (*see recipe, page 273*)

1   10-inch plain or spinach flour tortilla

    Nonstick cooking spray

½   cup shredded cheddar cheese (2 ounces)

½   cup shredded cooked chicken or turkey

¼   cup chopped avocado

2   to 3 fresh small jalapeño chile peppers, seeded and thinly sliced (see note, page 263)

½   cup bottled salsa

1 Lightly coat one side of tortilla with cooking spray. Sprinkle half of the cheese evenly on half the surface of the unsprayed side of the tortilla. Top with chicken, avocado, and jalapeño. Add a little salsa and sprinkle with remaining cheese. Fold tortilla over filling.

2 Heat a heavy skillet or griddle over medium heat. Cook quesadilla about 1 to 2 minutes per side or until cheese melts and tortilla is lightly browned. Cut into 6 wedges. Serve warm with remaining salsa.

Chicken Quesadillas

PREP: 15 minutes
COOK: 2 to 4 minutes
MAKES: 6 appetizer servings

NUTRITION FACTS per serving:

CALORIES 97
TOTAL FAT 6 g total fat (3 g sat. fat)
CHOLESTEROL 20 mg
PROTEIN 7 g
CARBOHYDRATE 5 g
FIBER 1 g
SODIUM 145 mg

EXCHANGES ½ Starch, ½ Meat, ½ Fat

1 cup sweet Marsala wine

⅓ cup orange juice

2 tablespoons packed brown sugar

3 ounces reduced-fat cream cheese (Neufchâtel), softened (about ⅓ cup)

1 ounce blue cheese, crumbled (¼ cup)

1 tablespoon milk

6 fresh figs or 3 pears

1 tablespoon sliced almonds, chopped and toasted

1 In a medium saucepan combine wine, orange juice, and sugar. Bring to boiling; reduce heat. Boil gently, uncovered, about 15 minutes or until reduced to about ⅓ cup.

2 Meanwhile, in a small bowl stir together cream cheese, blue cheese, and milk. Cut each fig into quarters, leaving fig attached at the bottom. (Or cut pears in half and core.) Drizzle some Marsala mixture onto each of 6 dessert plates. Top each plate with a fig. Spread fig open slightly. Spoon some of the cheese mixture into each fig and sprinkle with almonds. (Or spoon some cheese mixture onto each pear half and sprinkle with almonds.)

Blue Cheese-Stuffed Figs

START TO FINISH: 25 minutes
MAKES: 6 servings

NUTRITION FACTS per serving:

CALORIES 181
TOTAL FAT 6 g total fat (3 g sat. fat)
CHOLESTEROL 14 mg
PROTEIN 4 g
CARBOHYDRATE 19 g
FIBER 2 g
SODIUM 144 mg

EXCHANGES 1½ Fruit, 1 Fat

8 8-inch round spring roll wrappers

8 ounces fresh or frozen cooked, peeled, and deveined shrimp, coarsely chopped (1⅓ cups)

1 small head Bibb lettuce, cored and shredded (2 cups)

1 cup shredded carrots (2 medium)

¼ cup sliced green onions (2)

2 tablespoons snipped fresh cilantro

5 tablespoons purchased peanut dipping sauce

2 tablespoons seasoned rice vinegar

1 Place some warm water in a shallow dish. Dip each spring roll wrapper in warm water; place between damp paper towels for 10 minutes.

2 Meanwhile, for filling, in a large bowl combine shrimp, lettuce, carrots, green onions, and cilantro. Add 2 tablespoons of the peanut dipping sauce and 1 tablespoon of the rice vinegar. Toss ingredients to coat.

3 For the dipping sauce, in a small bowl stir together the remaining 3 tablespoons peanut sauce and 1 tablespoon rice vinegar; set aside.

4 Place about ½ cup of the filling about ½ inch from the bottom edge of 1 of the moistened spring roll wrappers. Fold the bottom edge of the wrapper over the filling. Fold in sides. Roll up. Repeat with remaining filling and spring roll wrappers. Cut in half. Serve with dipping sauce.

Asian Spring Rolls

START TO FINISH: 30 minutes
MAKES: 4 servings (8 rolls)

NUTRITION FACTS per serving:

CALORIES 214
TOTAL FAT 4 g total fat (1 g sat. fat)
CHOLESTEROL 111 mg
PROTEIN 15 g
CARBOHYDRATE 29 g
FIBER 2 g
SODIUM 524 mg

EXCHANGES 2 Vegetable, 1 Starch, 1½ Meat

Picadillo Chicken Pizzettas

PREP: 25 minutes   **BAKE:** 20 minutes
OVEN: 425°F   **MAKES:** 24 servings

NUTRITION FACTS per serving:

CALORIES 87
TOTAL FAT 4 g total fat (1 g sat. fat)
CHOLESTEROL 15 mg
PROTEIN 6 g
CARBOHYDRATE 8 g
FIBER 1 g
SODIUM 226 mg

EXCHANGES ½ Starch, ½ Meat

- 1 6- or 6½-ounce package pizza crust mix
- 1 cup bottled salsa
- ¼ teaspoon ground cinnamon
- ¼ teaspoon ground cumin
- 2 cups sliced or chopped cooked chicken or turkey
- ½ cup dried cranberries or raisins
- ½ cup pitted green olives coarsely chopped
- ¼ cup sliced green onions or chopped onion
- 1 tablespoon sliced almonds
- 1 cup shredded Manchego or Monterey Jack cheese (4 ounces)
- 1 tablespoon snipped fresh cilantro

1 Prepare pizza crust according to package directions. Pat dough into a greased 15×10×1-inch baking pan (crust will be thin). Bake in a 425°F oven for 5 minutes.

2 In a small bowl combine salsa, cinnamon, and cumin; spread evenly over crust. Top with chicken, cranberries, olives, onions, and almonds. Sprinkle with cheese.

3 Bake for 15 minutes or until edges of crust are golden. Remove from oven; sprinkle with snipped cilantro. Cut into 12 squares; cut each piece in half diagonally.

2   cups dried Chinese egg noodles or fine egg noodles (4 ounces)

¼   teaspoon ground ginger

⅓   cup bottled stir-fry sauce

1   cup fresh sugar snap peas or pea pods, tips and stems removed and cut up

1   cup sliced fresh shiitake mushrooms

1   small red sweet pepper, cut into bite-size strips

2   teaspoons peanut oil or cooking oil

5   ounces cooked chicken breast, cut in strips (about 1 cup)

2   tablespoons broken cashews

1 Cook noodles according to package directions. Drain; set aside. Stir ginger into the bottled stir-fry sauce; set aside.

2 In a large skillet cook and stir peas, mushrooms, and sweet pepper in hot oil over medium-high heat for 3 to 5 minutes or until crisp-tender. Add cooked noodles, chicken, stir-fry sauce, and cashews; heat through.

Ginger Noodle Bowl

START TO FINISH: 25 minutes
MAKES: 3 servings

NUTRITION FACTS per serving:

CALORIES 362
TOTAL FAT 10 g total fat (2 g sat. fat)
CHOLESTEROL 77 mg
PROTEIN 25 g
CARBOHYDRATE 42 g
FIBER 4 g
SODIUM 734 mg

EXCHANGES 2 Vegetable, 2 Starch, 2 Meat, 1½ Fat

Coffee-Crusted Sirloin

PREP: 15 minutes   **STAND:** 15 minutes
GRILL: 14 minutes   **MAKES:** 4 servings

NUTRITION FACTS per serving:

- -

CALORIES 213
TOTAL FAT 9 g total fat (4 g sat. fat)
CHOLESTEROL 83 mg
PROTEIN 25 g
CARBOHYDRATE 7 g
FIBER 0 g
SODIUM 319 mg

EXCHANGES ½ Milk, 3 Meat

1	pound boneless beef top sirloin steak, cut 1 inch thick
¼	cup balsamic vinegar
2	teaspoons finely ground coffee beans
1	tablespoon brown sugar
¼	teaspoon salt
1	small shallot, finely chopped (2 teaspoons)
1	tablespoon butter or margarine
2	teaspoons all-purpose flour
½	cup reduced-sodium chicken broth
¼	cup half-and-half or light cream
⅛	teaspoon black pepper

1 Trim fat from steak. Place steak in a shallow dish. Pour 2 tablespoons of the balsamic vinegar over steak. Cover and let stand at room temperature for 15 minutes, turning once. In a small bowl combine the ground coffee beans, brown sugar, and salt. Drain steak, discarding vinegar in dish. Press coffee mixture into both sides of the steak.

2 Place steak on the rack of an uncovered grill directly over medium coals. Grill to desired doneness, turning once. (Allow 14 to 18 minutes for medium-rare doneness [145°F] or 18 to 22 minutes for medium doneness [160°F].)

3 Meanwhile, in a small saucepan cook shallot in hot butter for 2 to 3 minutes or until tender. Stir in flour. Add chicken broth. Cook and stir until thickened and bubbly. Cook and stir for 1 minute more. Remove from heat. Stir in half-and-half and pepper. Stir in the remaining 2 tablespoons balsamic vinegar.

4 To serve, slice steak. Serve sauce with steak.

- 4   beef tenderloin steaks, cut 1 inch thick (about 1 pound total)
- 3   tablespoons cognac or brandy
- ½   teaspoon coarsely ground black pepper
- 1   cup sliced fresh mushrooms
- 1   tablespoon finely chopped shallot
- 1   tablespoon butter or margarine
- ½   cup beef broth
- ¼   cup fat-free half-and-half
- 2   tablespoons Dijon-style mustard
- 1   tablespoon all-purpose flour

1 Trim fat from steaks. Place in a shallow dish. Pour 2 tablespoons of the cognac over the steaks. Cover and let stand at room temperature for 15 minutes, turning once. Drain steaks, discarding cognac in dish. Sprinkle pepper over both sides of each steak.

2 Place steaks on the rack of an uncovered grill directly over medium coals. Grill to desired doneness, turning once. (Allow 11 to 15 minutes for medium-rare doneness [145°F] or 14 to 18 minutes for medium doneness [160°F].)

3 Meanwhile, in a small saucepan cook mushrooms and shallot in butter for 3 to 4 minutes or until tender. Stir in beef broth and remaining 1 tablespoon cognac. Bring to boiling; reduce heat. Boil gently, uncovered, for 5 minutes.

4 In a small bowl stir together the half-and-half, mustard, and flour until smooth. Stir into broth mixture. Cook and stir until thickened and bubbly. Cook and stir for 1 minute more. Serve sauce over steaks.

Filet Mignon with Cognac Sauce

PREP: 10 minutes   **STAND:** 15 minutes
GRILL: 11 minutes   **MAKES:** 4 servings

NUTRITION FACTS per serving:

CALORIES 258
TOTAL FAT 11 g total fat (5 g sat. fat)
CHOLESTEROL 65 mg
PROTEIN 25 g
CARBOHYDRATE 4 g
FIBER 0 g
SODIUM 375 mg

EXCHANGES 1 Vegetable, 3½ Meat

1 slice bacon, chopped

4 4-ounce beef tenderloin steaks, cut 1 inch thick

Salt

Black pepper

3 cups very thinly sliced fresh Swiss chard leaves (4 ounces)

½ teaspoon dried thyme, crushed

⅛ teaspoon salt

⅛ teaspoon black pepper

1 Preheat broiler. In a large skillet cook bacon over medium heat until crisp. Remove from skillet, reserving drippings. Crumble bacon; set aside. Remove skillet from heat; set aside.

2 Season steaks with salt and pepper. Place steaks on the unheated rack of a broiler pan. Broil 4 to 5 inches from the heat until desired doneness, turning once halfway through broiling time. (Allow 12 to 14 minutes for medium-rare doneness [145°F] or 15 to 18 minutes for medium doneness [160°F].)

3 Meanwhile, cook and stir Swiss chard in drippings in skillet over medium heat for 4 to 6 minutes or just until tender. Stir in reserved bacon, thyme, the ⅛ teaspoon salt, and the ⅛ teaspoon pepper. To serve, spoon Swiss chard mixture on top of the steaks.

Chard-Topped Steaks

PREP: 20 minutes   **BROIL:** 12 minutes
MAKES: 4 servings

NUTRITION FACTS per serving:

CALORIES 208
TOTAL FAT 11 g total fat (4 g sat. fat)
CHOLESTEROL 60 mg
PROTEIN 25 g
CARBOHYDRATE 1 g
FIBER 1 g
SODIUM 363 mg

EXCHANGES 3½ Meat

3 tablespoons Pickapeppa Sauce*

1 clove garlic, minced

⅛ teaspoon dried thyme, crushed

1 1-pound boneless pork top loin
roast (single loin)

2 large sweet potatoes, peeled and
cut in ¾-inch pieces (1 to
1¼ pounds total)

1 recipe Mango-Jicama Salsa

Fresh cilantro sprigs (optional)

1 In a small bowl combine 2 tablespoons of
the Pickapeppa Sauce, the garlic, and thyme;
set aside.

2 Trim fat from roast. Brush garlic mixture on
all sides of roast. Place roast on a rack in a
shallow roasting pan. Roast in a 325°F oven for
45 minutes.

3 Meanwhile, in a medium saucepan cook sweet
potatoes in boiling, lightly salted water about
8 minutes or just until tender; drain. Toss sweet
potatoes with remaining 1 tablespoon Pickapeppa
Sauce. Place sweet potatoes around roast in pan.
Continue roasting for 30 to 45 minutes more or
until pork juices run clear (160°F).

4 To serve, slice pork. Serve sliced pork with
sweet potatoes and Mango-Jicama Salsa. If
desired, garnish with cilantro.

Mango-Jicama Salsa: Drain one 8-ounce
can pineapple tidbits (juice pack), reserving
2 tablespoons of the juice. In a medium bowl
combine pineapple; reserved pineapple juice;
1 cup peeled, chopped jicama; 1 medium mango,
peeled, seeded, and chopped; 1 large tomato,
seeded and chopped; 1 green onion, sliced; 1 or
2 fresh jalapeño chile peppers, seeded and finely
chopped (see note, page 263); 1 tablespoon lime
juice; and ⅛ teaspoon salt. Cover and refrigerate
until serving time or up to 24 hours.

*Note: If you can't find Pickapeppa Sauce,
substitute 3 tablespoons Worcestershire sauce
mixed with a dash of bottled hot pepper sauce.

Caribbean Pork with Sweet Potatoes

PREP: 30 minutes   **ROAST:** 1¼ hours
OVEN: 325°F   **MAKES:** 4 servings

NUTRITION FACTS per serving:

CALORIES 390
TOTAL FAT 6 g total fat (2 g sat. fat)
CHOLESTEROL 66 mg
PROTEIN 28 g
CARBOHYDRATE 55 g
FIBER 6 g
SODIUM 231 mg

EXCHANGES 1 Vegetable, 1 Fruit,
2 Starch, 3 Meat

8   lamb rib chops, cut 1 inch thick

¼   teaspoon salt

¼   teaspoon black pepper

½   cup balsamic vinegar

¼   cup honey

4   teaspoons reduced-sodium soy sauce

     Fresh rosemary sprigs (optional)

1 Trim fat from chops. Season chops with salt and pepper. Place chops in a plastic bag set in a shallow dish. In a small bowl stir together balsamic vinegar, honey, and soy sauce. Pour over chops; seal the bag. Marinate in the refrigerator for at least 4 hours or up to 24 hours, turning the bag occasionally.

2 Drain lamb, reserving marinade. Pour marinade into a heavy small saucepan. Bring to boiling; reduce heat. Boil gently, uncovered, about 12 minutes or until reduced to about ⅓ cup; set aside. (Glaze will thicken as it cools. If it gets too thick to brush, reheat over low heat.)

3 Place chops on the rack of an uncovered grill directly over medium coals. Grill to desired doneness, turning and brushing once with glaze halfway through grilling. (Allow 12 to 14 minutes for medium-rare doneness [145°F] or 15 to 17 minutes for medium doneness [160°F].) Discard any remaining glaze. If desired, garnish with rosemary sprigs.

Balsamic-Glazed Lamb Chops

PREP: 10 minutes
MARINATE: 4 to 24 hours
COOK: 12 minutes   **GRILL:** 12 minutes
MAKES: 4 servings

NUTRITION FACTS per serving:

CALORIES 372
TOTAL FAT 13 g total fat (5 g sat. fat)
CHOLESTEROL 111 mg
PROTEIN 35 g
CARBOHYDRATE 27 g
FIBER 0 g
SODIUM 461 mg

EXCHANGES 1½ Fruit, 5 Meat

4   skinless, boneless chicken breast halves (about 1¼ pounds total)

Black pepper

2   to 3 ounces fontina cheese, crumbled or sliced

½   cup canned roasted red sweet peppers cut into strips

12   fresh sage leaves

¼   cup all-purpose flour

1   tablespoon olive oil

2   cups dry white wine

Fresh sage leaves (optional)

1 Place each chicken breast half, boned side up, between 2 pieces of plastic wrap. Working from the center to the edges, pound lightly with the flat side of a meat mallet to ¼-inch thickness. Remove plastic wrap. Sprinkle chicken lightly with black pepper. Layer cheese, sweet pepper strips, and sage in the center of each breast. Fold in sides; roll up into a spiral, pressing the edges to seal. Roll in flour.

2 In a medium nonstick skillet heat the oil over medium heat. Cook chicken about 5 minutes, turning to brown all sides. Remove chicken from skillet. Drain off any fat.

3 In the same skillet bring wine to boiling; reduce heat. Simmer, uncovered, about 4 minutes or until 1 cup liquid remains. Return chicken to skillet. Cover and simmer for 7 to 8 minutes or until internal temperature of chicken registers 170°F using an instant-read thermometer.

4 Transfer chicken to a serving plate; cover to keep warm. Strain remaining cooking liquid; return to skillet. Bring to boiling; reduce heat. Simmer, uncovered, until mixture measures ½ cup. Serve over stuffed chicken breasts. If desired, garnish with fresh sage leaves.

Tuscany Stuffed Chicken Breasts

PREP: 30 minutes   **COOK:** 16 minutes
MAKES: 4 servings

NUTRITION FACTS per serving:

CALORIES 359
TOTAL FAT 10 g total fat (4 g sat. fat)
CHOLESTEROL 98 mg
PROTEIN 38 g
CARBOHYDRATE 8 g
FIBER 1 g
SODIUM 196 mg

EXCHANGES ½ Starch, 5 Meat

1 large fresh poblano chile pepper (see note, page 263)

1 large clove garlic

Nonstick cooking spray

⅓ cup fine dry bread crumbs

1 tablespoon chili powder

1 teaspoon ground cumin

4 skinless, boneless chicken breast halves (1¼ to 1½ pounds total)

1 beaten egg

⅔ cup chopped tomato (1 medium)

½ cup chopped tomatillo or tomato

¼ cup chopped onion

2 tablespoons snipped fresh cilantro

Chicken with Poblano Salsa

PREP: 30 minutes
BAKE: 20 minutes + 15 minutes
OVEN: 450°/375°F
MAKES: 4 servings

NUTRITION FACTS per serving:

CALORIES 233
TOTAL FAT 5 g total fat (1 g sat. fat)
CHOLESTEROL 135 mg
PROTEIN 36 g
CARBOHYDRATE 11 g
FIBER 2 g
SODIUM 294 mg

EXCHANGES 1 Vegetable, 4½ Meat

1 To roast poblano pepper and garlic, quarter the pepper, removing seeds and membranes. Place pepper pieces and unpeeled garlic clove on a foil-lined baking sheet. Bake, uncovered, in a 450°F oven for 20 to 25 minutes or until the skin on pepper pieces is charred. Remove garlic; set aside to cool. Bring up the edges of foil and seal around the pepper pieces. Let pepper stand for 20 minutes to steam. Peel pepper pieces and garlic. Chop pepper; mash garlic.

2 Meanwhile, coat a 2-quart rectangular baking dish with nonstick cooking spray; set aside. In a shallow dish combine the bread crumbs, chili powder, and cumin. Dip chicken into egg; dip into bread crumb mixture to coat. Arrange chicken in prepared baking dish. Bake, uncovered, in a 375°F oven for 15 to 20 minutes or until chicken is tender and no longer pink (170°).

3 For salsa, in a medium bowl combine the poblano pepper, garlic, the ⅔ cup tomato, tomatillo or additional tomato, onion, and cilantro. To serve, slice chicken and spoon salsa over slices.

- 4 skinless, boneless chicken breast halves (1¼ to 1½ pounds total)
- 1 tablespoon lemon juice
- 1 tablespoon olive oil
- 1 tablespoon snipped fresh oregano or 1 teaspoon dried oregano, crushed
- ¼ teaspoon black pepper
- 2 cloves garlic, minced
- 3 medium cucumbers, seeded and cut into ½-inch pieces
- 2 medium tomatoes, cut into ½-inch pieces
- ½ cup chopped red onion (1 medium)
  Mixed salad greens (optional)
- ⅓ cup bottled reduced-calorie creamy cucumber salad dressing
- ½ cup crumbled feta cheese
- ¼ cup chopped pitted kalamata olives or ripe olives

1 Place chicken in a plastic bag set in a shallow dish. For marinade, in a small bowl combine lemon juice, oil, oregano, pepper, and garlic. Pour over chicken; seal bag. Marinate in the refrigerator for at least 4 hours or up to 24 hours, turning bag occasionally.

2 Meanwhile, in a medium bowl toss together cucumbers, tomatoes, and red onion.

3 Drain chicken, discarding marinade. Place chicken on the rack of an uncovered grill directly over medium coals. Grill for 12 to 15 minutes or until tender and no longer pink (170°F), turning once.

4 Transfer chicken to a cutting board; cut into bite-size pieces. Toss with cucumber mixture. If desired, serve on greens. Drizzle salad dressing over. Sprinkle with feta cheese and olives.

Grilled Greek Chicken Salad

PREP: 30 minutes
MARINATE: 4 to 24 hours
GRILL: 12 minutes   **MAKES:** 4 servings

NUTRITION FACTS per serving:

CALORIES 328
TOTAL FAT 13 g total fat (3 g sat. fat)
CHOLESTEROL 95 mg
PROTEIN 37 g
CARBOHYDRATE 14 g
FIBER 3 g
SODIUM 629 mg

EXCHANGES 3 Vegetable, 4½ Meat

Tilapia with Chili Cream Sauce

START TO FINISH: 25 minutes
MAKES: 4 servings

NUTRITION FACTS per serving:

CALORIES 187
TOTAL FAT 4 g total fat (2 g sat. fat)
CHOLESTEROL 60 mg
PROTEIN 23 g
CARBOHYDRATE 12 g
FIBER 1 g
SODIUM 258 mg

EXCHANGES ½ Milk, ½ Starch, 2½ Meat

1 pound fresh or frozen tilapia or other firm-flesh fish fillets, ½ to 1 inch thick
2 tablespoons cornmeal
2 tablespoons all-purpose flour
Nonstick cooking spray
1 teaspoon cooking oil
2 teaspoons butter or margarine
2 teaspoons all-purpose flour
1 teaspoon chili powder
¼ teaspoon salt
¼ teaspoon ground cumin
¾ cup fat-free half-and-half
2 tablespoons snipped fresh parsley or cilantro (optional)
Lime slices (optional)

1 Thaw fish, if frozen. Rinse fish; pat dry. Cut into 4 serving-size portions. Stir together cornmeal and the 2 tablespoons flour. Sprinkle over both sides of fish. Lightly coat a 12-inch nonstick skillet with cooking spray. Add oil to skillet. Heat over medium-high heat. Add fish pieces. Cook pieces over medium to medium-high heat for 2 to 3 minutes per side or until fish flakes easily when tested with a fork. Remove fish from skillet. Keep warm.

2 Melt butter in the same skillet. Stir in the 2 teaspoons flour, chili powder, salt, and cumin. Stir in half-and-half. Cook and stir until thickened and bubbly. Cook and stir for 1 minute more. To serve, spoon sauce over fish. If desired, sprinkle with parsley; garnish with lime slices.

3   tablespoons raspberry vinegar

2   tablespoons salad oil

1   tablespoon honey

1   10-ounce package torn mixed
     Italian-blend salad greens

1   medium star fruit (carambola),
     thinly sliced

½   small red onion, thinly sliced

     Fresh raspberries (optional)

1 In a screw-top jar combine vinegar, oil, and honey. Cover and shake well.

2 In a large bowl toss salad greens with star fruit and onion. Shake dressing well and pour over salad mixture. Toss lightly to coat. If desired, garnish with a few fresh raspberries.

Star Fruit Salad with Raspberry Vinaigrette

START TO FINISH: 15 minutes
MAKES: 6 servings

NUTRITION FACTS per serving:

CALORIES 66
TOTAL FAT 5 g total fat (1 g sat. fat)
CHOLESTEROL 0 mg
PROTEIN 1 g
CARBOHYDRATE 6 g
FIBER 1 g
SODIUM 5 mg

EXCHANGES ½ Fruit, 1 Fat

1 pound fresh green beans, trimmed

1 16-ounce can sliced beets, well drained and cut in thin bite-size strips

2 tablespoons orange juice

2 tablespoons olive oil

1 tablespoon balsamic vinegar

2 teaspoons bottled roasted minced garlic

⅛ teaspoon salt

Purchased mixed salad greens

Coarsely ground black pepper (optional)

1 In a large covered saucepan cook green beans in a small amount of lightly salted boiling water about 15 minutes or until almost tender. Add beets; cook for 2 to 3 minutes more or until beets are heated through. Drain and keep warm.

2 Meanwhile, for dressing,* in a screw-top jar combine orange juice, oil, balsamic vinegar, garlic, and salt. Cover and shake well. Pour dressing over warm beans and beets. To serve, arrange beans, beets, and salad greens on 4 plates. If desired, sprinkle salads with pepper.

*Note: In place of the homemade dressing, you can substitute a bottled garlic salad dressing or stir the roasted minced garlic into an Italian salad dressing.

Warm Beet Salad with Garlic Dressing

START TO FINISH: 30 minutes
MAKES: 4 servings

NUTRITION FACTS per serving:

CALORIES 132
TOTAL FAT 7 g total fat (1 g sat. fat)
CHOLESTEROL 0 mg
PROTEIN 3 g
CARBOHYDRATE 16 g
FIBER 6 g
SODIUM 223 mg

EXCHANGES 3 Vegetable, 1½ Fat

On the divider: Beef Tenderloin with Onion Cherry-Chutney (*see recipe, page 294*)

- 2 pounds fresh or frozen large shrimp in shells
- ¼ cup finely chopped fresh Anaheim chile pepper (see note, page 263)
- ½ teaspoon finely shredded lime peel
- ¼ cup lime juice
- 2 tablespoons olive oil
- 2 tablespoons finely chopped green onion
- 1 to 2 tablespoons snipped fresh cilantro or parsley
- ½ teaspoon sugar
- ½ teaspoon salt
- ¼ teaspoon black pepper
- 2 cloves garlic, minced
  Crushed ice or lettuce leaves (optional)
  Lime wedges (optional)

1 Thaw shrimp, if frozen. Peel and devein shrimp, leaving tails intact if desired. In a large saucepan bring 4 cups water to boiling. Add shrimp. Simmer, uncovered, for 1 to 3 minutes or until shrimp turn opaque, stirring occasionally. Drain; rinse under cold running water and drain again. Set aside.

2 In a heavy plastic bag set in a medium bowl combine chile pepper, lime peel, lime juice, olive oil, onion, cilantro, sugar, salt, black pepper, and garlic; mix well. Place cooked shrimp in the bag; seal bag. Turn bag to coat shrimp with marinade mixture. Marinate in the refrigerator for 2 to 3 hours, turning the bag occasionally.

3 To serve, drain the shrimp, discarding the marinade. If desired, serve shrimp in ice-filled glasses or on a lettuce-lined platter and accompany with lime wedges.

Fiesta Shrimp Appetizers

PREP: 40 minutes
MARINATE: 2 to 3 hours
MAKES: 10 appetizer servings

NUTRITION FACTS per serving:

CALORIES 87
TOTAL FAT 3 g total fat (0 g sat. fat)
CHOLESTEROL 103 mg
PROTEIN 14 g
CARBOHYDRATE 1 g
FIBER 0 g
SODIUM 159 mg

EXCHANGES 2 Meat, ½ Fat

3/4 cup all-purpose flour

3/4 cup rye flour

1 tablespoon caraway seeds

1/2 teaspoon baking powder

1/2 teaspoon salt

1/2 teaspoon ground cumin

1/4 teaspoon ground coriander

1/4 cup butter, cut into 4 pieces

1/3 cup milk

1 beaten egg white

Cumin-Caraway Crackers

PREP: 20 minutes   **STAND:** 5 minutes
BAKE: 15 minutes   **OVEN:** 350°F
MAKES: 40 crackers

NUTRITION FACTS per cracker:

CALORIES 27
TOTAL FAT 1 g total fat (1 g sat. fat)
CHOLESTEROL 3 mg
PROTEIN 1 g
CARBOHYDRATE 3 g
FIBER 0 g
SODIUM 49 mg

EXCHANGES 1/2 Starch

1 In a food processor bowl combine all-purpose flour, rye flour, caraway seeds, baking powder, salt, cumin, and coriander. Add butter; cover and process until blended. Add milk; process just until mixture forms a dough (if necessary, add an additional 1 tablespoon milk).

2 Transfer dough to a floured surface; let stand for 5 minutes. Roll to 1/8-inch thickness; cut with a 2-inch round or other shape cutter or use a knife to cut into desired shapes. Transfer cutouts to an ungreased baking sheet. Brush lightly with egg white. Using a fork, prick crackers all over.

3 Bake in a 350°F oven for 15 to 17 minutes or until crisp. Cool completely on wire racks; store in an airtight container.

14 to 16 medium cremini and/or
    button mushrooms
    (2-inch diameter)

4   green onions, sliced

1   clove garlic, minced

1   tablespoon butter or margarine

2   ounces blue cheese, crumbled
    (½ cup)

⅓   cup toasted pine nuts

1 Remove mushroom stems; chop stems to make about 1 cup. Set caps aside. In a large skillet cook mushroom stems, green onions, and garlic in butter over medium heat for 5 minutes or until mushroom stems are tender. Remove from heat. Stir in cheese and pine nuts.

2 Place mushroom caps, stem sides up, in a 15×10×1-inch baking pan. Spoon about 1 tablespoon cheese mixture into each.

3 Bake in a 400°F oven for 12 to 15 minutes or until mushrooms are tender.

Make-ahead directions: Prepare as above through step 2. Cover and chill up to 2 hours. Bake as directed above.

Mushrooms Stuffed with Blue Cheese

PREP: 30 minutes   **BAKE:** 12 minutes
OVEN: 400°F
MAKES: 14 to 16 servings

NUTRITION FACTS per serving:

CALORIES 50
TOTAL FAT 4 g total fat (2 g sat. fat)
CHOLESTEROL 5 mg
PROTEIN 3 g
CARBOHYDRATE 2 g
FIBER 0 g
SODIUM 67 mg

EXCHANGES 1 Vegetable, ½ Fat

Stuffed Cherry Tomatoes

PREP: 45 minutes   **MAKES:** 30 appetizers

NUTRITION FACTS per appetizer:

CALORIES 29
TOTAL FAT 2 g total fat (1 g sat. fat)
CHOLESTEROL 2 mg
PROTEIN 1 g
CARBOHYDRATE 1 g
FIBER 0 g
SODIUM 16 mg

EXCHANGES ½ Fat

30	cherry tomatoes (1-inch diameter)
1	cup firmly packed fresh basil leaves
½	cup firmly packed fresh flat-leaf parsley leaves
¼	cup pine nuts, toasted
1	large clove garlic, quartered
⅛	teaspoon black pepper
2	tablespoons olive oil
4	ounces goat cheese (chèvre), crumbled (1 cup)
	Fresh basil leaves (optional)

1 Slice off the top of each tomato. Cut a thin slice off the bottom of each tomato so they stand level. Scoop out tomatoes from the top using a small, narrow spoon or melon baller. Turn upside down on paper towels to drain.

2 For pesto, in a blender container or food processor bowl combine 1 cup basil, the parsley, pine nuts, garlic, and pepper. Cover and blend or process with several on/off turns until a paste forms, stopping machine several times and scraping the sides. With the machine running slowly, gradually add oil and blend or process to the consistency of soft butter. Transfer to a small bowl and stir in the goat cheese.

3 Spoon pesto mixture into a small self-sealing plastic bag. Snip a small hole in one corner of the bag. Seal bag. Squeeze pesto into the tomato shells. Place filled tomatoes on a serving plate. If desired, garnish with small basil leaves.

Make-ahead directions: Prepare as above through step 3. Cover and chill up to 4 hours.

12   thin half-slices of orange, lemon, or lime

Water

3   cups orange juice, chilled

3   cups apricot nectar, chilled

2   cups ice cubes

1   750-milliliter bottle sparkling water, chilled

1 For citrus ice cubes, place a thin half-slice of orange, lemon, or lime in each compartment of an ice cube tray, with one end of the slice extending above the tray about ¾ inch. Fill tray with water and freeze for 2 hours or until firm.

2 Pour orange juice and apricot nectar over plain ice cubes in a large (11-cup) glass pitcher or punch bowl. Add sparkling water, stirring gently. Place a citrus ice cube in each punch cup. Pour or ladle juice mixture into cup.

Golden Sparklers

PREP: 15 minutes   **FREEZE:** 2 hours
MAKES: about 20 (½ -cup) servings

NUTRITION FACTS per serving:

CALORIES 38
TOTAL FAT 0 g total fat (0 g sat. fat)
CHOLESTEROL 0 mg
PROTEIN 0 g
CARBOHYDRATE 9 g
FIBER 0 g
SODIUM 9 mg

EXCHANGES ½ Fruit

6 cups water

4 teaspoons sugar

1 1-inch piece fresh ginger, thinly sliced

8 lemon peel strips (2½×1 inch each)

8 green tea bags

Lemon slices (optional)

1 In a large saucepan combine the water, sugar, ginger, and lemon peel strips. Bring to boiling; reduce heat. Simmer, uncovered, for 10 minutes. Remove ginger and lemon strips with a slotted spoon and discard.

2 Place tea bags in a teapot; immediately add simmering water mixture. Cover and let stand 3 to 5 minutes. Remove tea bags and discard. Serve immediately in mugs. If desired, garnish with lemon slices.

Ginger-Lemon Tea

START TO FINISH: 25 minutes
MAKES: 6 (8-ounce) servings

NUTRITION FACTS per serving:

CALORIES 13
TOTAL FAT 0 g total fat (0 g sat. fat)
CHOLESTEROL 0 mg
PROTEIN 0 g
CARBOHYDRATE 3 g
FIBER 0 g
SODIUM 7 mg

EXCHANGES Free

1   cup frozen loose-pack raspberries, slightly thawed

2   cups brewed tea

2   cups cranberry-raspberry drink

1   cup prepared lemonade

¼   cup water

3   whole allspice

1   lemon, cut into thin wedges

Fresh raspberries (optional)

1 In a medium saucepan slightly mash the 1 cup raspberries with a potato masher. Stir in the tea, cranberry-raspberry drink, lemonade, the water, and allspice. Bring to boiling; reduce heat. Simmer, uncovered, for 10 minutes. Strain and discard the fruit pulp and spices.

2 Serve in mugs with lemon wedges and, if desired, additional fresh raspberries.

Mulled Raspberry Tea

START TO FINISH: 15 minutes
MAKES: 6 (about 7-ounce) servings

NUTRITION FACTS per serving:

CALORIES 74
TOTAL FAT 0 g total fat (0 g sat. fat)
CHOLESTEROL 0 mg
PROTEIN 0 g
CARBOHYDRATE 18 g
FIBER 1 g
SODIUM 15 mg

EXCHANGES 1 Fruit

1   2- to 2½-pound beef tenderloin roast

2   teaspoons dried thyme, crushed

3   cloves garlic, minced

½   teaspoon salt

¼   teaspoon black pepper

1   cup chopped onion (1 large)

1   cup chopped red and/or yellow sweet pepper (1 large)

1   tablespoon olive oil or cooking oil

2   medium apples, cored and chopped (about 1⅓ cups)

⅓   cup dried tart cherries

¼   cup red wine vinegar

3   tablespoons packed brown sugar

Beef Tenderloin with Onion-Cherry Chutney

PREP: 20 minutes   **ROAST:** 35 minutes
STAND: 30 minutes   **OVEN:** 425°F
MAKES: 10 servings

NUTRITION FACTS per serving:

CALORIES 212
TOTAL FAT 8 g total fat (2 g sat. fat)
CHOLESTEROL 54 mg
PROTEIN 20 g
CARBOHYDRATE 15 g
FIBER 2 g
SODIUM 169 mg

EXCHANGES 1 Fruit, 2½ Meat

1 Place roast on a rack in a shallow roasting pan. In a small bowl stir together 1½ teaspoons of the thyme, 2 of the minced garlic cloves (1 teaspoon), salt, and black pepper. Rub onto surface of the meat. Insert an oven-going meat thermometer into thickest portion of roast. Roast, uncovered, in a 425°F oven; for medium rare, allow 35 to 40 minutes or until the thermometer registers 140°F. Remove the roast from the oven; cover with foil and let stand for 15 minutes before carving. The meat's temperature will rise 5°F during the time it stands for a final doneness temperature of 145°F.

2 Meanwhile, for chutney, in a medium saucepan cook the onion, sweet pepper, and remaining garlic in hot oil until onion is tender. Add apples and cherries; cook and stir for 2 minutes. Add vinegar, brown sugar, and remaining thyme; boil gently, uncovered, for 10 to 12 minutes or until most of the liquid is evaporated. Remove from heat; cover and let stand for 30 minutes. Slice meat and serve with chutney.

1   4- to 5-pound whole turkey breast

¼   teaspoon salt

⅛   teaspoon black pepper

3   tablespoons frozen orange juice concentrate, thawed

2   tablespoons honey

2   teaspoons snipped fresh thyme

2   teaspoons cornstarch

2   teaspoons cold water

1   cup reduced-sodium chicken broth

    Orange slices, fresh cranberries, fresh thyme, and leaf lettuce (optional)

1 Sprinkle turkey with the salt and pepper. Place turkey, bone side down, on rack in shallow roasting pan. Insert an oven-going meat thermometer into thickest portion of turkey breast, making sure it does not touch bone.

2 In a small bowl combine 2 tablespoons of the orange juice concentrate, the honey, and thyme. Set aside.

3 Roast turkey, uncovered, in a 325°F oven for 1½ to 2¼ hours or until juices run clear and turkey is no longer pink (170°F), brushing with the orange juice concentrate mixture the last 15 minutes of roasting. Transfer turkey to a cutting board; cover with foil and let stand 10 to 15 minutes before carving.

4 Meanwhile, in a small saucepan stir together cornstarch and water until smooth; stir in broth and remaining 1 tablespoon orange juice concentrate. Cook and stir until slightly thickened and bubbly; cook and stir for 2 minutes more. Season to taste with additional salt and pepper. Serve sauce with turkey. If desired, garnish with orange slices, cranberries, fresh thyme sprigs, and lettuce.

Orange Roasted Turkey

PREP: 20 minutes   **ROAST:** 1½ hours
STAND: 10 minutes   **OVEN:** 325°F
MAKES: 10 servings

NUTRITION FACTS per serving:

CALORIES 274
TOTAL FAT 11 g total fat (3 g sat. fat)
CHOLESTEROL 105 mg
PROTEIN 36 g
CARBOHYDRATE 6 g
FIBER 0 g
SODIUM 193 mg

EXCHANGES ½ Fruit, 5 Meat

1   8-pound cooked ham
    (shank portion)
    Whole cloves
½   cup packed brown sugar
¼   cup chutney
¼   cup plum jam
1   tablespoon Dijon-style mustard
1   clove garlic, minced
1   teaspoon rice vinegar
⅛   teaspoon bottled hot pepper
    sauce

1 Score ham by making shallow diagonal cuts in a diamond pattern. Stud with cloves. Place on a rack in a shallow roasting pan. Insert an oven-going meat thermometer in meat, making sure it does not touch bone. Bake in a 325°F oven about 1¾ hours.

2 For glaze, in medium saucepan combine brown sugar, chutney, jam, mustard, garlic, vinegar, and hot pepper sauce. Cook and stir over medium heat until mixture is bubbly.

3 Brush ham with some of the glaze. Bake about 30 minutes more or until thermometer registers 140°F. Reheat the remaining glaze, if necessary. Pass glaze with ham.

Chutney-Glazed Ham

PREP: 15 minutes   **BAKE:** 2¼ hours
OVEN: 325°F   **MAKES:** 20 servings

NUTRITION FACTS per serving:

CALORIES 211
TOTAL FAT 6 g total fat (2 g sat. fat)
CHOLESTEROL 59 mg
PROTEIN 26 g
CARBOHYDRATE 11 g
FIBER 0 g
SODIUM 1,410 mg

EXCHANGES ½ Fruit, 3½ Meat

2 pounds sweet potatoes (4 to 6 medium)

⅓ cup pure maple syrup or maple-flavored syrup

3 tablespoons coarse-grain Dijon-style mustard

2 tablespoons cooking oil

½ teaspoon salt

½ teaspoon freshly ground black pepper

½ cup fresh cranberries

1 Peel and cut the sweet potatoes into 1- to 1½-inch chunks. In a large bowl combine the maple syrup, mustard, oil, salt, and pepper; add sweet potatoes and cranberries. Toss to coat. Transfer the mixture to a 3-quart baking dish, spreading mixture evenly.

2 Bake, uncovered, in a 400°F oven for 30 to 35 minutes or until potatoes are glazed and tender, stirring twice.

Maple-Glazed Sweet Potatoes

PREP: 20 minutes **BAKE:** 30 minutes
OVEN: 400°F **MAKES:** 8 servings

NUTRITION FACTS per serving:

CALORIES 160
TOTAL FAT 4 g total fat (1 g sat. fat)
CHOLESTEROL 0 mg
PROTEIN 1 g
CARBOHYDRATE 30 g
FIBER 3 g
SODIUM 287 mg

EXCHANGES 2 Starch, ½ Fat

8 ounces parsnips, thinly sliced (about 2¼ cups)

8 ounces carrots, thinly sliced (about 2¼ cups)

2 medium, firm ripe pears, peeled and cut in ½-inch slices

¾ cup orange juice

⅓ cup dried cranberries

1 teaspoon grated fresh ginger or ½ teaspoon ground ginger

2 tablespoons brown sugar

1 tablespoon butter or margarine

1 In a large nonstick skillet combine parsnips, carrots, pears, orange juice, dried cranberries, and ginger. Bring to boiling; reduce heat to medium. Cook, uncovered, for 7 to 8 minutes or until vegetables are crisp-tender and most of the liquid has evaporated, stirring occasionally.

2 Add brown sugar and butter, stirring until butter melts. Cook, uncovered, for 2 to 3 minutes more or until vegetables are glazed.

Autumn Vegetable Medley

START TO FINISH: 35 minutes
MAKES: 6 side-dish servings

NUTRITION FACTS per serving:

CALORIES 148
TOTAL FAT 3 g total fat (1 g sat. fat)
CHOLESTEROL 5 mg
PROTEIN 1 g
CARBOHYDRATE 32 g
FIBER 5 g
SODIUM 41 mg

EXCHANGES 1 Vegetable, 1 Fruit, ½ Starch, ½ Fat

1   12-ounce package fresh cranberries (3 cups)

¾   cup apple juice

½   cup sugar

1   tablespoon lemon juice

1   teaspoon dried minced onion

½   teaspoon dried rosemary, crushed

2   medium pears, cored and chopped (2 cups)

Fresh rosemary sprig (optional)

1 In a medium saucepan combine cranberries, apple juice, sugar, lemon juice, onion, and rosemary. Bring to boiling; reduce heat. Cook, uncovered, over medium heat about 5 minutes or until cranberries pop.

2 Add pears and cook, uncovered, 2 minutes more or just until pears are tender. Serve warm with turkey, ham, or roast pork. If desired, garnish with a rosemary sprig.

Make-ahead directions: Prepare as above. Cool, cover, and chill relish up to 1 day.

Cranberry-Pear Relish

START TO FINISH: 20 minutes
MAKES: 12 (about ¼-cup) servings

NUTRITION FACTS per serving:

CALORIES 69
TOTAL FAT 0 g total fat (0 g sat. fat)
CHOLESTEROL 0 mg
PROTEIN 0 g
CARBOHYDRATE 18 g
FIBER 2 g
SODIUM 1 mg

EXCHANGES 1 Other Carbo.

2 cups all-purpose flour

1 cup granulated sugar

1 tablespoon finely chopped crystallized ginger

2½ teaspoons baking powder

½ teaspoon baking soda

½ teaspoon ground nutmeg

¼ teaspoon salt

1 cup canned pumpkin

½ cup milk

2 eggs

⅓ cup shortening

1 cup coarsely chopped pitted dates

1 recipe Spiced Glaze

Crystallized ginger, chopped (optional)

Ginger-Date Pumpkin Loaves

PREP: 25 minutes   **BAKE:** 35 minutes
STAND: Overnight   **OVEN:** 350°F
MAKES: 5 small loaves (25 servings) or
2 large loaves (24 servings)

NUTRITION FACTS per serving:

CALORIES 127
TOTAL FAT 3 g total fat (1 g sat. fat)
CHOLESTEROL 17 mg
PROTEIN 2 g
CARBOHYDRATE 23 g
FIBER 1 g
SODIUM 97 mg

EXCHANGES ½ Fruit, 1 Starch

1 Grease five 4½×2½×1½-inch loaf pans or two 8×4×2-inch loaf pans; set aside. In a large mixing bowl combine 1 cup of the flour, the granulated sugar, the 1 tablespoon ginger, the baking powder, baking soda, nutmeg, and salt. Add pumpkin, milk, eggs, and shortening. Beat with an electric mixer on low to medium speed for 30 seconds. Beat on high speed for 2 minutes, scraping side of bowl occasionally. Add the remaining flour; beat until well mixed. Stir in dates.

2 Spoon the batter into prepared pans. Bake in a 350°F oven until wooden toothpicks inserted near centers comes out clean. (Allow 35 to 40 minutes for 4½×2½×1½-inch loaves or about 45 minutes for 8×4×2-inch loaves.) Cool in pans on wire racks for 10 minutes. Remove from pans. Cool completely on wire racks. Wrap bread and store overnight before slicing. Drizzle with Spiced Glaze before serving. If desired, sprinkle top with additional chopped crystallized ginger.

Spiced Glaze: In a small bowl stir together ½ cup sifted powdered sugar and ⅛ teaspoon ground ginger. Stir in enough water (2 to 3 teaspoons) to make drizzling consistency.

- 1   8-ounce package pitted whole dates, snipped
- 1½   cups boiling water
- 1   cup all-purpose flour
- 1   cup whole wheat flour
- 1   teaspoon baking soda
- 1   teaspoon baking powder
- ½   teaspoon salt
- 1   slightly beaten egg
- 1   teaspoon vanilla
- ½   cup sliced almonds, toasted and coarsely chopped

1 Place dates in a medium bowl. Pour the boiling water over dates. Let stand about 20 minutes or until dates are softened and mixture has cooled slightly.

2 Lightly grease bottom and ½ inch up sides of an 8×4×2-inch loaf pan; set aside. In a large bowl stir together all-purpose flour, whole wheat flour, baking soda, baking powder, and salt. Stir the egg and vanilla into the cooled date mixture. Add the date mixture and the almonds to the flour mixture; stir until well mixed (mixture will be thick).

3 Spoon batter evenly into prepared pan. Bake in a 350°F oven for 50 to 55 minutes or until a wooden toothpick inserted near the center comes out clean. Cool in pan on wire rack for 10 minutes. Remove from pan. Cool completely on a wire rack. Wrap and store overnight before slicing.

Date-Nut Bread

PREP: 15 minutes
STAND: 20 minutes + overnight
BAKE: 50 minutes   **OVEN:** 350°F
MAKES: 1 loaf (16 servings)

NUTRITION FACTS per serving:

CALORIES 119
TOTAL FAT 3 g total fat (0 g sat. fat)
CHOLESTEROL 13 mg
PROTEIN 3 g
CARBOHYDRATE 22 g
FIBER 3 g
SODIUM 182 mg

EXCHANGES ½ Fruit, 1 Starch

2   pink or red grapefruit

2   navel oranges

4   cups Belgian endive leaves

4   cups torn curly endive or escarole

1   small jicama, peeled and cut in thin bite-size strips (about 2 cups)

1   recipe Citrus-Dijon Dressing

1 Peel and section grapefruit and oranges over a bowl, reserving any juices for the dressing.

2 Place greens on individual salad plates. Arrange fruit and jicama on top of greens. Drizzle Citrus-Dijon Dressing over salads. Serve immediately.

Citrus-Dijon Dressing: In a screw-top jar combine reserved grapefruit and orange juices, ⅓ cup salad oil, 1 teaspoon finely shredded lemon peel, ¼ cup lemon juice, 1 tablespoon Dijon-style mustard, 2 teaspoons sugar, and ¼ teaspoon black pepper. Cover and shake well.

Mixed Citrus Salad

START TO FINISH: 20 minutes
MAKES: 10 servings

NUTRITION FACTS per serving:

CALORIES 110
TOTAL FAT 8 g total fat (1 g sat. fat)
CHOLESTEROL 0 mg
PROTEIN 1 g
CARBOHYDRATE 11 g
FIBER 2 g
SODIUM 42 mg

EXCHANGES 1 Vegetable, ½ Fruit, 1½ Fat

- ½ medium honeydew melon, peeled, seeded, and cut into bite-size pieces (2 cups)
- 2 medium tart apples, cored, halved lengthwise, and cut into bite-size pieces
- 2 medium nectarines or peaches, pitted and thinly sliced
- ¼ cup vanilla low-fat yogurt
- 3 tablespoons apricot jam
- ½ teaspoon ground ginger or nutmeg
- 1 cup red raspberries

1 In a large bowl combine melon, apples, and nectarines. For dressing, in a small bowl stir together yogurt, jam, and spice.

2 Add dressing to fruit mixture; toss to coat. Spoon into dishes or glasses. Top with raspberries. Serve immediately.

Honeydew and Apple Salad

START TO FINISH: 15 minutes
MAKES: 6 servings

NUTRITION FACTS per serving:

CALORIES 109
TOTAL FAT 1 g total fat (0 g sat. fat)
CHOLESTEROL 1 mg
PROTEIN 1 g
CARBOHYDRATE 27 g
FIBER 3 g
SODIUM 16 mg

EXCHANGES 2 Fruit

Cranberry Twist Bread

PREP: 30 minutes   **RISE:** 1½ hours
BAKE: 25 minutes   **OVEN:** 375°F
MAKES: 16 servings

NUTRITION FACTS per serving:

CALORIES 136
TOTAL FAT 3 g total fat (2 g sat. fat)
CHOLESTEROL 19 mg
PROTEIN 3 g
CARBOHYDRATE 24 g
FIBER 1 g
SODIUM 102 mg

EXCHANGES 1½ Starch, ½ Fat

2¾	**to 3 cups all-purpose flour**
1	**package active dry yeast**
¾	**cup milk**
⅓	**cup granulated sugar**
2	**tablespoons butter or margarine**
1	**egg**
½	**cup finely chopped fresh cranberries**
2	**tablespoons finely chopped pecans**
1½	**teaspoons finely shredded orange peel**
½	**teaspoon pumpkin pie spice**
1½	**teaspoons butter or margarine, melted**
1	**recipe Orange Icing**

1 In large bowl stir together 1 cup of the flour and yeast; set aside. In small saucepan heat and stir milk, 2 tablespoons of the sugar, the 2 tablespoons butter, and ½ teaspoon salt until warm (120°F to 130°F). Add milk mixture to flour mixture; add egg. Beat with an electric mixer on low to medium speed for 30 seconds, scraping bowl. Beat on high speed 3 minutes. Stir in as much remaining flour as you can.

2 Turn out dough onto a floured surface. Knead in enough remaining flour to make a soft dough that is smooth and elastic (3 to 5 minutes). Shape dough into a ball. Place in a lightly greased bowl; turn once. Cover; let rise until double (1 to 1½ hours). For filling, in small bowl stir together cranberries, remaining sugar, pecans, peel, and spice; set aside.

3 Punch down dough. Turn out onto lightly floured surface. Cover; let rest 10 minutes. Roll dough into a 14×10-inch rectangle. Brush with melted butter. Spread filling over dough. Starting from a long side, roll dough into a spiral. Seal seam. Place, seam side down, and cut roll in half lengthwise. Place cut sides up, side by side, on greased baking sheet. Loosely twist halves together, keeping cut sides up. Pinch ends to seal. Cover; let rise in a warm place until nearly double (about 30 minutes).

4 Bake in a 375°F oven about 25 minutes or until golden brown. Cool on wire rack. Drizzle with Orange Icing.

Orange Icing: Stir together ½ cup sifted powdered sugar and enough orange juice (2 to 3 teaspoons) for drizzling consistency.

Nonstick cooking spray

1½	cups all-purpose flour
¼	cup sugar
1	teaspoon ground ginger
1	teaspoon ground cinnamon
½	teaspoon baking powder
½	teaspoon baking soda
¼	teaspoon salt
½	cup water
⅓	cup full-flavored molasses
3	tablespoons butter or margarine, melted
2	egg whites
	Frozen light whipped dessert topping, thawed (optional)

1 Lightly coat an 8×8×2-inch baking pan with nonstick cooking spray; dust lightly with flour. Set aside.

2 In a large mixing bowl combine the 1½ cups flour, the sugar, ginger, cinnamon, baking powder, baking soda, and salt. Add the water, molasses, butter, and egg whites. Beat with an electric mixer on low to medium speed until combined. Beat on high speed for 2 minutes. Spread into prepared pan.

3 Bake in a 350°F oven about 20 minutes or until a wooden toothpick inserted near the center comes out clean. Cool in the pan on a wire rack for 10 minutes. Remove cake from pan. Serve warm and, if desired, with dessert topping.

Gingerbread

PREP: 15 minutes **BAKE:** 20 minutes
OVEN: 350°F **COOL:** 10 minutes
MAKES: 9 servings

NUTRITION FACTS per serving:

CALORIES 163
TOTAL FAT 4 g total fat (3 g sat. fat)
CHOLESTEROL 11 mg
PROTEIN 3 g
CARBOHYDRATE 28 g
FIBER 1 g
SODIUM 216 mg

EXCHANGES 2 Other Carbo., ½ Fat

1½ cups sugar

1 envelope unflavored gelatin

3¼ cups blood orange juice and/or orange juice

1½ cups buttermilk

1 teaspoon vanilla

1 In a medium saucepan combine sugar and gelatin. Stir in 2 cups of the orange juice. Cook and stir until sugar and gelatin dissolve. Remove from heat. Stir in the remaining orange juice, the buttermilk, and vanilla.

2 Transfer to a 4-quart ice cream freezer; freeze according to manufacturer's directions. Ripen for 4 hours.*

*Note: Ripening homemade sherbet is not essential, but it improves the texture and slows down melting. To ripen in a traditional-style ice cream freezer, after churning, remove the lid and dasher and cover the top of the freezer can with waxed paper or foil. Plug the hole in the lid with a small piece of cloth; replace the lid. Pack outer freezer bucket with enough ice and rock salt to cover the top of the freezer can (use 4 cups ice to 1 cup salt). Let sherbet stand about 4 hours. When using an ice cream freezer with an insulated freezer bowl, transfer the sherbet to a covered freezerproof container and ripen in your regular freezer about 4 hours (or follow the manufacturer's recommendations).

Blood Orange Sherbet

PREP: 40 minutes
FREEZE: According to manufacturer's directions
RIPEN: 4 hours   **MAKES:** 16 servings

NUTRITION FACTS per serving:

CALORIES 104
TOTAL FAT 0 g (0 g sat. fat)
CHOLESTEROL 1 mg
PROTEIN 1 g
CARBOHYDRATE 24 g
FIBER 0 g
SODIUM 26 mg

EXCHANGES 1½ Other Carbo.

3   cups strawberry or raspberry sorbet, softened

2   cups low-fat or light chocolate ice cream

1   tablespoon orange liqueur or orange juice

2   cups fresh raspberries, blueberries, blackberries, and/or strawberries

    Fresh mint sprigs (optional)

1 Line a 2-quart bowl with plastic wrap. Press sorbet on bottom and two-thirds up the sides of the bowl to form a shell. Cover and freeze at least 1 hour.

2 Soften chocolate ice cream. Gently stir in orange liqueur or orange juice. Spoon into the center of the sorbet shell, pressing down to remove air bubbles. Cover and freeze for at least 4 hours.

3 Unmold frozen mixture. Remove plastic wrap. Serve with berries. If desired, garnish with mint.

Frozen Berry-Orange Bombe

PREP: 15 minutes
FREEZE: 1 hour + 4 hours
MAKES: 10 servings

NUTRITION FACTS per serving:

CALORIES 123
TOTAL FAT 1 g total fat (1 g sat. fat)
CHOLESTEROL 2 mg
PROTEIN 1 g
CARBOHYDRATE 27 g
FIBER 1 g
SODIUM 17 mg

EXCHANGES 2 Other Carbo.

1¼ cups apricot nectar

⅓ cup snipped dried apricots

2 tablespoons dried tart red cherries or dried cranberries

4 medium, firm red pears

2 tablespoons sugar

¼ teaspoon ground nutmeg

½ teaspoon vanilla

⅛ teaspoon ground cardamom

Baked Red Pears

PREP: 15 minutes **BAKE:** 40 minutes
OVEN: 350°F **MAKES:** 4 servings

NUTRITION FACTS per serving:

CALORIES 206
TOTAL FAT 1 g total fat (0 g sat. fat)
CHOLESTEROL 0 mg
PROTEIN 1 g
CARBOHYDRATE 52 g
FIBER 6 g
SODIUM 4 mg

EXCHANGES 1 Fruit, 2½ Other Carbo.

1 In a small saucepan combine apricot nectar, apricots, and cherries or cranberries. Bring to boiling. Remove from heat; let stand for 5 minutes. Drain fruit, reserving liquid.

2 Meanwhile, cut off tops of pears; set aside. Core pears almost through to bottom. Place pears and pear tops in a 2-quart square baking dish. In a small bowl combine drained fruit mixture, sugar, and nutmeg. Spoon into centers of pears. In another small bowl combine reserved liquid, vanilla, and cardamom; pour over and around pears.

3 Cover and bake in a 350°F oven for 20 minutes. Uncover; bake for 20 to 25 minutes more or until pears are tender, basting pears occasionally with cooking liquid.

4 To serve, place tops on pears; spoon liquid over pears. Serve warm.

Chapter 18

Index & Metric

How Recipes Are Analyzed

The Better Homes and Gardens® Test Kitchen uses nutrition-analysis software to determine the nutritional value of a single serving of a recipe. Here are some factors to keep in mind regarding each analysis:

- Analyses do not include optional ingredients.

- The first serving size listed is analyzed when a range is given. For example, if a recipe makes 4 to 6 servings, the Nutrition Facts are based on 4 servings.

- When ingredient choices (such as butter or margarine) appear in a recipe, the first one mentioned is used for analysis.

- When milk is a recipe ingredient, the analysis has been calculated using fat-free (skim) milk unless otherwise noted.

- The exchanges, listed for every recipe along with the Nutrition Facts, are based on the exchange list developed by the American Dietetic Association and the American Diabetes Association.

NUTRITION NOTE

Note on Sodium: For this cookbook, the goal was to keep the sodium levels at a reasonable level that would allow you to stay under the recommended limit of 2,400 mg a day. But for recipes that have high-sodium ingredients, such as ham or other processed foods, the sodium levels are relatively high—1,000 mg or more. This only occurs in a small number of recipes but is something to watch for if you have hypertension and have been told to follow a low-sodium diet.

METRIC INFORMATION

The charts on this page provide a guide for converting measurements from the U.S. customary system, which is used throughout this book, to the metric system.

Product Differences

Most of the ingredients called for in the recipes in this book are available in most countries. However, some are known by different names. Here are some common American ingredients and their possible counterparts:

- Sugar (white) is granulated, fine granulated, or castor sugar.
- Powdered sugar is icing sugar.
- All-purpose flour is enriched, bleached or unbleached white household flour. When self-rising flour is used in place of all-purpose flour in a recipe that calls for leavening, omit the leavening agent (baking soda or baking powder) and salt.
- Light-colored corn syrup is golden syrup.
- Cornstarch is cornflour.
- Baking soda is bicarbonate of soda.
- Vanilla or vanilla extract is vanilla essence.
- Green, red, or yellow sweet peppers are capsicums or bell peppers.
- Golden raisins are sultanas.

Volume and Weight

The United States traditionally uses cup measures for liquid and solid ingredients. The chart below shows the approximate imperial and metric equivalents. If you are accustomed to weighing solid ingredients, the following approximate equivalents will be helpful.

- 1 cup butter, castor sugar, or rice = 8 ounces = ½ pound = 250 grams
- 1 cup flour = 4 ounces = ¼ pound = 125 grams
- 1 cup icing sugar = 5 ounces = 150 grams

Canadian and U.S. volume for a cup measure is 8 fluid ounces (237 ml), but the standard metric equivalent is 250 ml.

1 British imperial cup is 10 fluid ounces.

In Australia, 1 tablespoon equals 20 ml, and there are 4 teaspoons in the Australian tablespoon.

Spoon measures are used for smaller amounts of ingredients. Although the size of the tablespoon varies slightly in different countries, for practical purposes and for recipes in this book, a straight substitution is all that's necessary. Measurements made using cups or spoons always should be level unless stated otherwise.

Common Weight Range Replacements

IMPERIAL / U.S.	METRIC
½ ounce	15 g
1 ounce	25 g or 30 g
4 ounces (¼ pound)	115 g or 125 g
8 ounces (½ pound)	225 g or 250 g
16 ounces (1 pound)	450 g or 500 g
1¼ pounds	625 g
1½ pounds	750 g
2 pounds or 2¼ pounds	1,000 g or 1 Kg

Oven Temperature Equivalents

FAHRENHEIT SETTING	CELSIUS SETTING*	GAS SETTING
300°F	150°C	Gas Mark 2 (very low)
325°F	160°C	Gas Mark 3 (low)
350°F	180°C	Gas Mark 4 (moderate)
375°F	190°C	Gas Mark 5 (moderate)
400°F	200°C	Gas Mark 6 (hot)
425°F	220°C	Gas Mark 7 (hot)
450°F	230°C	Gas Mark 8 (very hot)
475°F	240°C	Gas Mark 9 (very hot)
500°F	260°C	Gas Mark 10 (extremely hot)
Broil	Broil	Grill

*Electric and gas ovens may be calibrated using celsius. However, for an electric oven, increase celsius setting 10 to 20 degrees when cooking above 160°C. For convection or forced air ovens (gas or electric) lower the temperature setting 25°F/10°C when cooking at all heat levels.

Baking Pan Sizes

IMPERIAL / U.S.	METRIC
9×1½-inch round cake pan	22- or 23×4-cm (1.5 L)
9×1½-inch pie plate	22- or 23×4-cm (1 L)
8×8×2-inch square cake pan	20×5-cm (2 L)
9×9×2-inch square cake pan	22- or 23×4.5-cm (2.5 L)
11×7×1½-inch baking pan	28×17×4-cm (2 L)
2-quart rectangular baking pan	30×19×4.5-cm (3 L)
13×9×2-inch baking pan	34×22×4.5-cm (3.5 L)
15×10×1-inch jelly roll pan	40×25×2-cm
9×5×3-inch loaf pan	23×13×8-cm (2 L)
2-quart casserole	2 L

U.S. / Standard Metric Equivalents

⅛ teaspoon = 0.5 ml	
¼ teaspoon = 1 ml	
½ teaspoon = 2 ml	
1 teaspoon = 5 ml	
1 tablespoon = 15 ml	
2 tablespoons = 25 ml	
¼ cup = 2 fluid ounces = 50 ml	
⅓ cup = 3 fluid ounces = 75 ml	
½ cup = 4 fluid ounces = 125 ml	
⅔ cup = 5 fluid ounces = 150 ml	
¾ cup = 6 fluid ounces = 175 ml	
1 cup = 8 fluid ounces = 250 ml	
2 cups = 1 pint = 500 ml	
1 quart = 1 litre